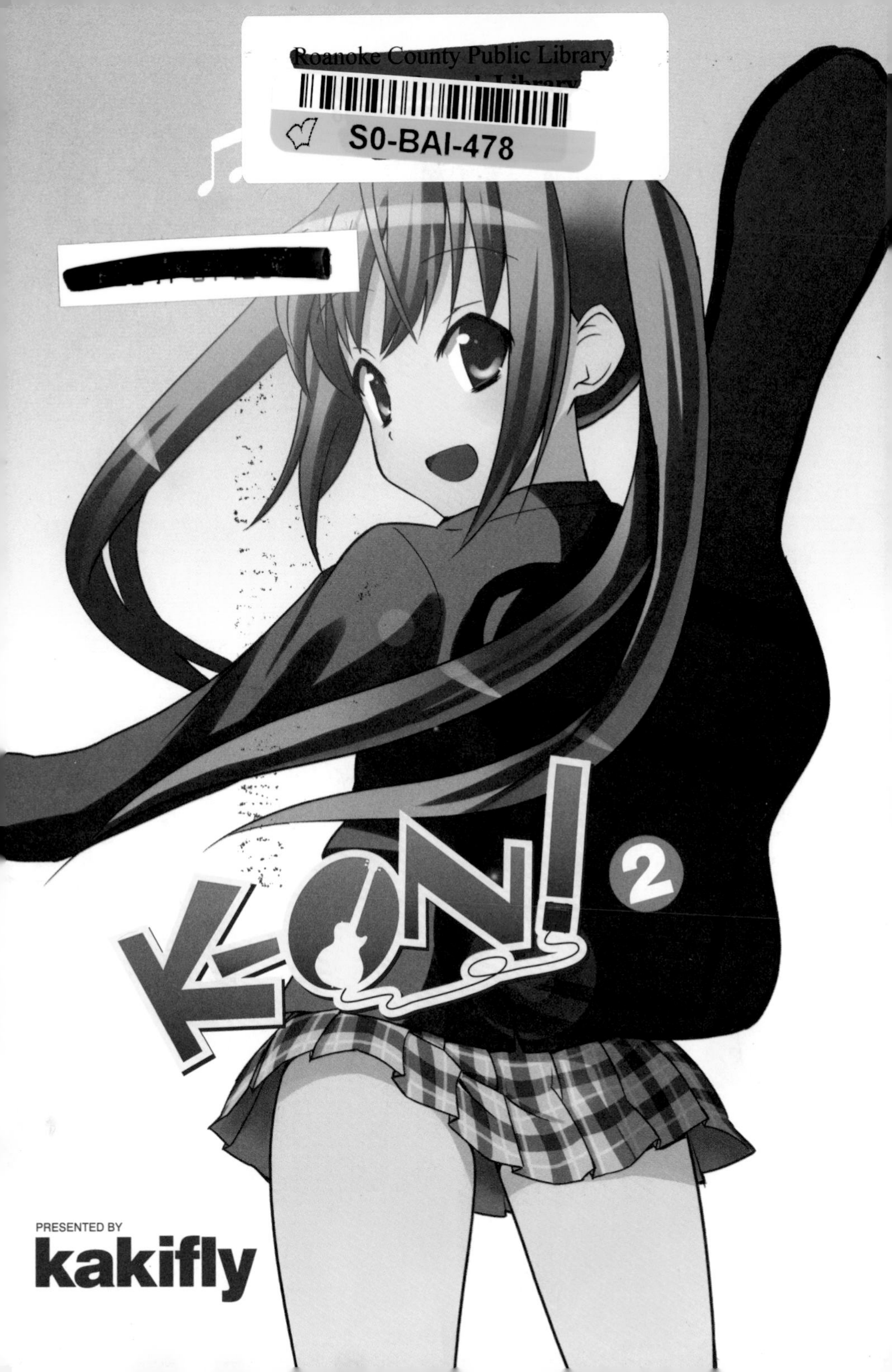
K-ON! 2
PRESENTED BY
kakifly

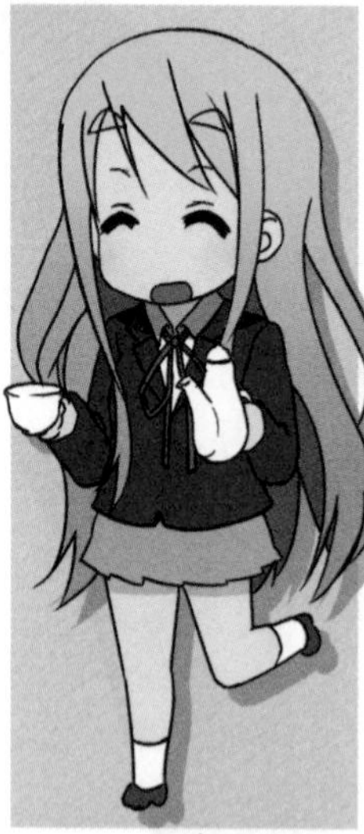

TSUMUGI KOTOBUKI
KEYBOARD

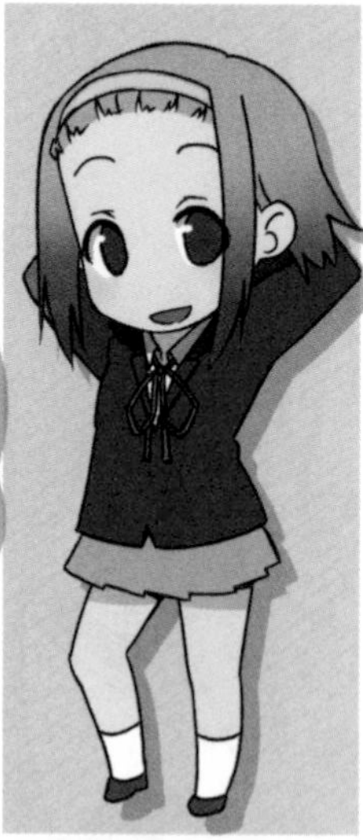

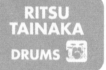

RITSU TAINAKA
DRUMS

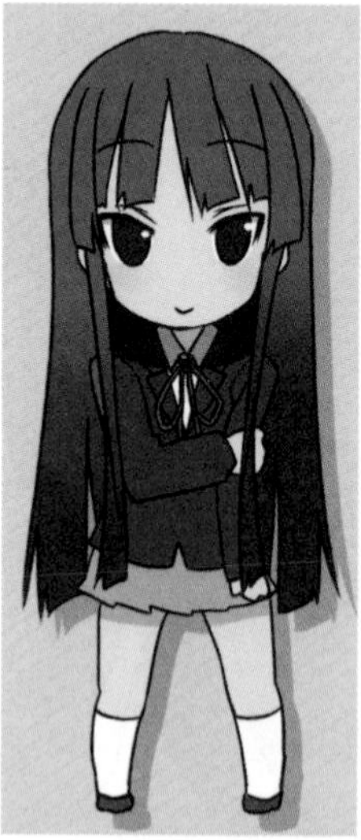

MIO AKIYAMA
BASS

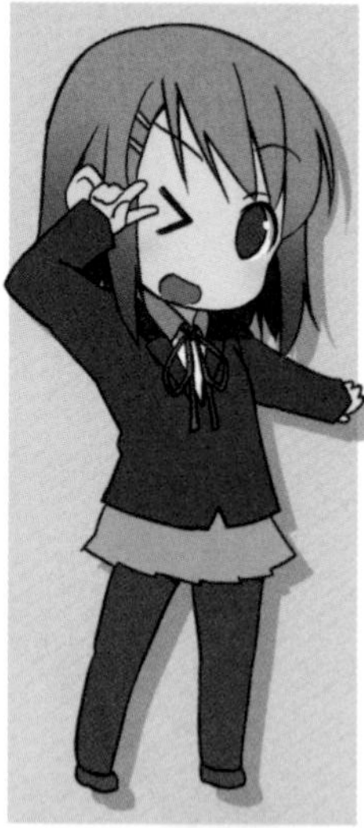

YUI HIRASAWA
GUITAR

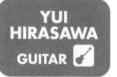

C H A R A C T E R S

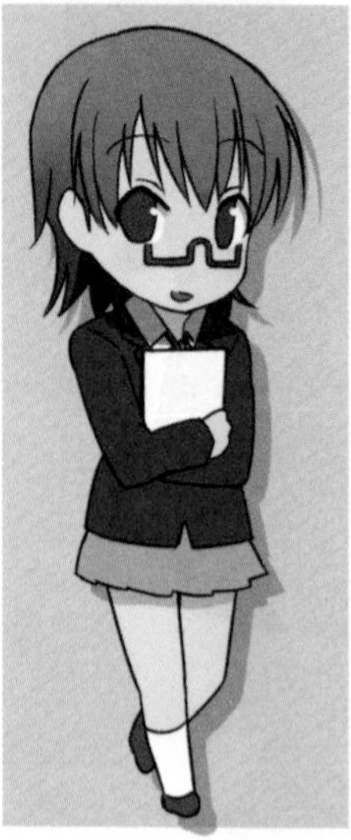

NODOKA MANABE
YUI'S FRIEND

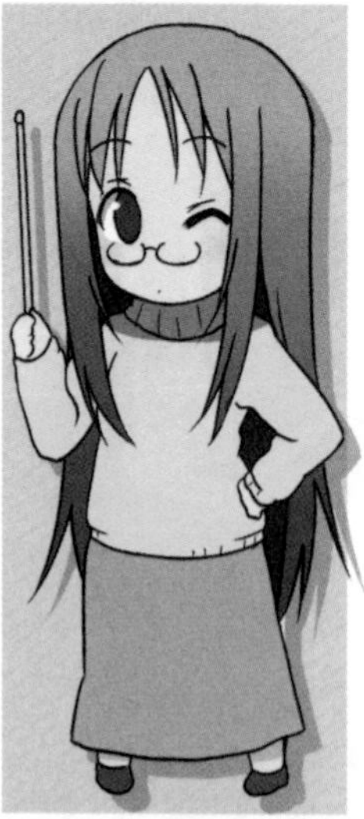

SAWAKO YAMANAKA
TEACHER

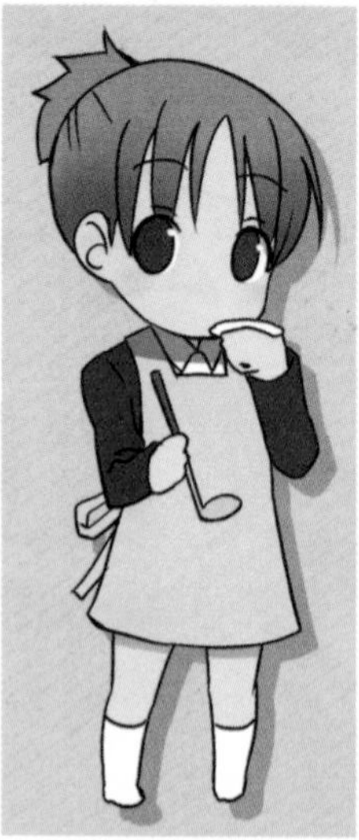

UI HIRASAWA
YUI'S YOUNGER SISTER

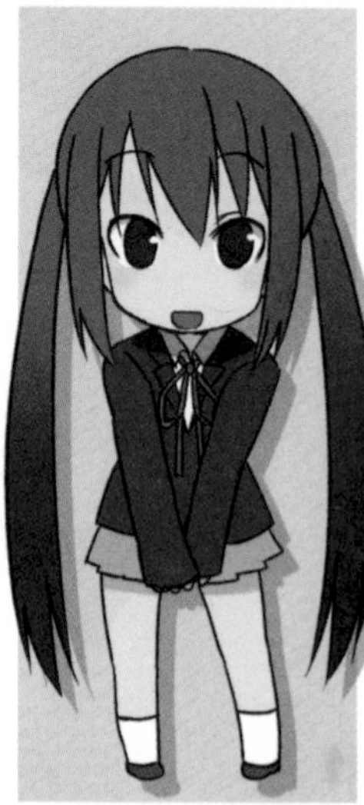

AZUSA NAKANO
NEW STUDENT

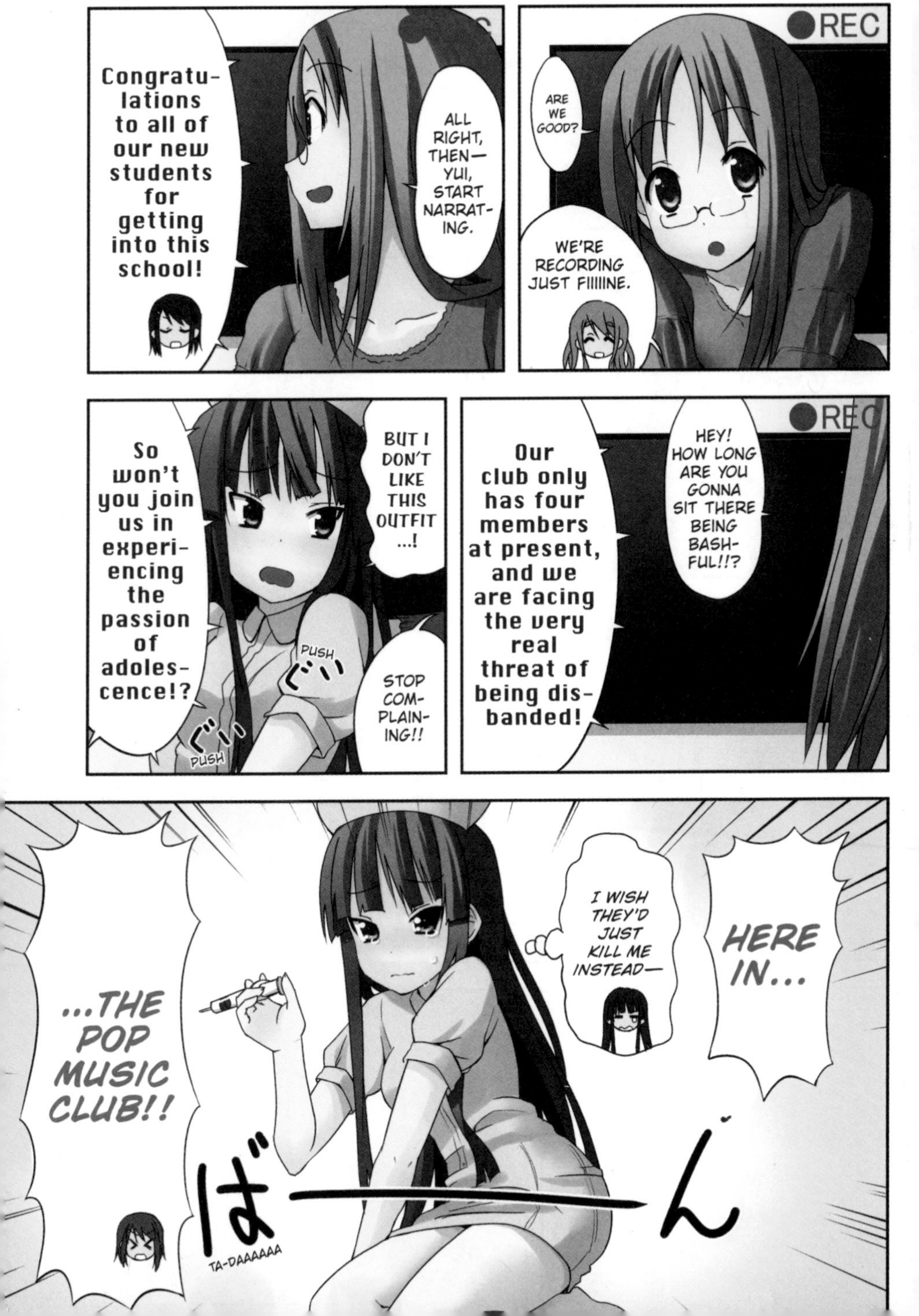
REC
ARE WE GOOD?
WE'RE RECORDING JUST FIIIIINE.
ALL RIGHT, THEN— YUI, START NARRATING.
Congratulations to all of our new students for getting into this school!
REC
HEY! HOW LONG ARE YOU GONNA SIT THERE BEING BASHFUL!!?
Our club only has four members at present, and we are facing the very real threat of being disbanded!
BUT I DON'T LIKE THIS OUTFIT ...!
STOP COMPLAINING!!
PUSH
So won't you join us in experiencing the passion of adolescence!?
PUSH
HERE IN...
I WISH THEY'D JUST KILL ME INSTEAD—
...THE POP MUSIC CLUB!!
ばーーん
TA-DAAAAAA

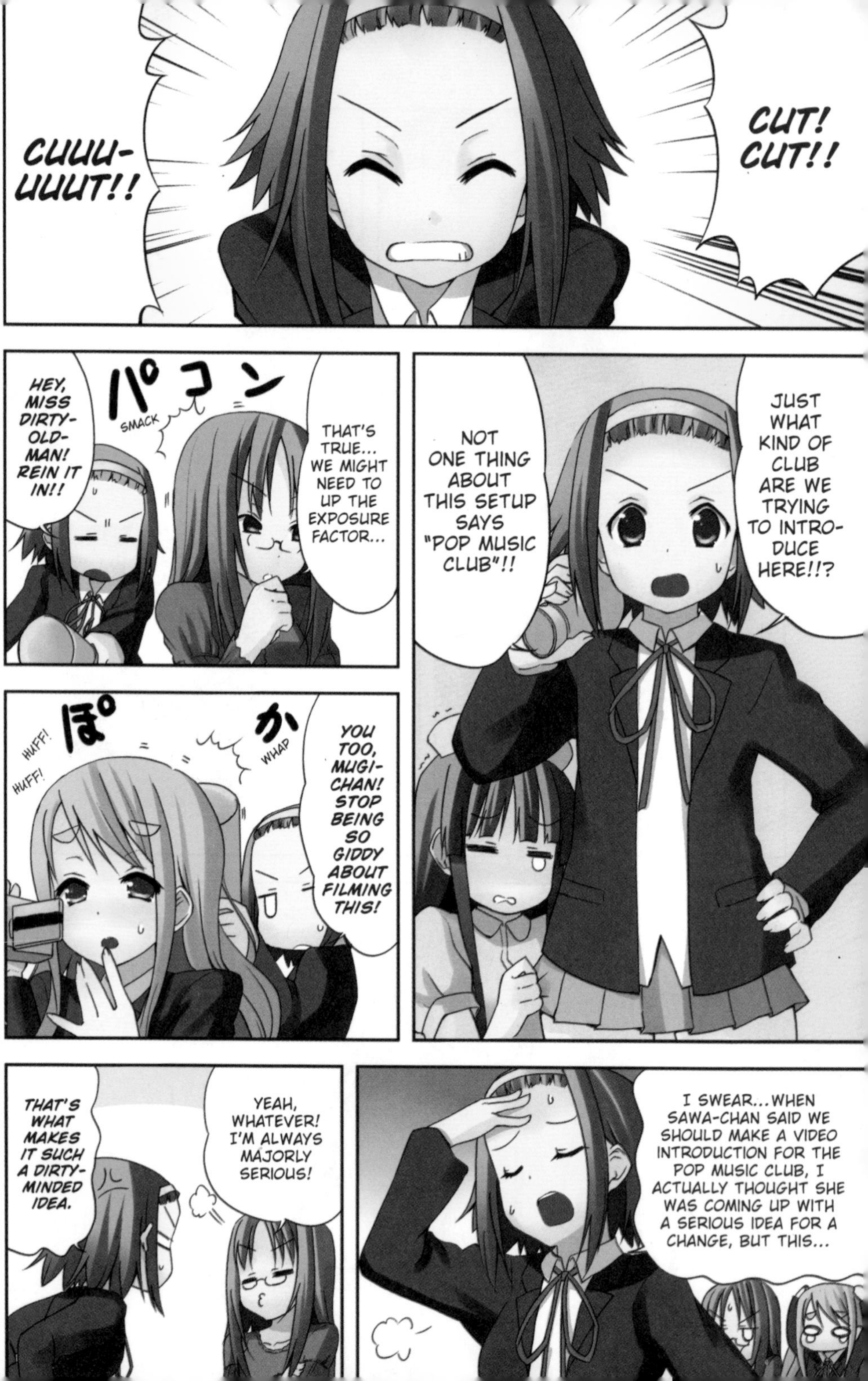
CUT! CUT!!
CUUUU-UUUT!!
JUST WHAT KIND OF CLUB ARE WE TRYING TO INTRO-DUCE HERE!!?
NOT ONE THING ABOUT THIS SETUP SAYS "POP MUSIC CLUB"!!
THAT'S TRUE... WE MIGHT NEED TO UP THE EXPOSURE FACTOR...
パコン
SMACK
HEY, MISS DIRTY-OLD-MAN! REIN IT IN!!
YOU TOO, MUGI-CHAN! STOP BEING SO GIDDY ABOUT FILMING THIS!
か
WHAP
ぽ
HUFF!
HUFF!
I SWEAR...WHEN SAWA-CHAN SAID WE SHOULD MAKE A VIDEO INTRODUCTION FOR THE POP MUSIC CLUB, I ACTUALLY THOUGHT SHE WAS COMING UP WITH A SERIOUS IDEA FOR A CHANGE, BUT THIS...
YEAH, WHATEVER! I'M ALWAYS MAJORLY SERIOUS!
THAT'S WHAT MAKES IT SUCH A DIRTY-MINDED IDEA.

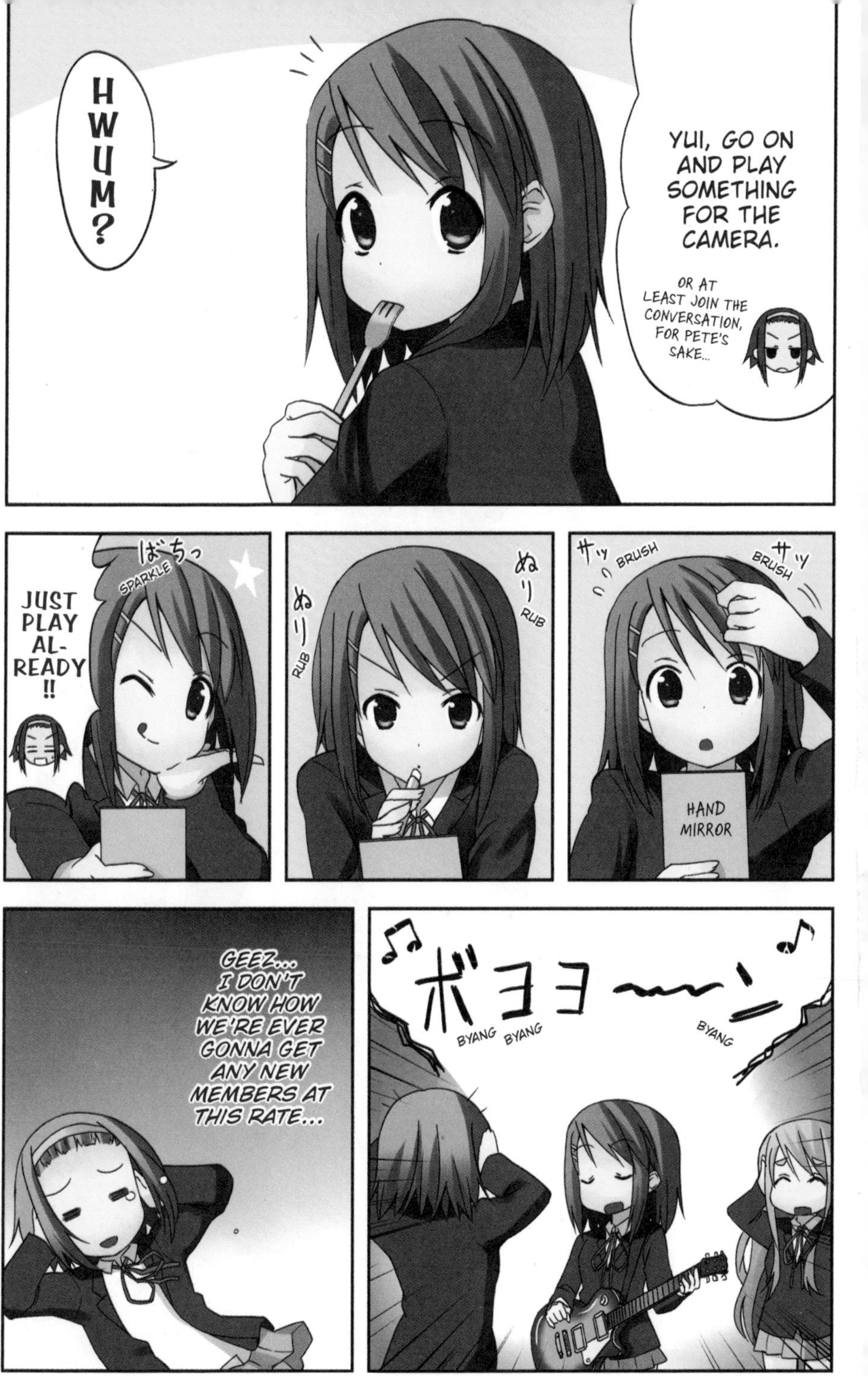
YUI, GO ON AND PLAY SOMETHING FOR THE CAMERA.
OR AT LEAST JOIN THE CONVERSATION, FOR PETE'S SAKE...
HWUM?
サッ BRUSH
サッ BRUSH
HAND MIRROR
ぬり RUB
ぬり RUB
ばちっ SPARKLE
JUST PLAY AL-READY!!
ボヨヨ〜ン
BYANG BYANG BYANG
GEEZ... I DON'T KNOW HOW WE'RE EVER GONNA GET ANY NEW MEMBERS AT THIS RATE...

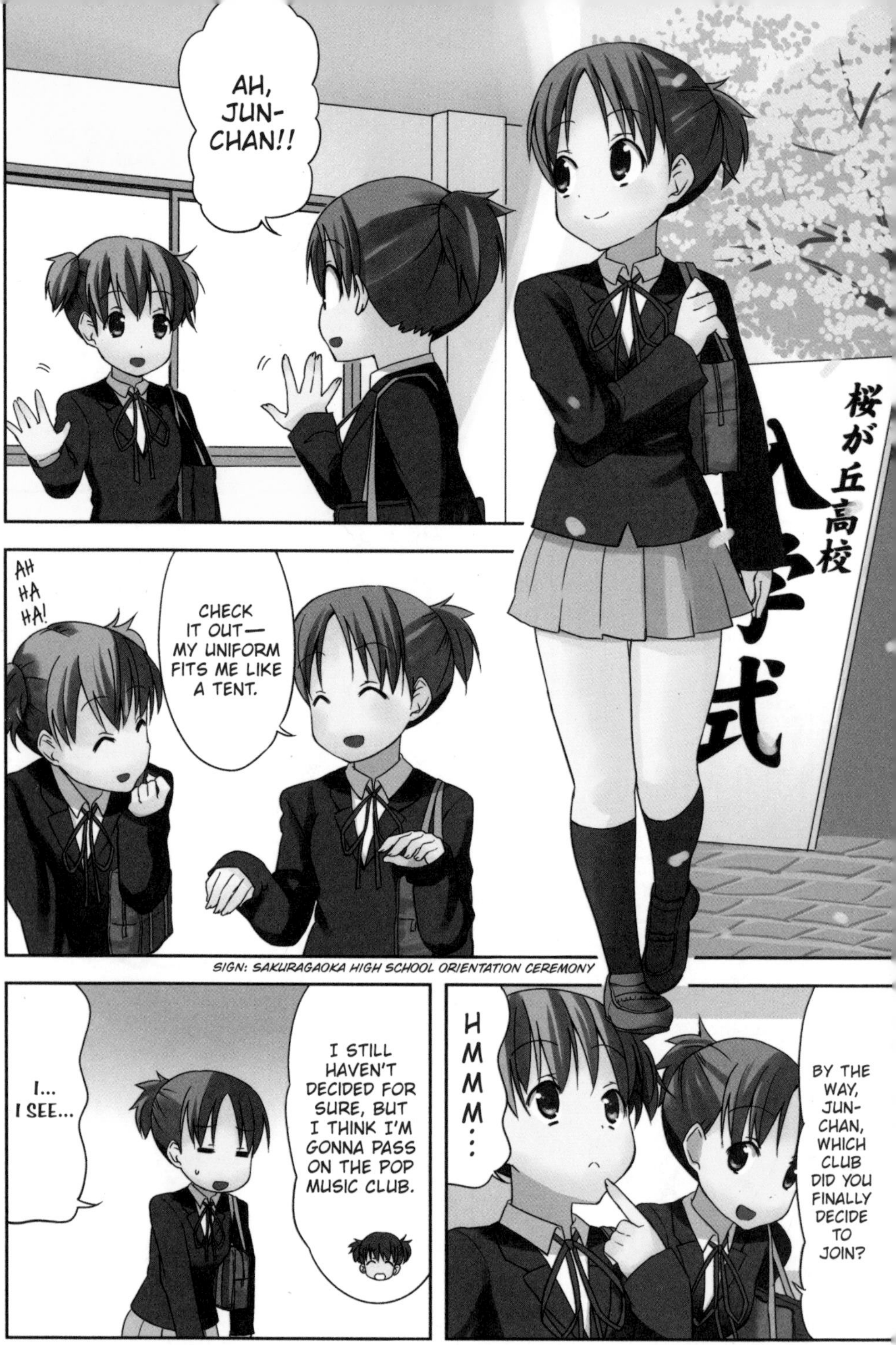
桜が丘高校
AH, JUN-CHAN!!
CHECK IT OUT— MY UNIFORM FITS ME LIKE A TENT.
AH HA HA!
BY THE WAY, JUN-CHAN, WHICH CLUB DID YOU FINALLY DECIDE TO JOIN?
HMMM...
I STILL HAVEN'T DECIDED FOR SURE, BUT I THINK I'M GONNA PASS ON THE POP MUSIC CLUB.
I... I SEE...
SIGN: SAKURAGAOKA HIGH SCHOOL ORIENTATION CEREMONY

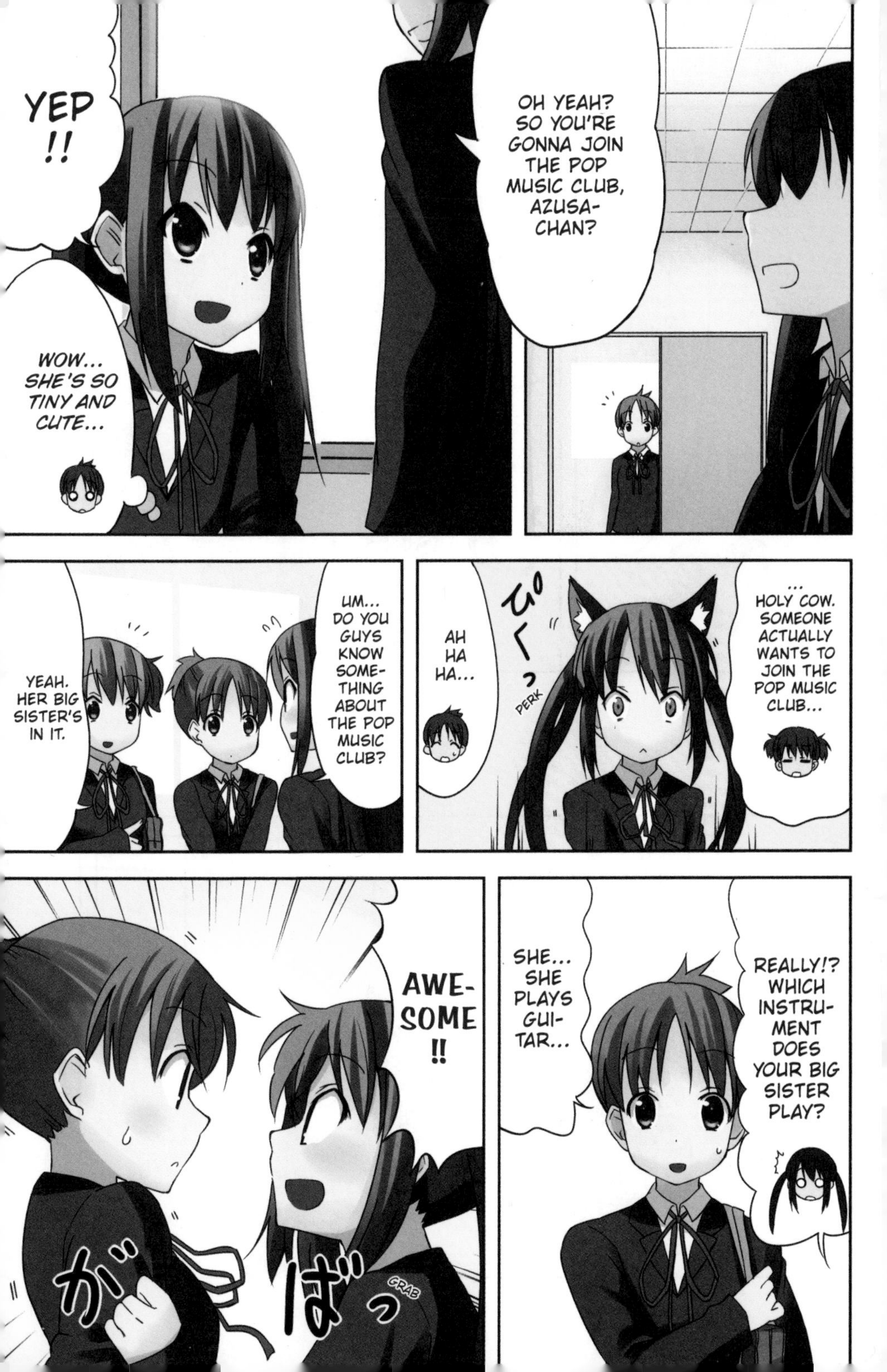
OH YEAH? SO YOU'RE GONNA JOIN THE POP MUSIC CLUB, AZUSA-CHAN?
YEP !!
WOW... SHE'S SO TINY AND CUTE...
... HOLY COW. SOMEONE ACTUALLY WANTS TO JOIN THE POP MUSIC CLUB...
ぴくっ
PERK
AH HA HA...
UM... DO YOU GUYS KNOW SOMETHING ABOUT THE POP MUSIC CLUB?
YEAH. HER BIG SISTER'S IN IT.
REALLY!? WHICH INSTRUMENT DOES YOUR BIG SISTER PLAY?
SHE... SHE PLAYS GUITAR...
AWESOME !!
がばっ
GRAB

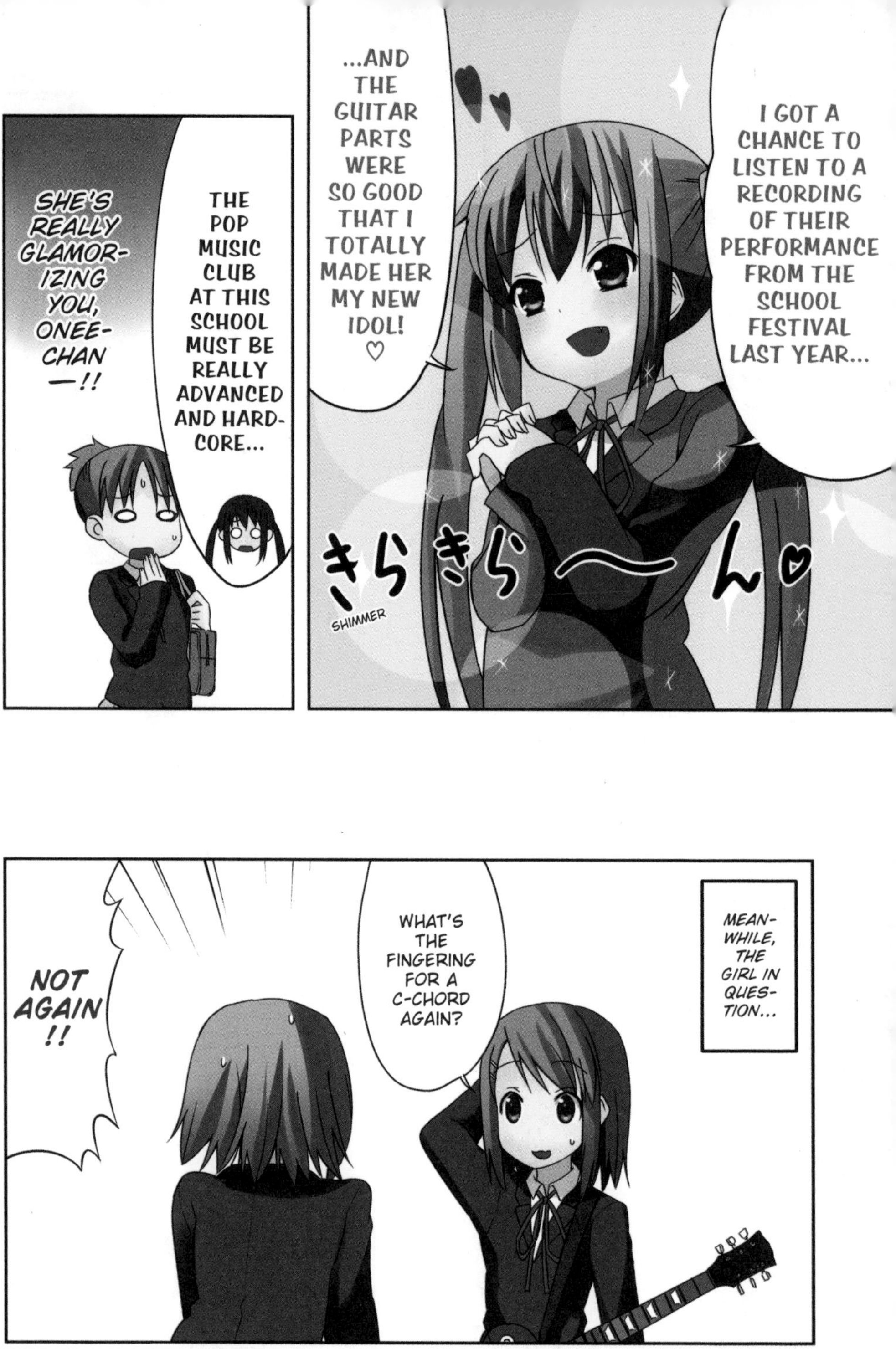
I GOT A CHANCE TO LISTEN TO A RECORDING OF THEIR PERFORMANCE FROM THE SCHOOL FESTIVAL LAST YEAR...
...AND THE GUITAR PARTS WERE SO GOOD THAT I TOTALLY MADE HER MY NEW IDOL! ♡
きらきら～ん♡
SHIMMER
THE POP MUSIC CLUB AT THIS SCHOOL MUST BE REALLY ADVANCED AND HARD-CORE...
SHE'S REALLY GLAMORIZING YOU, ONEE-CHAN—!!
MEANWHILE, THE GIRL IN QUESTION...
WHAT'S THE FINGERING FOR A C-CHORD AGAIN?
NOT AGAIN!!

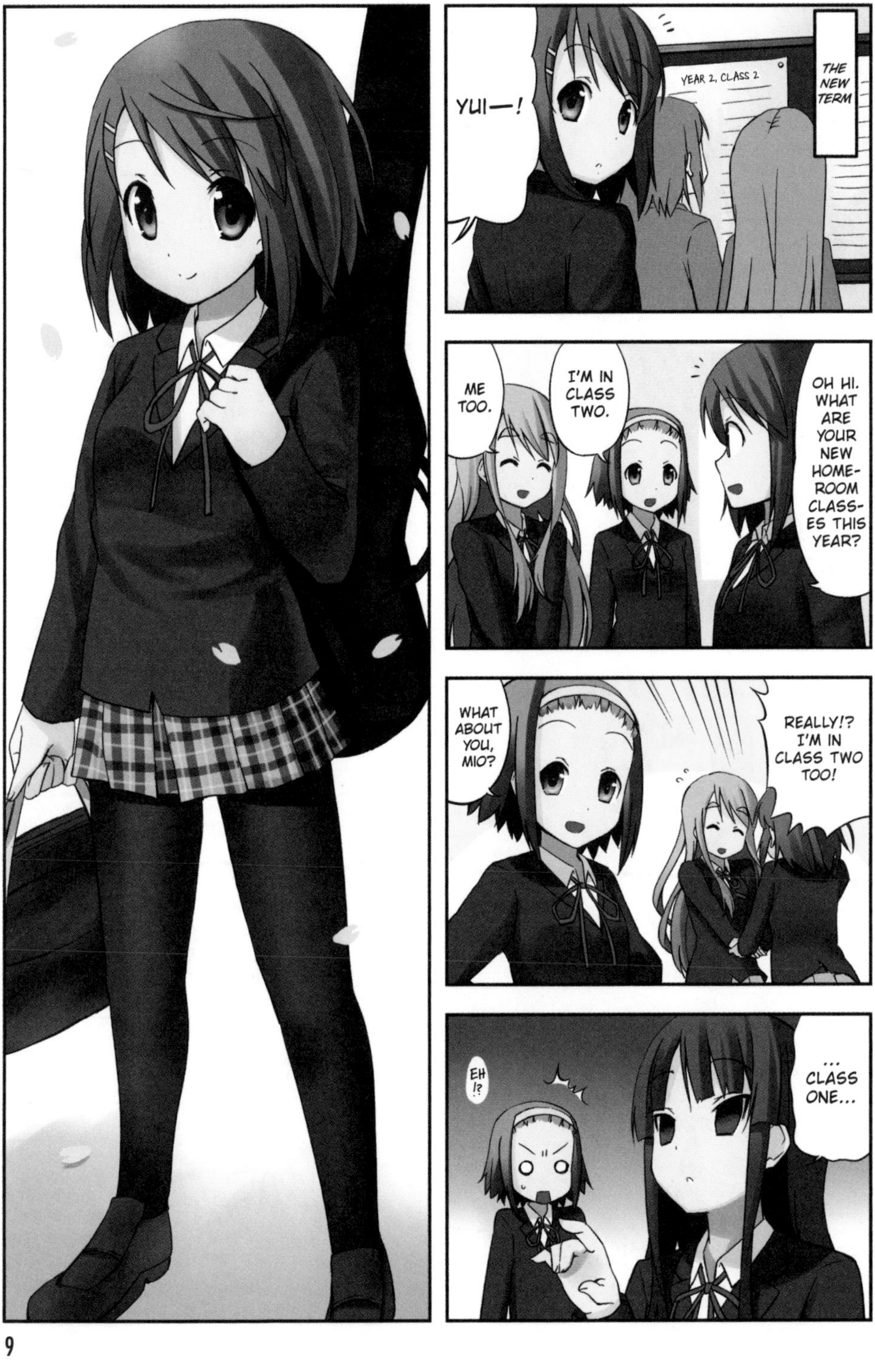
THE NEW TERM
YEAR 2, CLASS 2
YUI—!
OH HI. WHAT ARE YOUR NEW HOME-ROOM CLASSES THIS YEAR?
I'M IN CLASS TWO.
ME TOO.
REALLY!? I'M IN CLASS TWO TOO!
WHAT ABOUT YOU, MIO?
...CLASS ONE...
EH!?

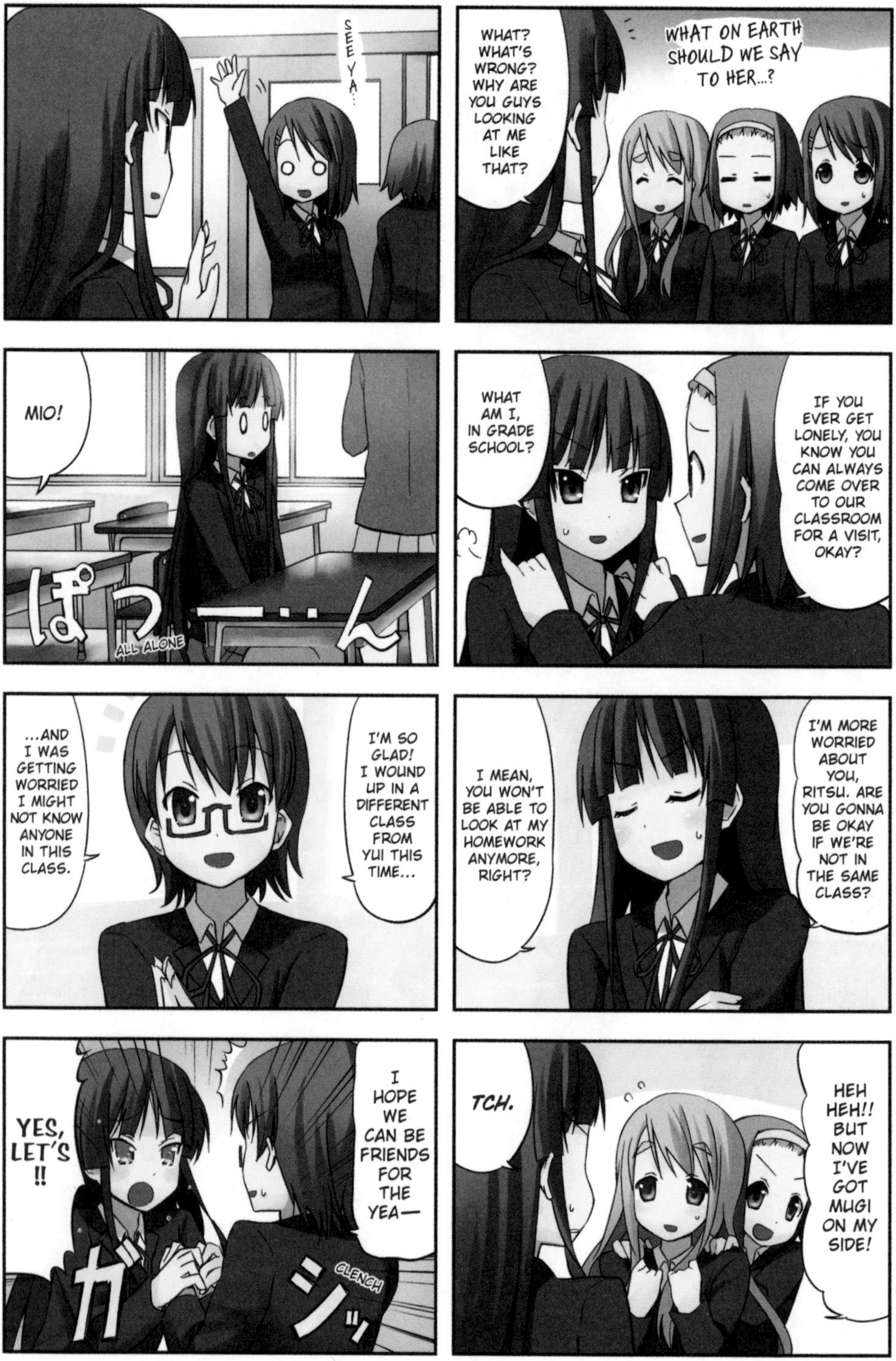
WHAT ON EARTH SHOULD WE SAY TO HER...?
WHAT? WHAT'S WRONG? WHY ARE YOU GUYS LOOKING AT ME LIKE THAT?
SEE YA...
IF YOU EVER GET LONELY, YOU KNOW YOU CAN ALWAYS COME OVER TO OUR CLASSROOM FOR A VISIT, OKAY?
WHAT AM I, IN GRADE SCHOOL?
MIO!
ぽつーん
ALL ALONE
I'M MORE WORRIED ABOUT YOU, RITSU. ARE YOU GONNA BE OKAY IF WE'RE NOT IN THE SAME CLASS?
I MEAN, YOU WON'T BE ABLE TO LOOK AT MY HOMEWORK ANYMORE, RIGHT?
I'M SO GLAD! I WOUND UP IN A DIFFERENT CLASS FROM YUI THIS TIME...
...AND I WAS GETTING WORRIED I MIGHT NOT KNOW ANYONE IN THIS CLASS.
HEH HEH!! BUT NOW I'VE GOT MUGI ON MY SIDE!
TCH.
I HOPE WE CAN BE FRIENDS FOR THE YEA—
YES, LET'S!!
ガシッ
CLENCH

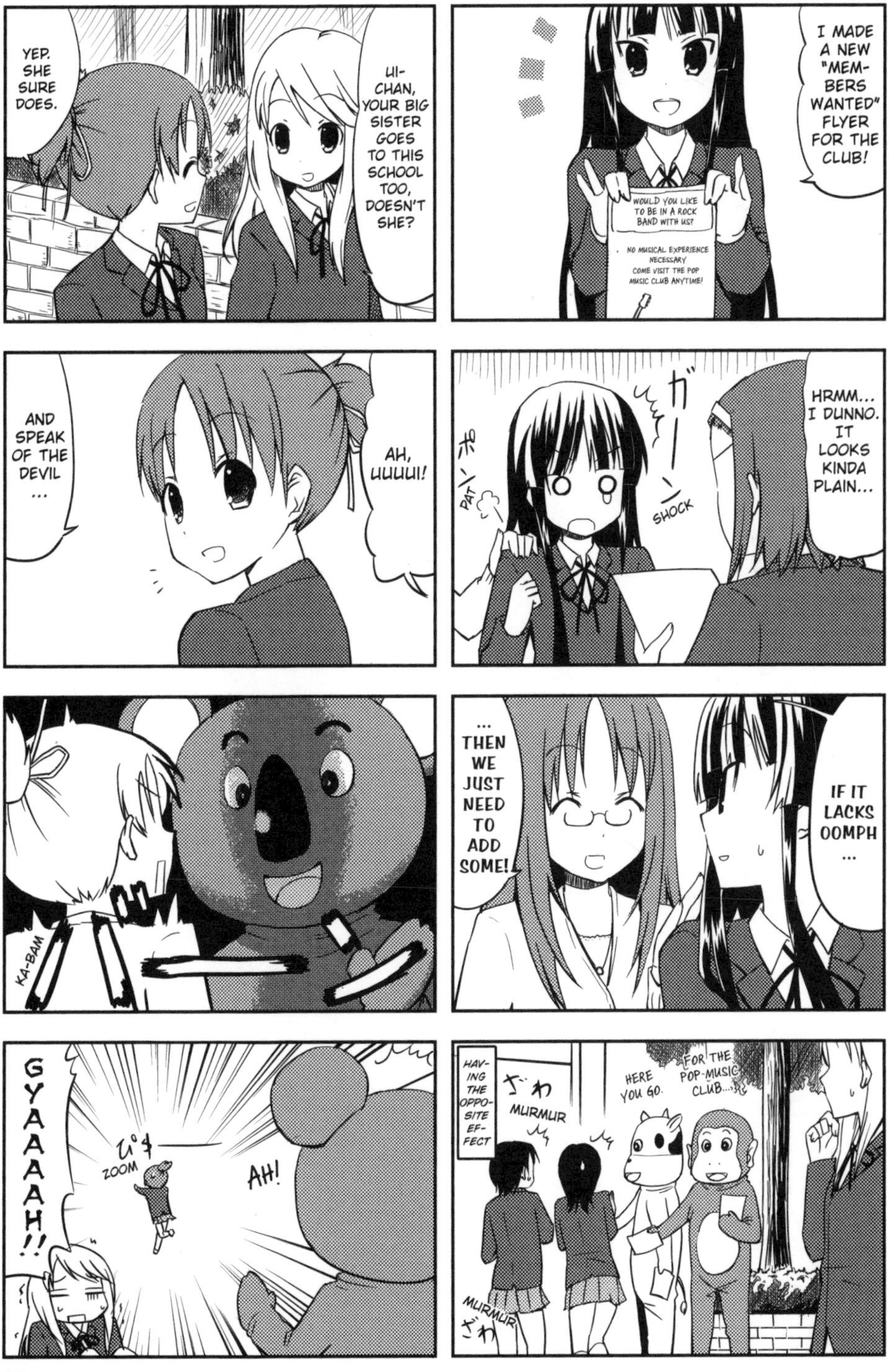

I MADE A NEW "MEMBERS WANTED" FLYER FOR THE CLUB!
WOULD YOU LIKE TO BE IN A ROCK BAND WITH US?
NO MUSICAL EXPERIENCE NECESSARY COME VISIT THE POP MUSIC CLUB ANYTIME!
UI-CHAN, YOUR BIG SISTER GOES TO THIS SCHOOL TOO, DOESN'T SHE?
YEP. SHE SURE DOES.
HRMM... I DUNNO. IT LOOKS KINDA PLAIN...
ガーン
SHOCK
ポン
PAT
AH, UUUUI!
AND SPEAK OF THE DEVIL...
IF IT LACKS OOMPH...
...THEN WE JUST NEED TO ADD SOME!
KA-BAM
HAVING THE OPPOSITE EFFECT
FOR THE POP-MUSIC CLUB...
HERE YOU GO.
ざわ
MURMUR
MURMUR
ざわ
AH!
ぴゅ—
ZOOM
GYAAAAAH!!

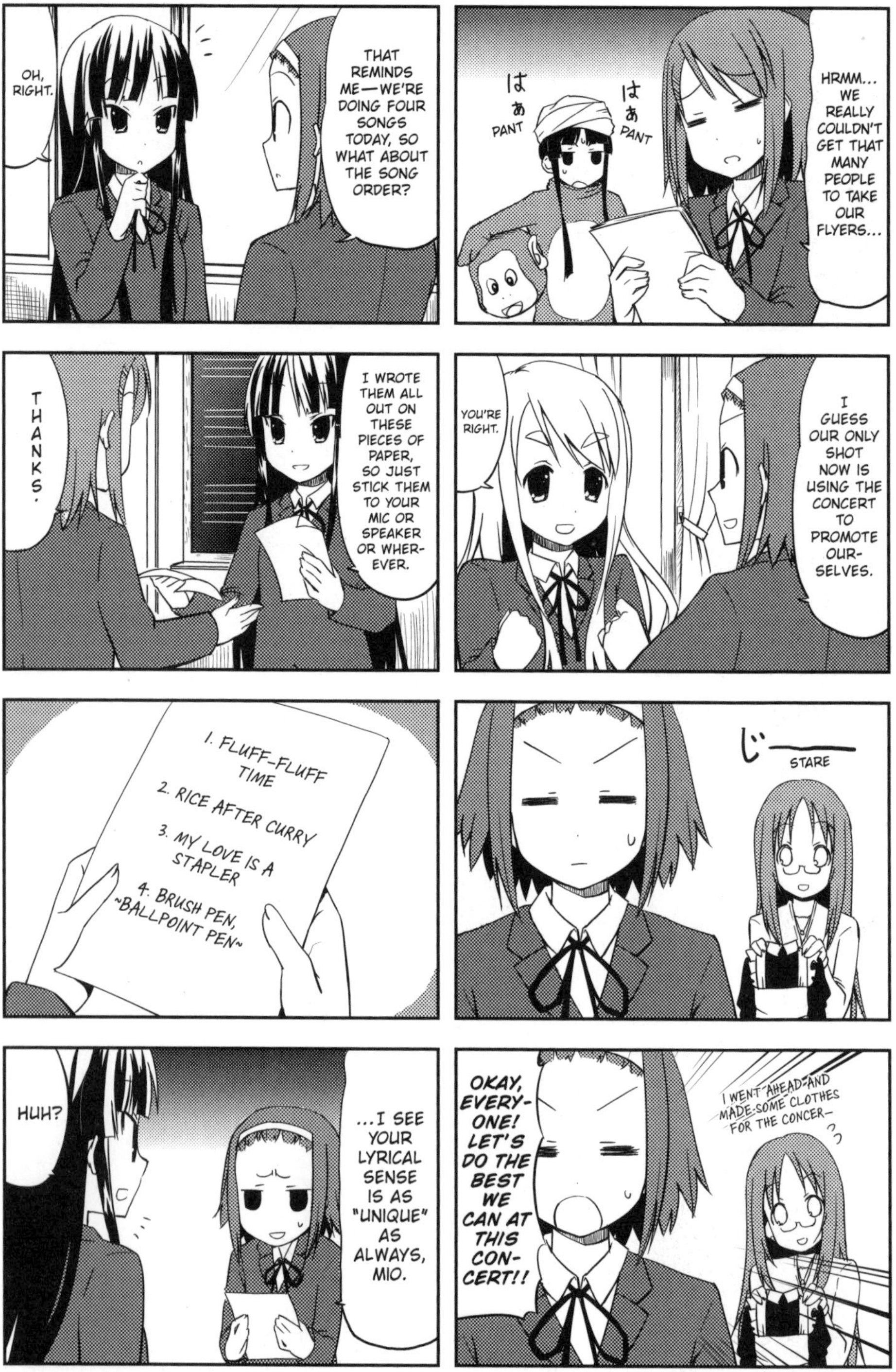
HRMM... WE REALLY COULDN'T GET THAT MANY PEOPLE TO TAKE OUR FLYERS...
はぁ PANT
はぁ PANT
I GUESS OUR ONLY SHOT NOW IS USING THE CONCERT TO PROMOTE OUR-SELVES.
YOU'RE RIGHT.
じーー STARE
OKAY, EVERY-ONE! LET'S DO THE BEST WE CAN AT THIS CON-CERT!!
I WENT AHEAD AND MADE SOME CLOTHES FOR THE CONCER—
THAT REMINDS ME—WE'RE DOING FOUR SONGS TODAY, SO WHAT ABOUT THE SONG ORDER?
OH, RIGHT.
I WROTE THEM ALL OUT ON THESE PIECES OF PAPER, SO JUST STICK THEM TO YOUR MIC OR SPEAKER OR WHER-EVER.
THANKS.
1. FLUFF-FLUFF TIME
2. RICE AFTER CURRY
3. MY LOVE IS A STAPLER
4. BRUSH PEN, ~BALLPOINT PEN~
...I SEE YOUR LYRICAL SENSE IS AS "UNIQUE" AS ALWAYS, MIO.
HUH?

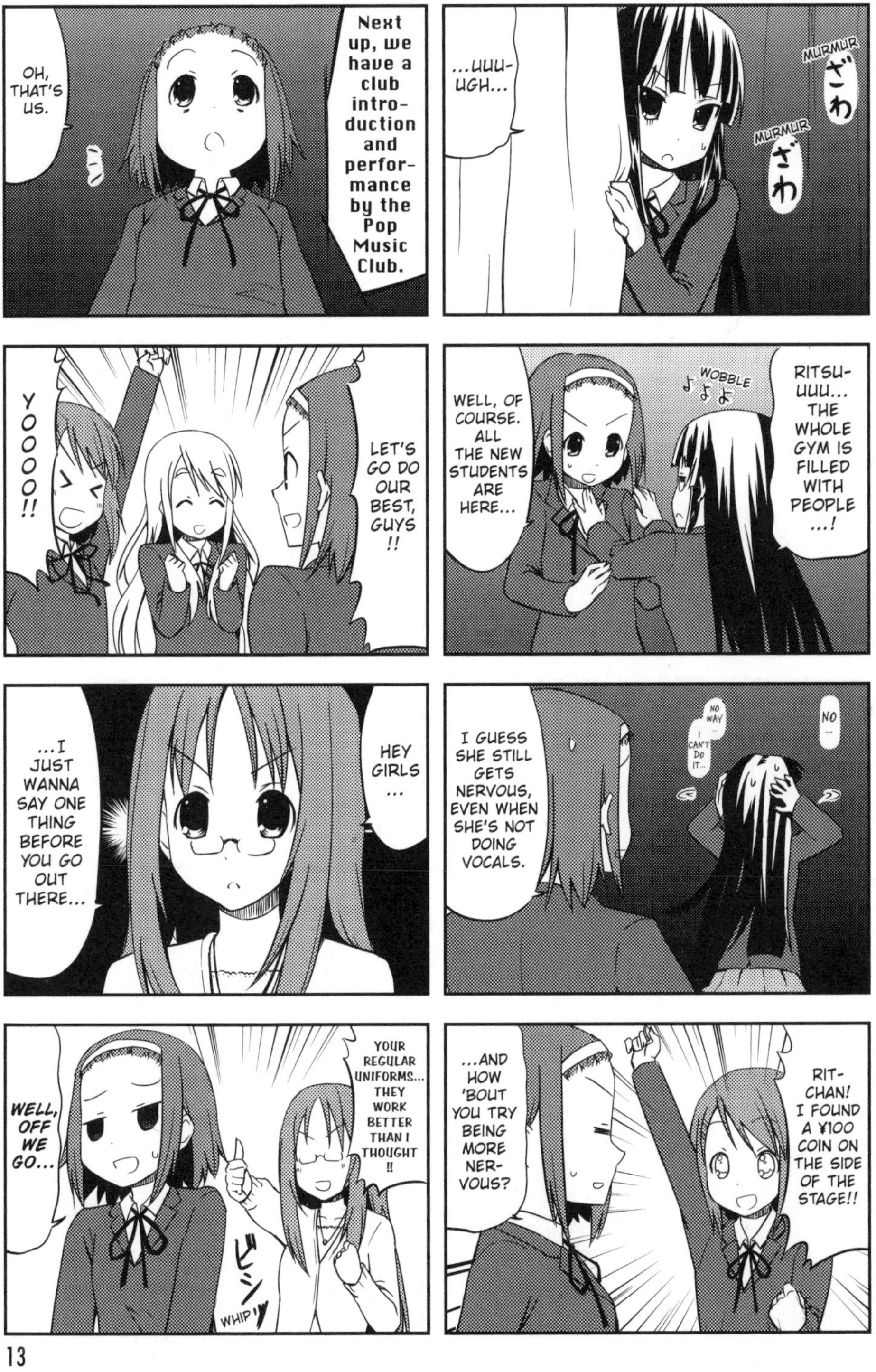
MURMUR ざわ
MURMUR ざわ
...UUU-UGH...
Next up, we have a club introduction and performance by the Pop Music Club.
OH, THAT'S US.
RITSU-UUU... THE WHOLE GYM IS FILLED WITH PEOPLE...!
WOBBLE よよよ
WELL, OF COURSE. ALL THE NEW STUDENTS ARE HERE...
LET'S GO DO OUR BEST, GUYS!!
YOOOOO!!
NO...
NO WAY...
I CAN'T DO IT...
I GUESS SHE STILL GETS NERVOUS, EVEN WHEN SHE'S NOT DOING VOCALS.
HEY GIRLS...
...I JUST WANNA SAY ONE THING BEFORE YOU GO OUT THERE...
RIT-CHAN! I FOUND A ¥100 COIN ON THE SIDE OF THE STAGE!!
...AND HOW 'BOUT YOU TRY BEING MORE NER-VOUS?
YOUR REGULAR UNIFORMS... THEY WORK BETTER THAN I THOUGHT!!
ビシッ WHIP!
WELL, OFF WE GO...

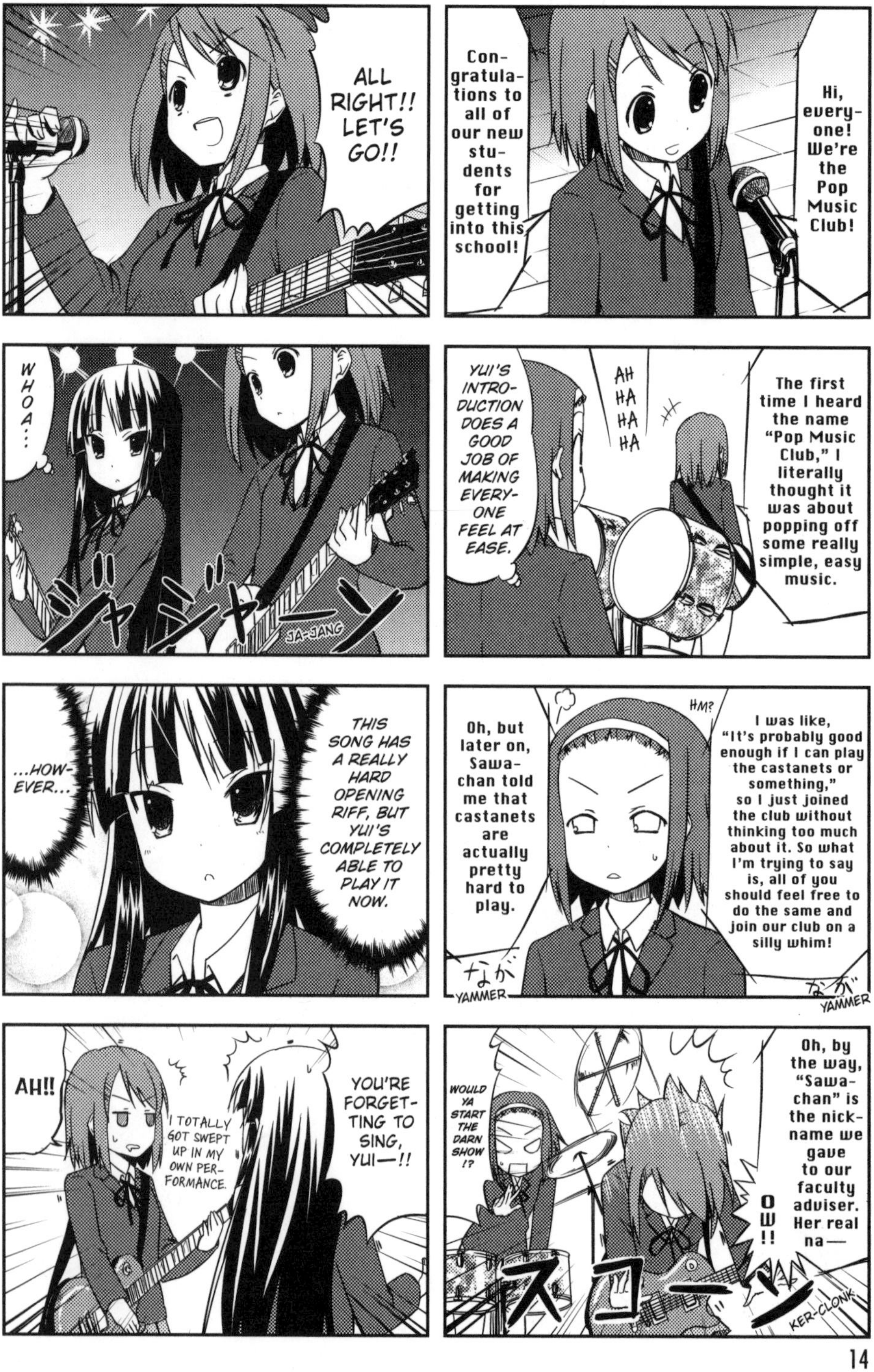
Hi, everyone! We're the Pop Music Club!
Congratulations to all of our new students for getting into this school!
ALL RIGHT!! LET'S GO!!
The first time I heard the name "Pop Music Club," I literally thought it was about popping off some really simple, easy music.
AH HA HA HA
YUI'S INTRODUCTION DOES A GOOD JOB OF MAKING EVERYONE FEEL AT EASE.
WHOA...
JA-JANG
HM?
I was like, "It's probably good enough if I can play the castanets or something," so I just joined the club without thinking too much about it. So what I'm trying to say is, all of you should feel free to do the same and join our club on a silly whim!
Oh, but later on, Sawa-chan told me that castanets are actually pretty hard to play.
なが
YAMMER
なが
YAMMER
THIS SONG HAS A REALLY HARD OPENING RIFF, BUT YUI'S COMPLETELY ABLE TO PLAY IT NOW.
...HOWEVER...
Oh, by the way, "Sawa-chan" is the nickname we gave to our faculty adviser. Her real na—
OW!!
WOULD YA START THE DARN SHOW!?
KER-CLONK
YOU'RE FORGETTING TO SING, YUI—!!
I TOTALLY GOT SWEPT UP IN MY OWN PERFORMANCE.
AH!!

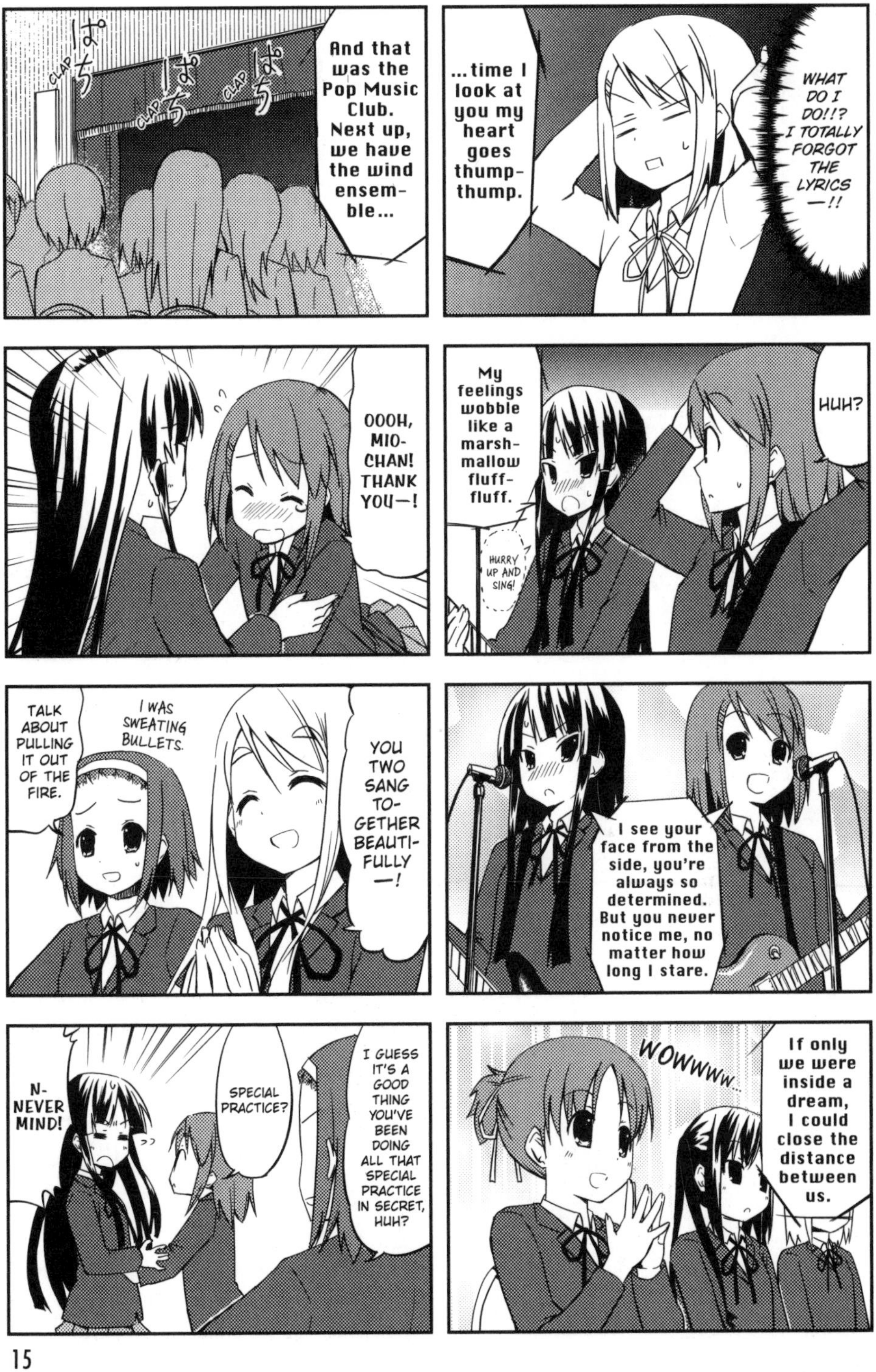
WHAT DO I DO!!? I TOTALLY FORGOT THE LYRICS—!!
...time I look at you my heart goes thump-thump.
HUH?
My feelings wobble like a marsh-mallow fluff-fluff.
HURRY UP AND SING!
I see your face from the side, you're always so determined. But you never notice me, no matter how long I stare.
If only we were inside a dream, I could close the distance between us.
WOWWWW...
ぱち CLAP
ぱち CLAP
ぱち CLAP
And that was the Pop Music Club. Next up, we have the wind ensem-ble...
OOOH, MIO-CHAN! THANK YOU—!
YOU TWO SANG TO-GETHER BEAUTI-FULLY—!
I WAS SWEATING BULLETS.
TALK ABOUT PULLING IT OUT OF THE FIRE.
I GUESS IT'S A GOOD THING YOU'VE BEEN DOING ALL THAT SPECIAL PRACTICE IN SECRET, HUH?
SPECIAL PRACTICE?
N-NEVER MIND!

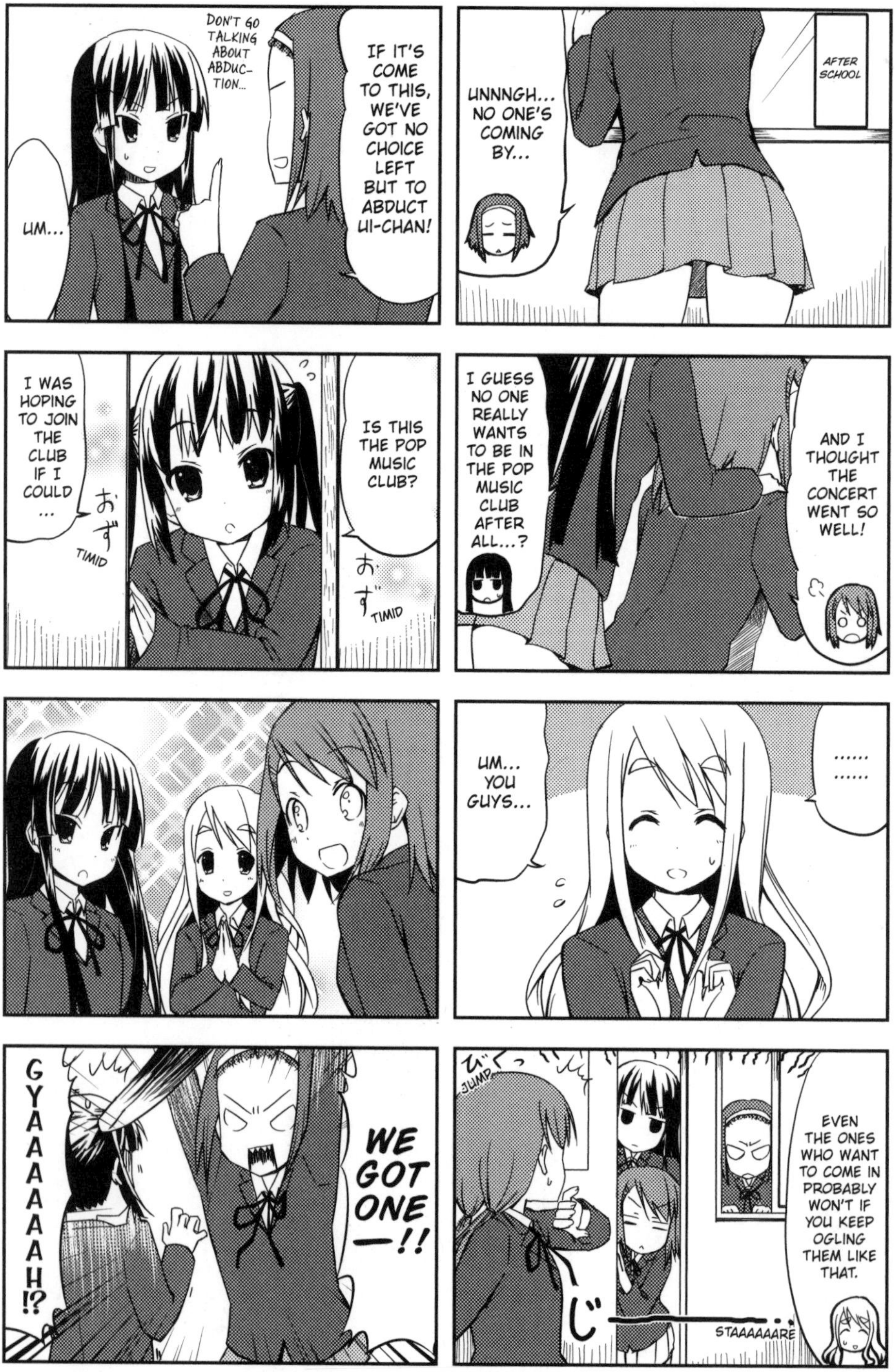

AFTER SCHOOL
UNNNGH... NO ONE'S COMING BY...
IF IT'S COME TO THIS, WE'VE GOT NO CHOICE LEFT BUT TO ABDUCT UI-CHAN!
DON'T GO TALKING ABOUT ABDUCTION...
UM...
AND I THOUGHT THE CONCERT WENT SO WELL!
I GUESS NO ONE REALLY WANTS TO BE IN THE POP MUSIC CLUB AFTER ALL...?
IS THIS THE POP MUSIC CLUB?
おず TIMID
I WAS HOPING TO JOIN THE CLUB IF I COULD...
おず TIMID
....
UM... YOU GUYS...
EVEN THE ONES WHO WANT TO COME IN PROBABLY WON'T IF YOU KEEP OGLING THEM LIKE THAT.
びくっ JUMP
じーーー STAAAAAARE
WE GOT ONE—!!
GYAAAAAAAH!?

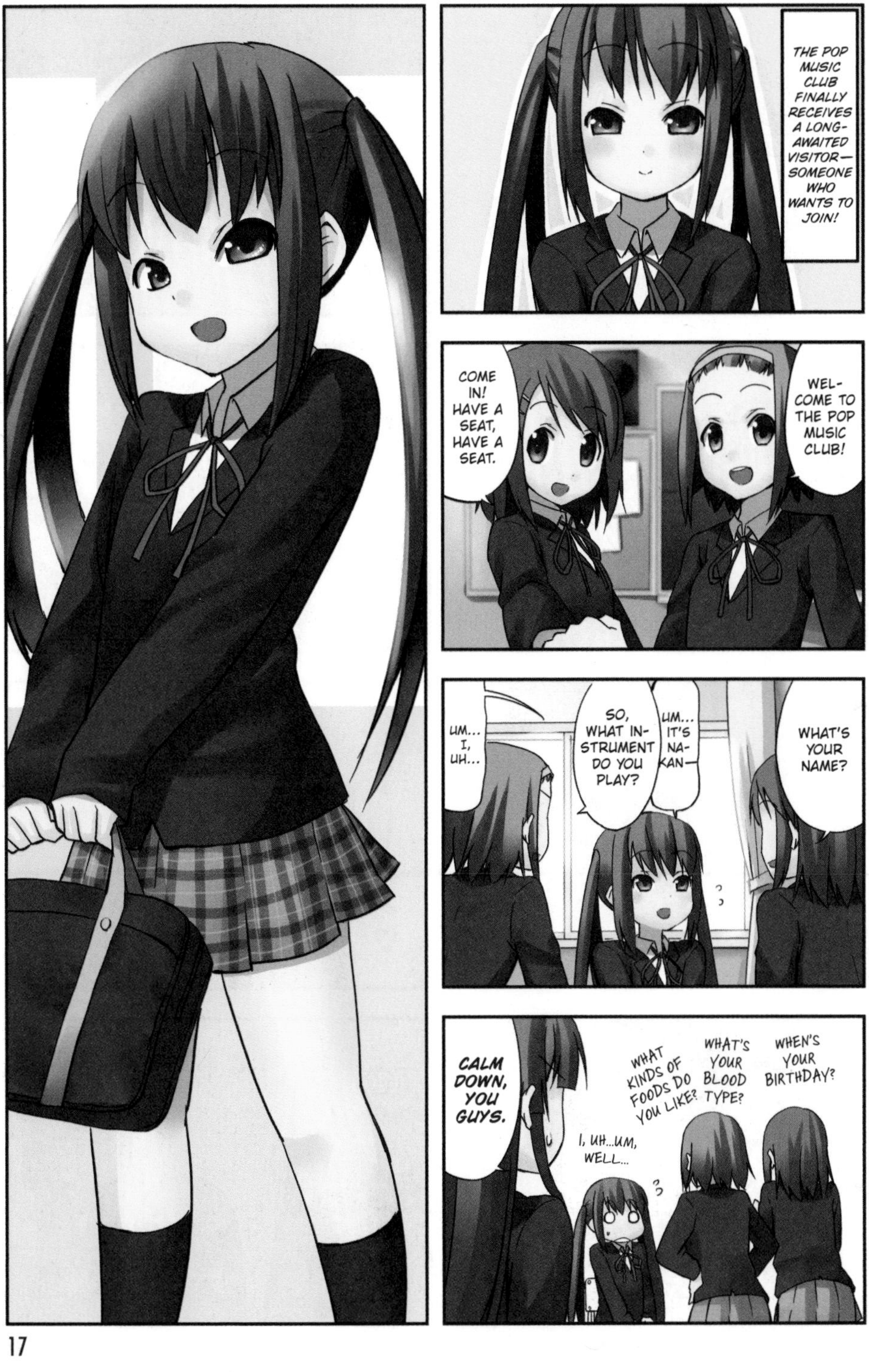
THE POP MUSIC CLUB FINALLY RECEIVES A LONG-AWAITED VISITOR—SOMEONE WHO WANTS TO JOIN!
WEL-COME TO THE POP MUSIC CLUB!
COME IN! HAVE A SEAT, HAVE A SEAT.
WHAT'S YOUR NAME?
UM... IT'S NA-KAN—
SO, WHAT IN-STRUMENT DO YOU PLAY?
UM... I, UH...
WHEN'S YOUR BIRTHDAY?
WHAT'S YOUR BLOOD TYPE?
WHAT KINDS OF FOODS DO YOU LIKE?
I, UH...UM, WELL...
CALM DOWN, YOU GUYS.

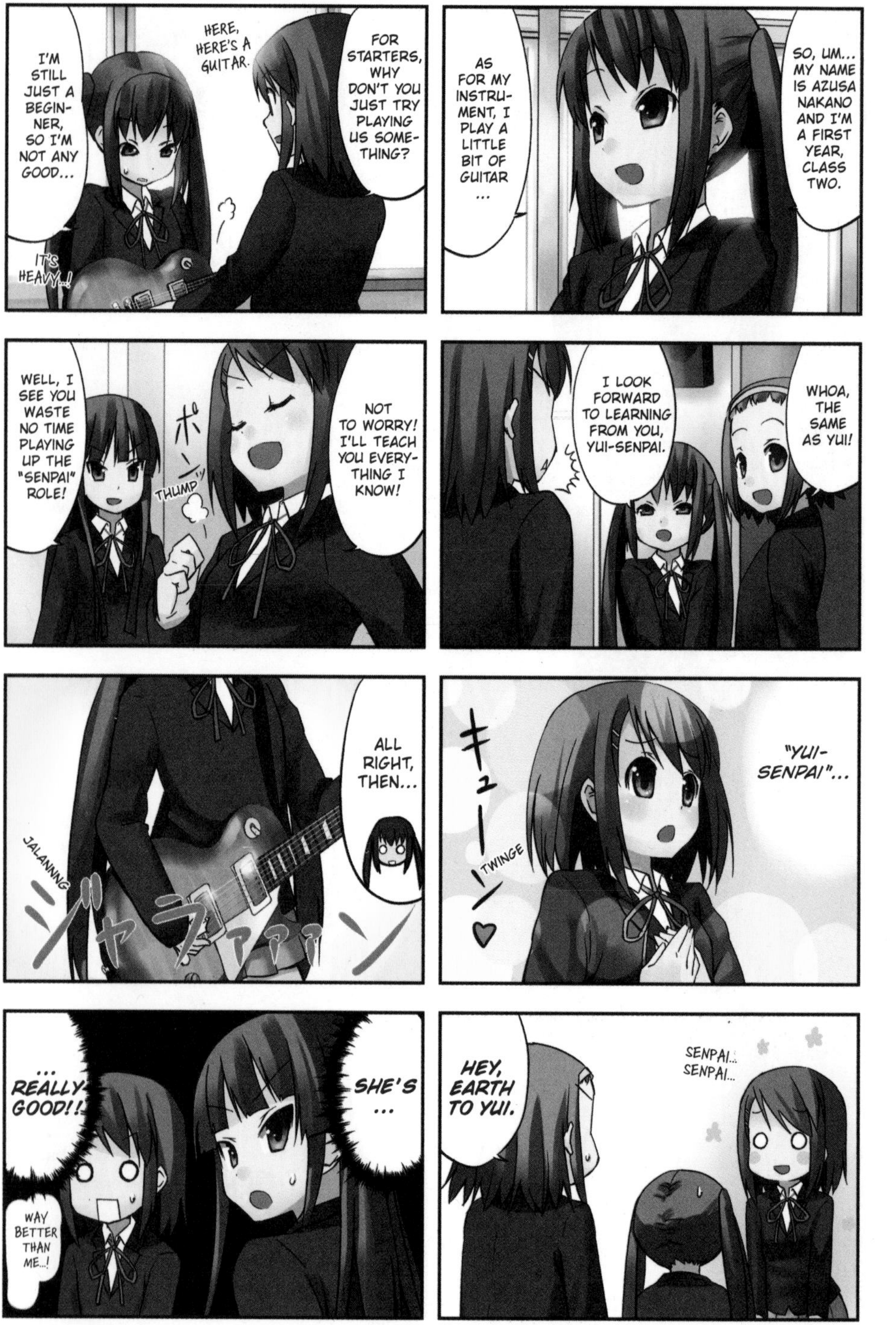
SO, UM... MY NAME IS AZUSA NAKANO AND I'M A FIRST YEAR, CLASS TWO.
AS FOR MY INSTRUMENT, I PLAY A LITTLE BIT OF GUITAR...
FOR STARTERS, WHY DON'T YOU JUST TRY PLAYING US SOMETHING?
HERE, HERE'S A GUITAR.
I'M STILL JUST A BEGINNER, SO I'M NOT ANY GOOD...
IT'S HEAVY...!
WHOA, THE SAME AS YUI!
I LOOK FORWARD TO LEARNING FROM YOU, YUI-SENPAI.
NOT TO WORRY! I'LL TEACH YOU EVERYTHING I KNOW!
ポン
THUMP
WELL, I SEE YOU WASTE NO TIME PLAYING UP THE "SENPAI" ROLE!
"YUI-SENPAI"...
キュー
TWINGE
ALL RIGHT, THEN...
ジャラァァァン
JALANNNG
SENPAI... SENPAI...
HEY, EARTH TO YUI.
SHE'S...
...REALLY GOOD!!
WAY BETTER THAN ME...!

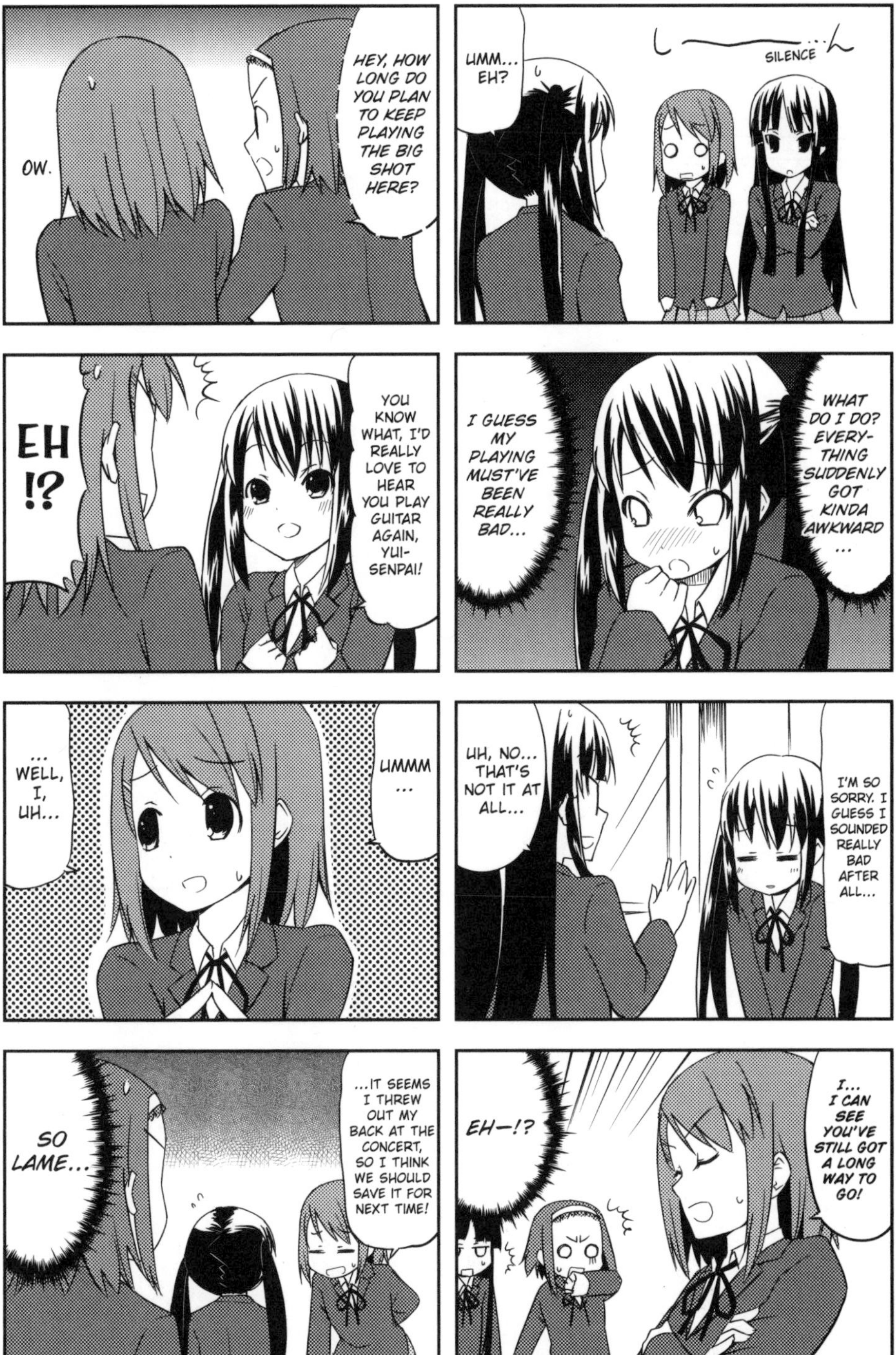
し——…ん
SILENCE
UMM... EH?
WHAT DO I DO? EVERY-THING SUDDENLY GOT KINDA AWKWARD...
I GUESS MY PLAYING MUST'VE BEEN REALLY BAD...
I'M SO SORRY. I GUESS I SOUNDED REALLY BAD AFTER ALL...
UH, NO... THAT'S NOT IT AT ALL...
I... I CAN SEE YOU'VE STILL GOT A LONG WAY TO GO!
EH—!?
HEY, HOW LONG DO YOU PLAN TO KEEP PLAYING THE BIG SHOT HERE?
OW.
YOU KNOW WHAT, I'D REALLY LOVE TO HEAR YOU PLAY GUITAR AGAIN, YUI-SENPAI!
EH !?
UMMM ...
... WELL, I, UH...
...IT SEEMS I THREW OUT MY BACK AT THE CONCERT, SO I THINK WE SHOULD SAVE IT FOR NEXT TIME!
SO LAME...

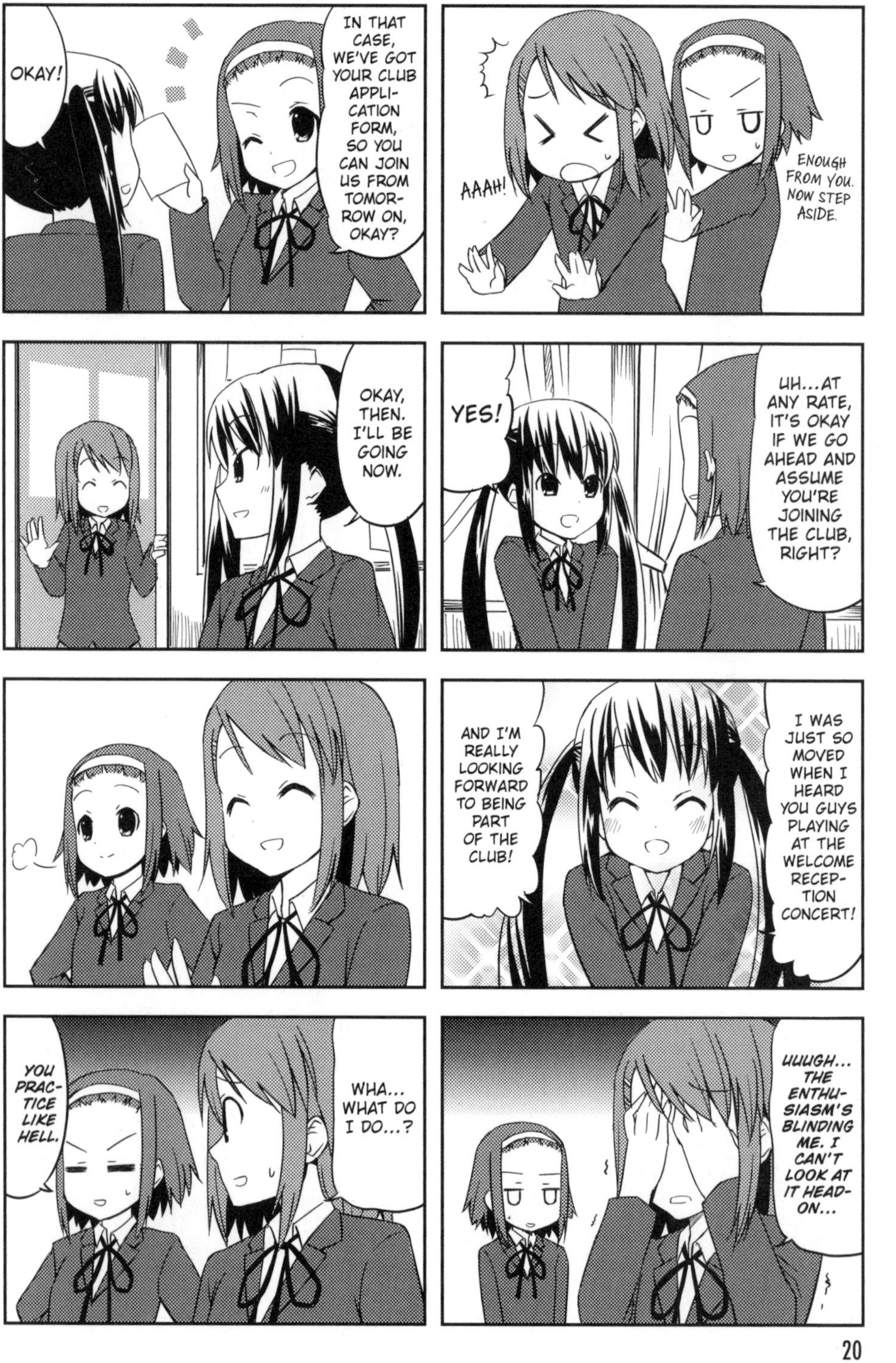
ENOUGH FROM YOU. NOW STEP ASIDE.
AAAH!
IN THAT CASE, WE'VE GOT YOUR CLUB APPLI-CATION FORM, SO YOU CAN JOIN US FROM TOMOR-ROW ON, OKAY?
OKAY!
UH...AT ANY RATE, IT'S OKAY IF WE GO AHEAD AND ASSUME YOU'RE JOINING THE CLUB, RIGHT?
YES!
OKAY, THEN. I'LL BE GOING NOW.
I WAS JUST SO MOVED WHEN I HEARD YOU GUYS PLAYING AT THE WELCOME RECEP-TION CONCERT!
AND I'M REALLY LOOKING FORWARD TO BEING PART OF THE CLUB!
UUUGH... THE ENTHU-SIASM'S BLINDING ME. I CAN'T LOOK AT IT HEAD-ON...
WHA... WHAT DO I DO...?
YOU PRAC-TICE LIKE HELL.

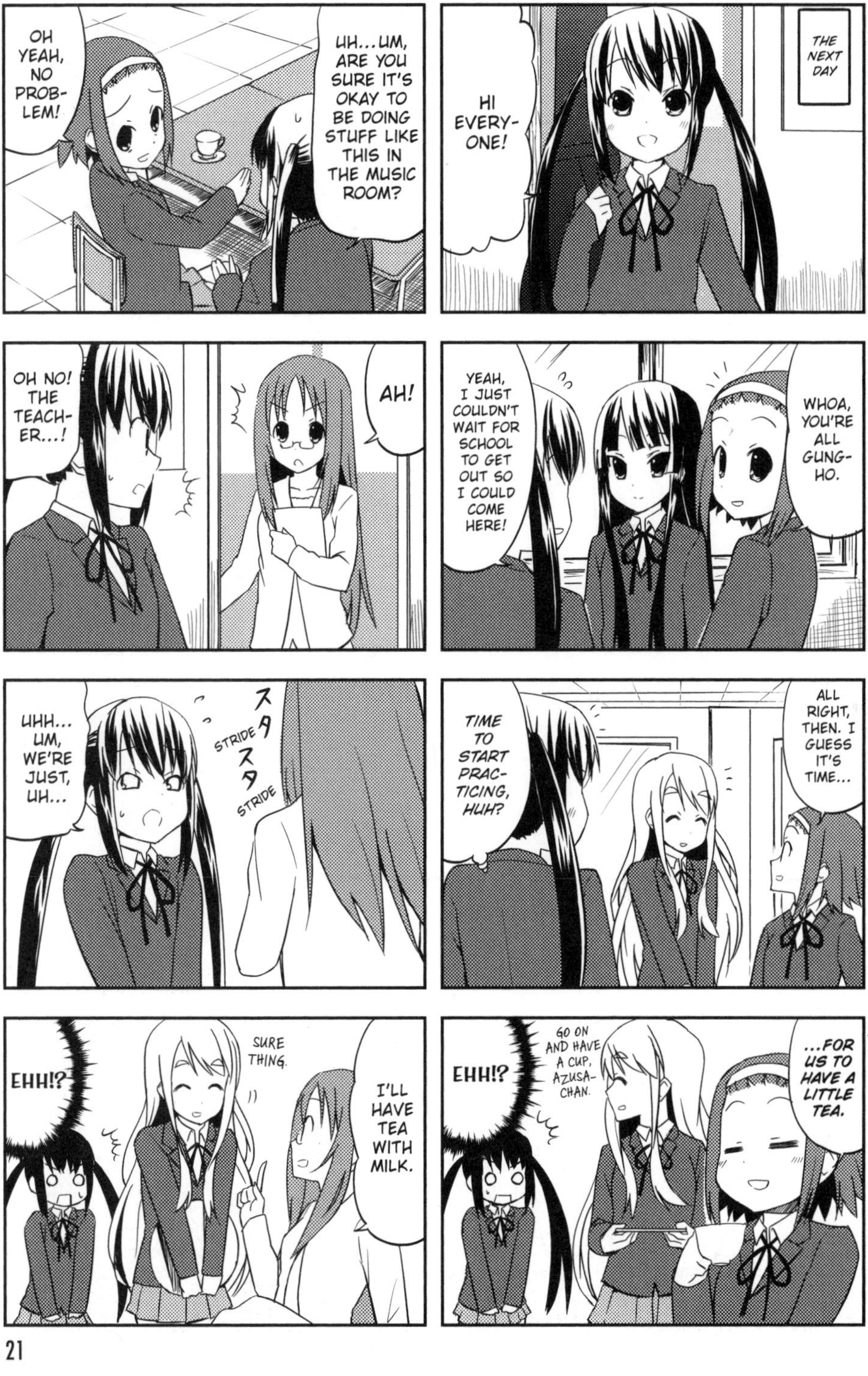
THE NEXT DAY
HI EVERYONE!
UH...UM, ARE YOU SURE IT'S OKAY TO BE DOING STUFF LIKE THIS IN THE MUSIC ROOM?
OH YEAH, NO PROBLEM!
WHOA, YOU'RE ALL GUNG-HO.
YEAH, I JUST COULDN'T WAIT FOR SCHOOL TO GET OUT SO I COULD COME HERE!
AH!
OH NO! THE TEACHER...!
ALL RIGHT, THEN. I GUESS IT'S TIME...
TIME TO START PRACTICING, HUH?
スタ STRIDE
スタ STRIDE
UHH... UM, WE'RE JUST, UH...
...FOR US TO HAVE A LITTLE TEA.
GO ON AND HAVE A CUP, AZUSA-CHAN.
EHH!?
I'LL HAVE TEA WITH MILK.
SURE THING.
EHH!?

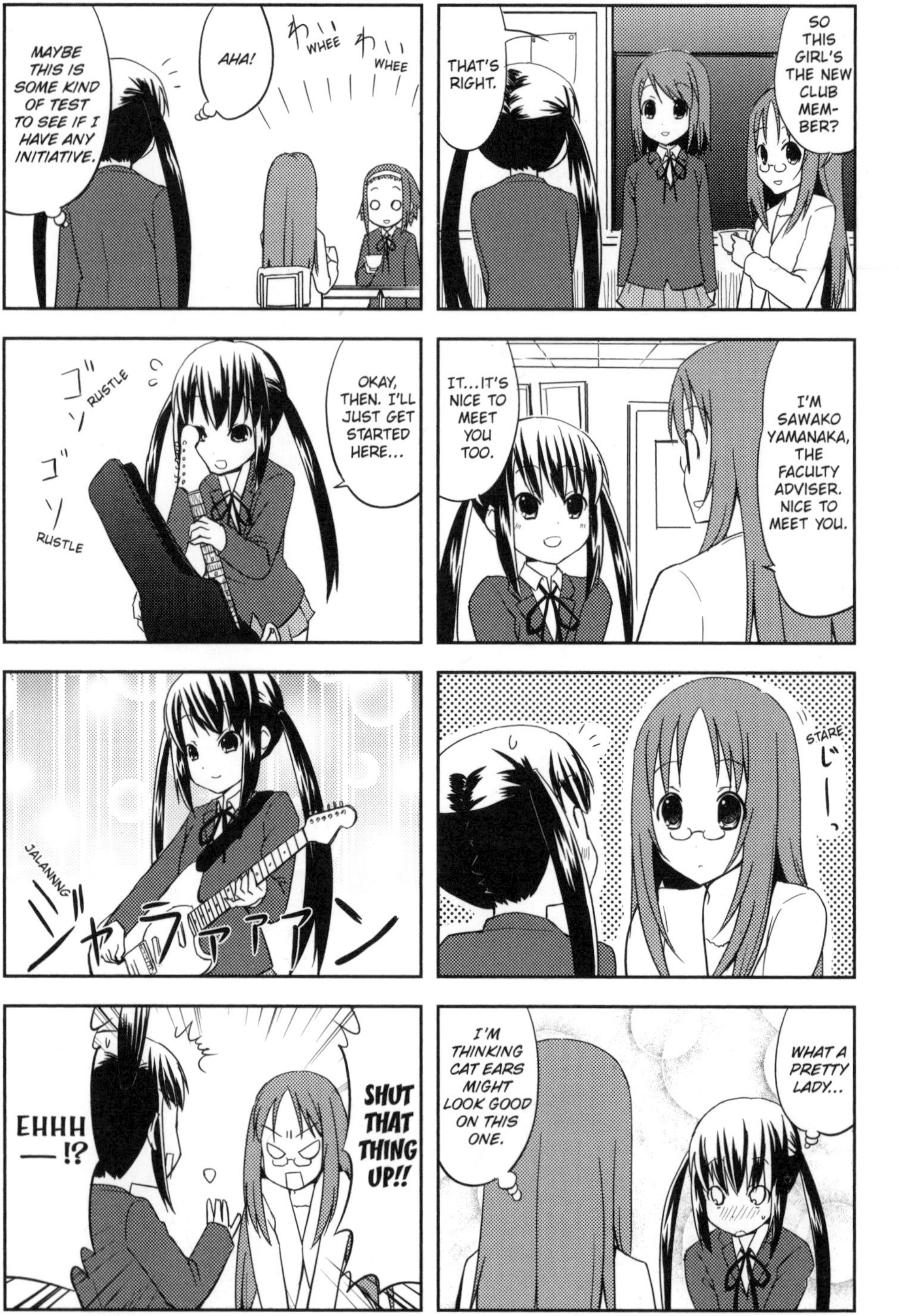
SO THIS GIRL'S THE NEW CLUB MEMBER?
THAT'S RIGHT.
わい WHEE
わい WHEE
AHA!
MAYBE THIS IS SOME KIND OF TEST TO SEE IF I HAVE ANY INITIATIVE.
I'M SAWAKO YAMANAKA, THE FACULTY ADVISER. NICE TO MEET YOU.
IT...IT'S NICE TO MEET YOU TOO.
OKAY, THEN. I'LL JUST GET STARTED HERE...
ゴソ RUSTLE
ゴソ RUSTLE
じーっ STARE
JALANNNG
ジャラァァアン
WHAT A PRETTY LADY...
I'M THINKING CAT EARS MIGHT LOOK GOOD ON THIS ONE.
SHUT THAT THING UP!!
EHHH—!?

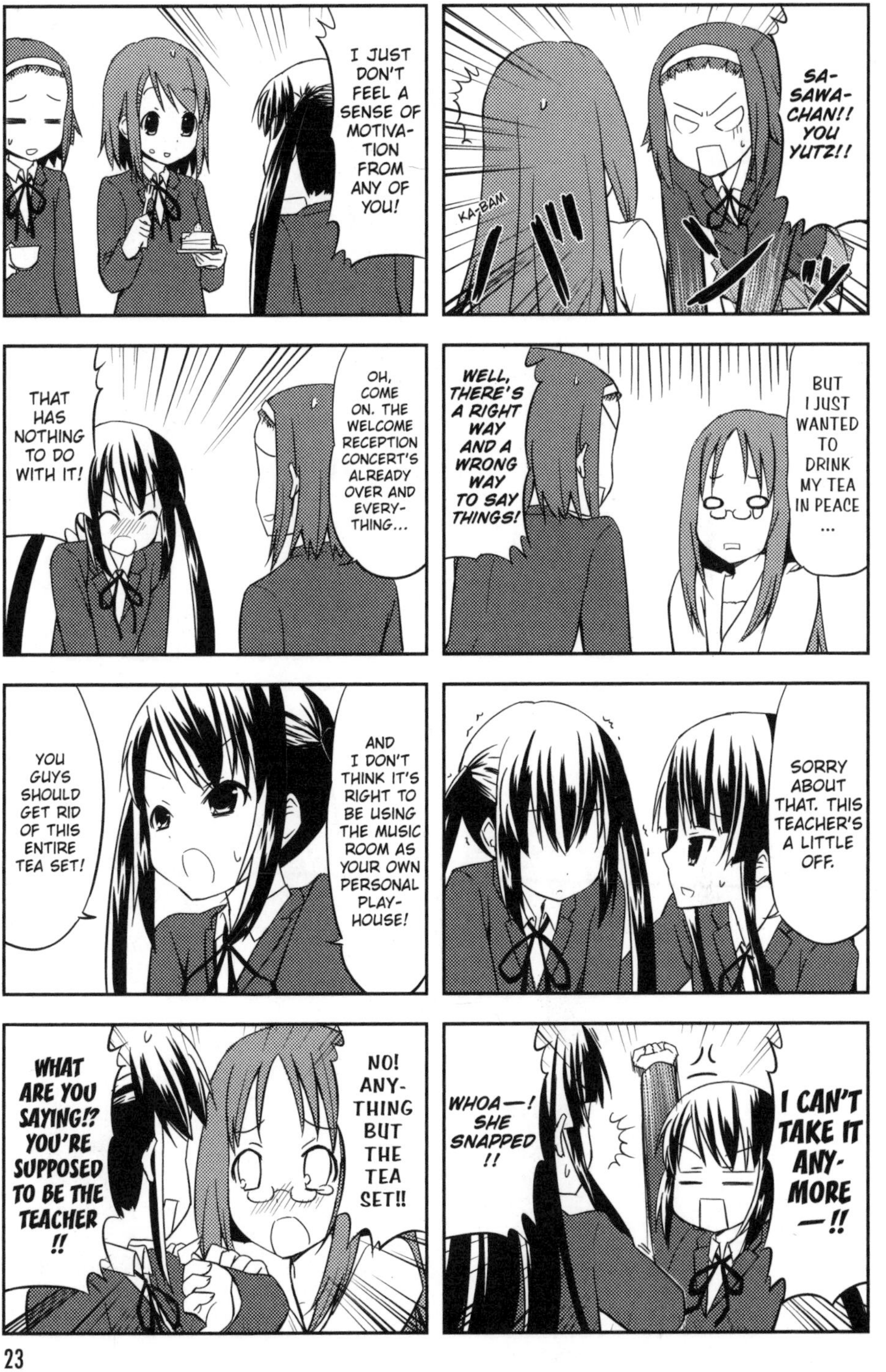
I JUST DON'T FEEL A SENSE OF MOTIVATION FROM ANY OF YOU!
OH, COME ON. THE WELCOME RECEPTION CONCERT'S ALREADY OVER AND EVERYTHING...
THAT HAS NOTHING TO DO WITH IT!
AND I DON'T THINK IT'S RIGHT TO BE USING THE MUSIC ROOM AS YOUR OWN PERSONAL PLAYHOUSE!
YOU GUYS SHOULD GET RID OF THIS ENTIRE TEA SET!
NO! ANYTHING BUT THE TEA SET!!
WHAT ARE YOU SAYING!? YOU'RE SUPPOSED TO BE THE TEACHER!!
SA-SAWA-CHAN!! YOU YUTZ!!
KA-BAM
BUT I JUST WANTED TO DRINK MY TEA IN PEACE...
WELL, THERE'S A RIGHT WAY AND A WRONG WAY TO SAY THINGS!
SORRY ABOUT THAT. THIS TEACHER'S A LITTLE OFF.
I CAN'T TAKE IT ANYMORE—!!
WHOA—! SHE SNAPPED!!

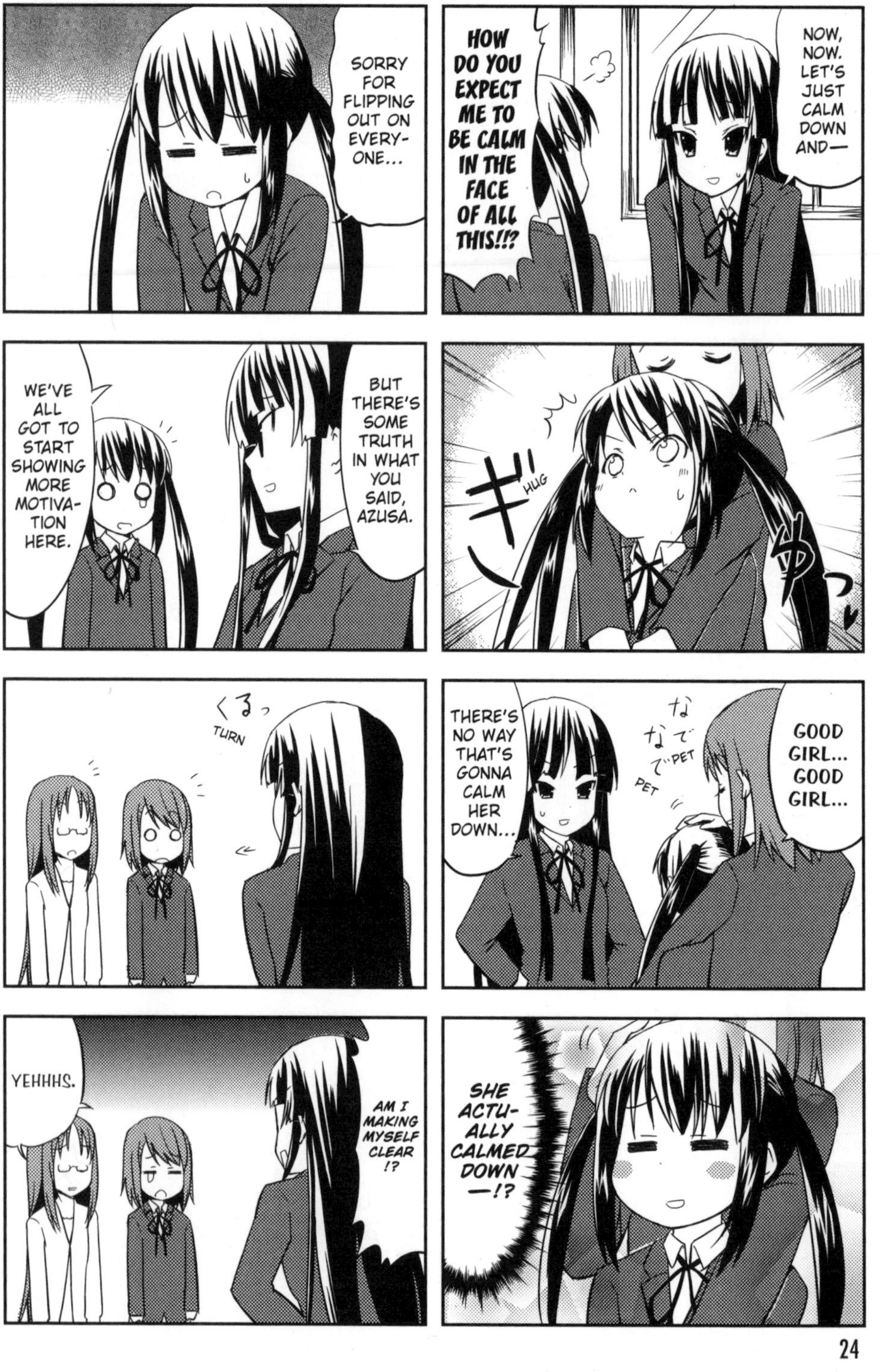
NOW, NOW. LET'S JUST CALM DOWN AND—
HOW DO YOU EXPECT ME TO BE CALM IN THE FACE OF ALL THIS!!?
SORRY FOR FLIPPING OUT ON EVERY-ONE...
HUG
BUT THERE'S SOME TRUTH IN WHAT YOU SAID, AZUSA.
WE'VE ALL GOT TO START SHOWING MORE MOTIVA-TION HERE.
GOOD GIRL... GOOD GIRL...
なでなで
PET PET
THERE'S NO WAY THAT'S GONNA CALM HER DOWN...
くるっ
TURN
SHE ACTU-ALLY CALMED DOWN—!?
AM I MAKING MYSELF CLEAR!?
YEHHHS.

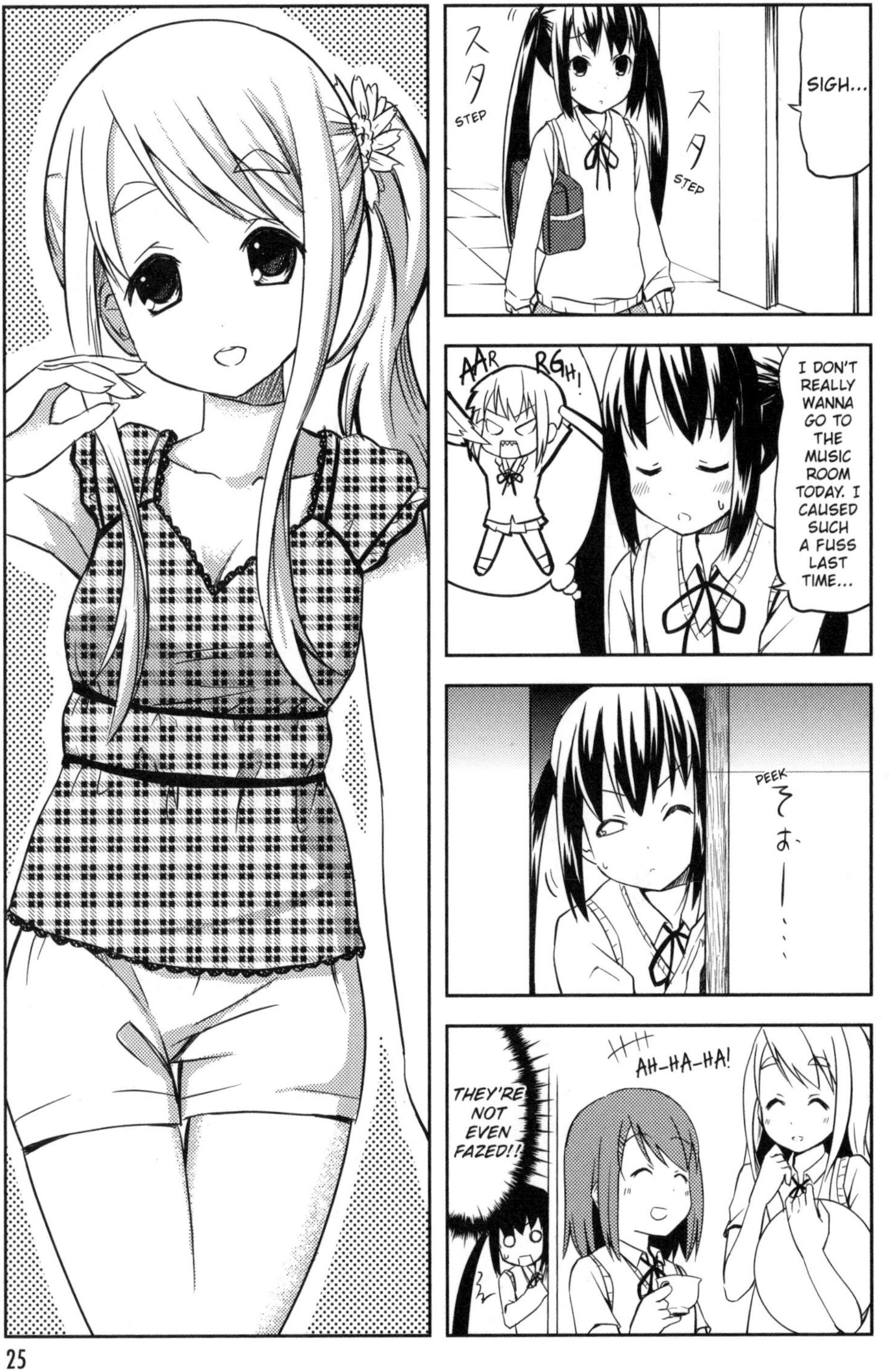
SIGH...
スタ
STEP
スタ
STEP
I DON'T REALLY WANNA GO TO THE MUSIC ROOM TODAY. I CAUSED SUCH A FUSS LAST TIME...
AARRGH!
PEEK
そぉー...
AH-HA-HA!
THEY'RE NOT EVEN FAZED!!

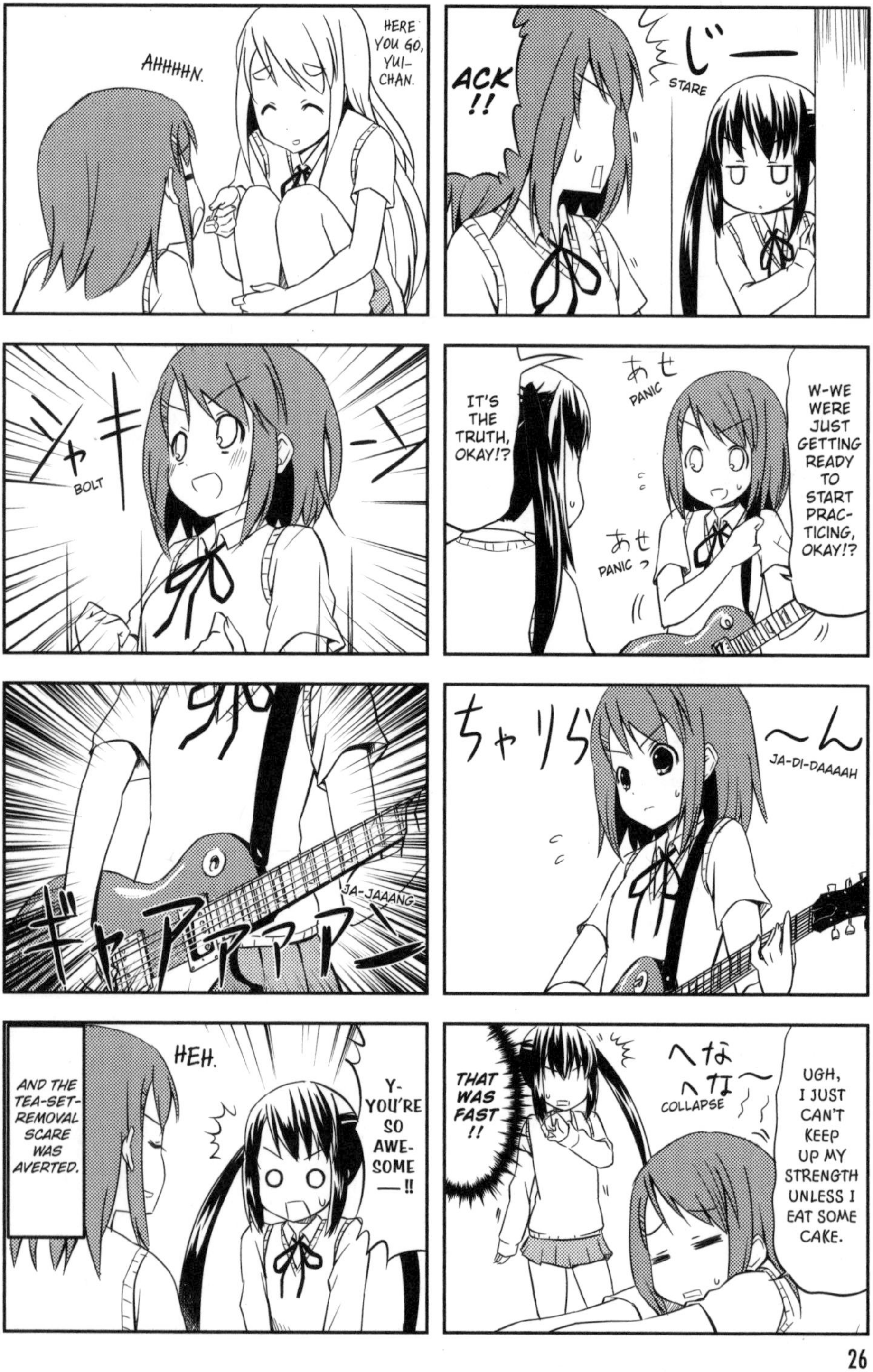
じー
STARE
ACK!!
HERE YOU GO, YUI-CHAN.
AHHHHN.
W-WE WERE JUST GETTING READY TO START PRACTICING, OKAY!?
あせ
PANIC
IT'S THE TRUTH, OKAY!?
あせ
PANIC
ジャキーン
BOLT
ちゃりら〜ん
JA-DI-DAAAAH
ギャアアアアン
JA-JAAANG
UGH, I JUST CAN'T KEEP UP MY STRENGTH UNLESS I EAT SOME CAKE.
へなへな〜
COLLAPSE
THAT WAS FAST!!
Y-YOU'RE SO AWESOME—!!
HEH.
AND THE TEA-SET-REMOVAL SCARE WAS AVERTED.

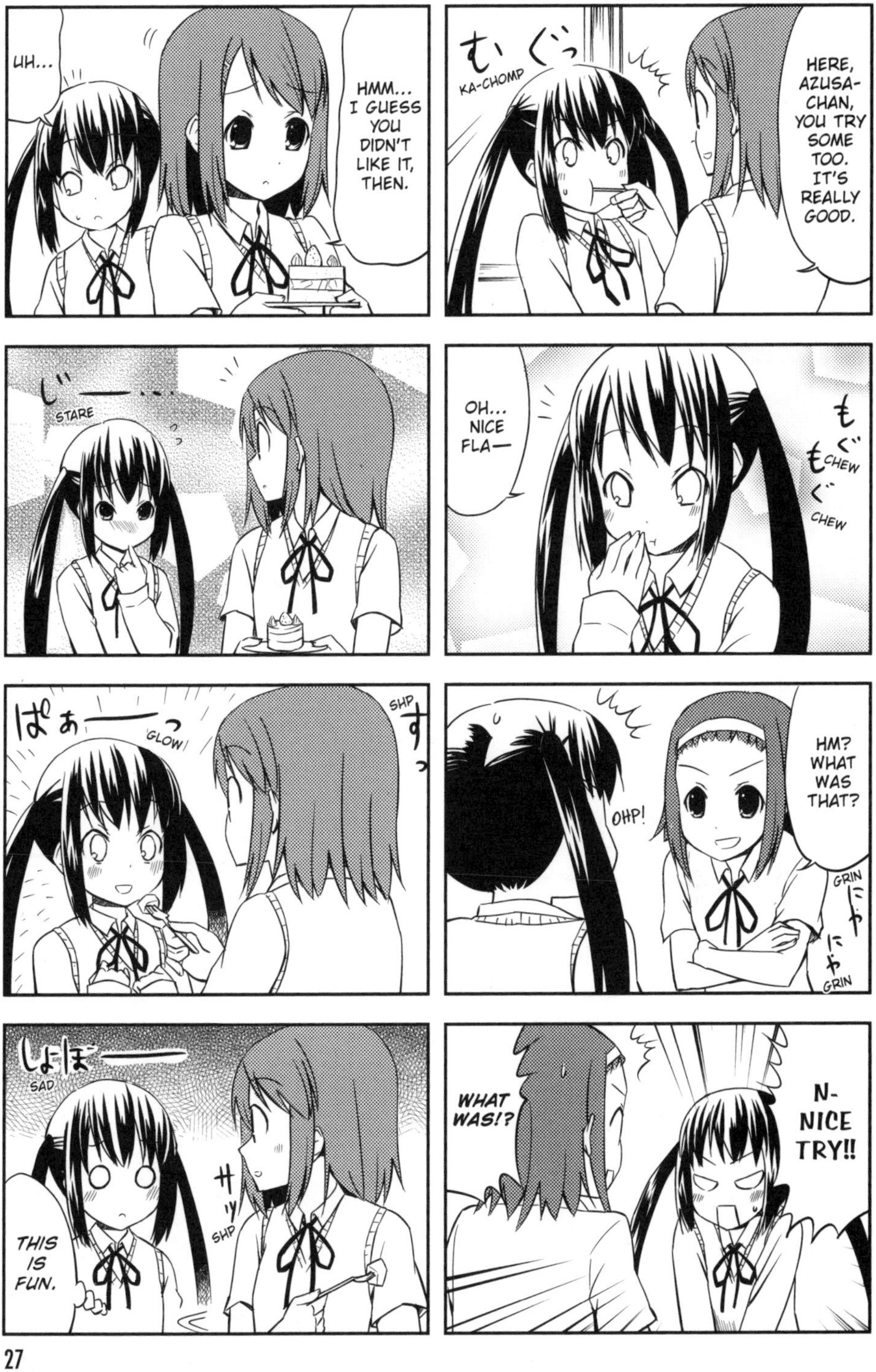
HERE, AZUSA-CHAN, YOU TRY SOME TOO. IT'S REALLY GOOD.
むぐっ
KA-CHOMP
HMM... I GUESS YOU DIDN'T LIKE IT, THEN.
UH...
もぐもぐ
CHEW CHEW
OH... NICE FLA—
じー...
STARE
HM? WHAT WAS THAT?
にやにや
GRIN GRIN
OHP!
すっ
SHP
ぱぁーっ
GLOW
N-NICE TRY!!
WHAT WAS!?
しょぼー
SAD
サッ
SHP
THIS IS FUN.

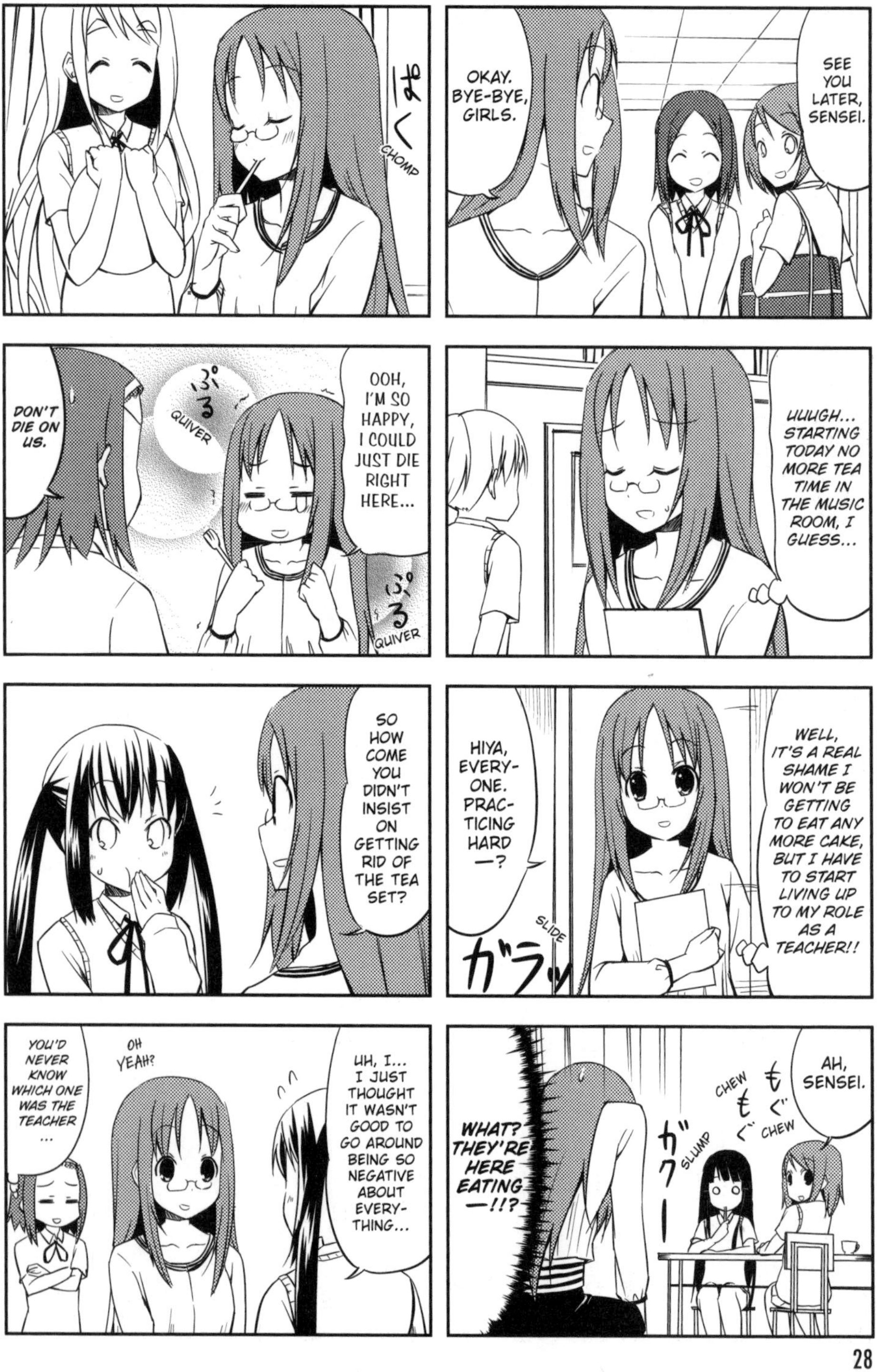
SEE YOU LATER, SENSEI.
OKAY. BYE-BYE, GIRLS.
UUUGH... STARTING TODAY NO MORE TEA TIME IN THE MUSIC ROOM, I GUESS...
WELL, IT'S A REAL SHAME I WON'T BE GETTING TO EAT ANY MORE CAKE, BUT I HAVE TO START LIVING UP TO MY ROLE AS A TEACHER!!
HIYA, EVERY-ONE. PRAC-TICING HARD—?
ガラッ
SLIDE
AH, SENSEI.
もぐもぐ
CHEW CHEW
ガクー
SLUMP
WHAT? THEY'RE HERE EATING—!!?
ぱく
CHOMP
OOH, I'M SO HAPPY, I COULD JUST DIE RIGHT HERE...
ぷる
QUIVER
ぷる
QUIVER
DON'T DIE ON US.
SO HOW COME YOU DIDN'T INSIST ON GETTING RID OF THE TEA SET?
UH, I... I JUST THOUGHT IT WASN'T GOOD TO GO AROUND BEING SO NEGATIVE ABOUT EVERY-THING...
OH YEAH?
YOU'D NEVER KNOW WHICH ONE WAS THE TEACHER...

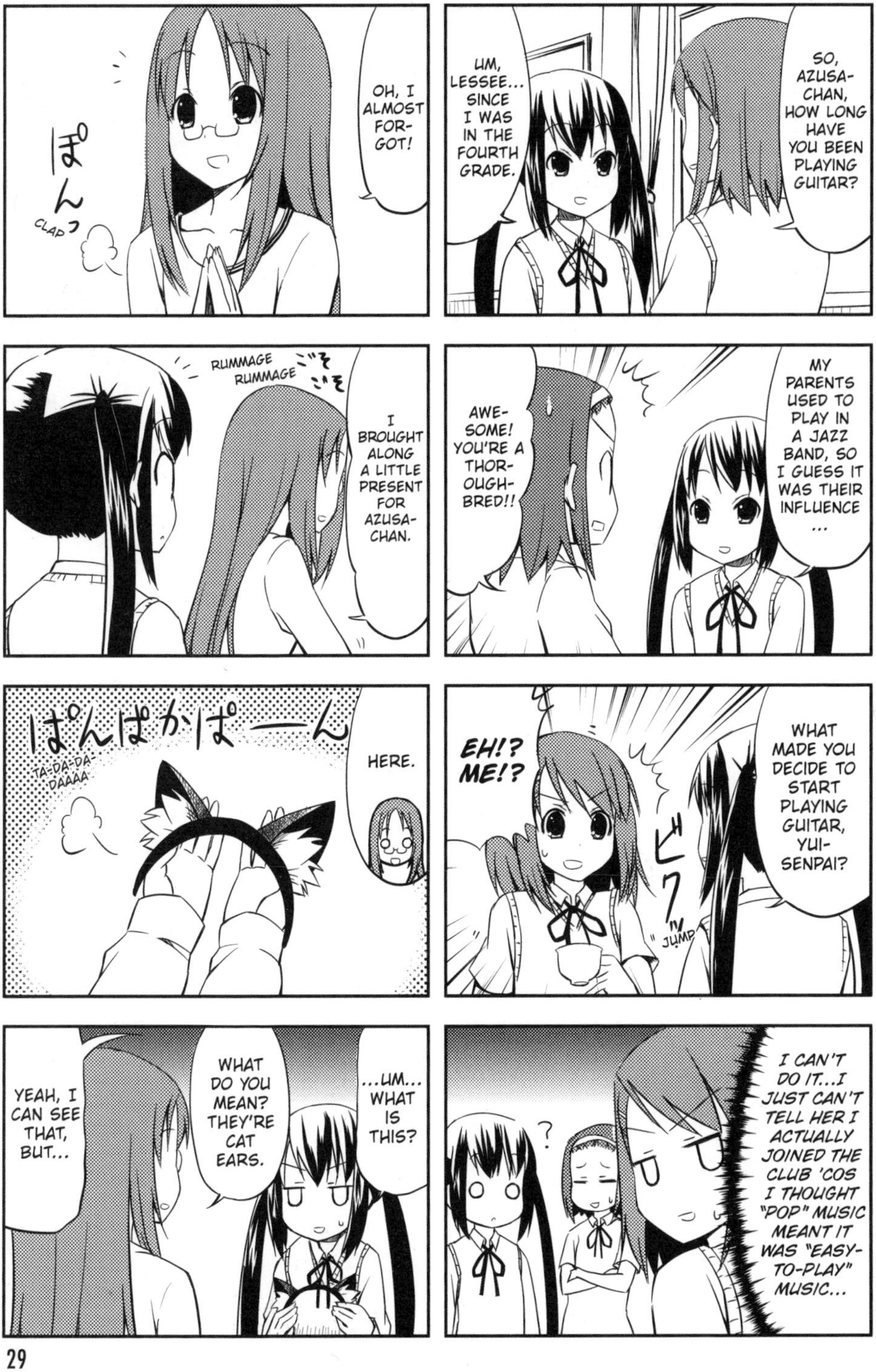
SO, AZUSA-CHAN, HOW LONG HAVE YOU BEEN PLAYING GUITAR?
UM, LESSEE... SINCE I WAS IN THE FOURTH GRADE.
OH, I ALMOST FOR-GOT!
ぽんっ
CLAP
MY PARENTS USED TO PLAY IN A JAZZ BAND, SO I GUESS IT WAS THEIR INFLUENCE...
AWE-SOME! YOU'RE A THOR-OUGH-BRED!!
I BROUGHT ALONG A LITTLE PRESENT FOR AZUSA-CHAN.
ごそごそ
RUMMAGE RUMMAGE
WHAT MADE YOU DECIDE TO START PLAYING GUITAR, YUI-SENPAI?
EH!? ME!?
ビクッ
JUMP
HERE.
ぱんぱかぱーん
TA-DA-DA-DAAAA
?
I CAN'T DO IT...I JUST CAN'T TELL HER I ACTUALLY JOINED THE CLUB 'COS I THOUGHT "POP" MUSIC MEANT IT WAS "EASY-TO-PLAY" MUSIC...
...UM... WHAT IS THIS?
WHAT DO YOU MEAN? THEY'RE CAT EARS.
YEAH, I CAN SEE THAT, BUT...

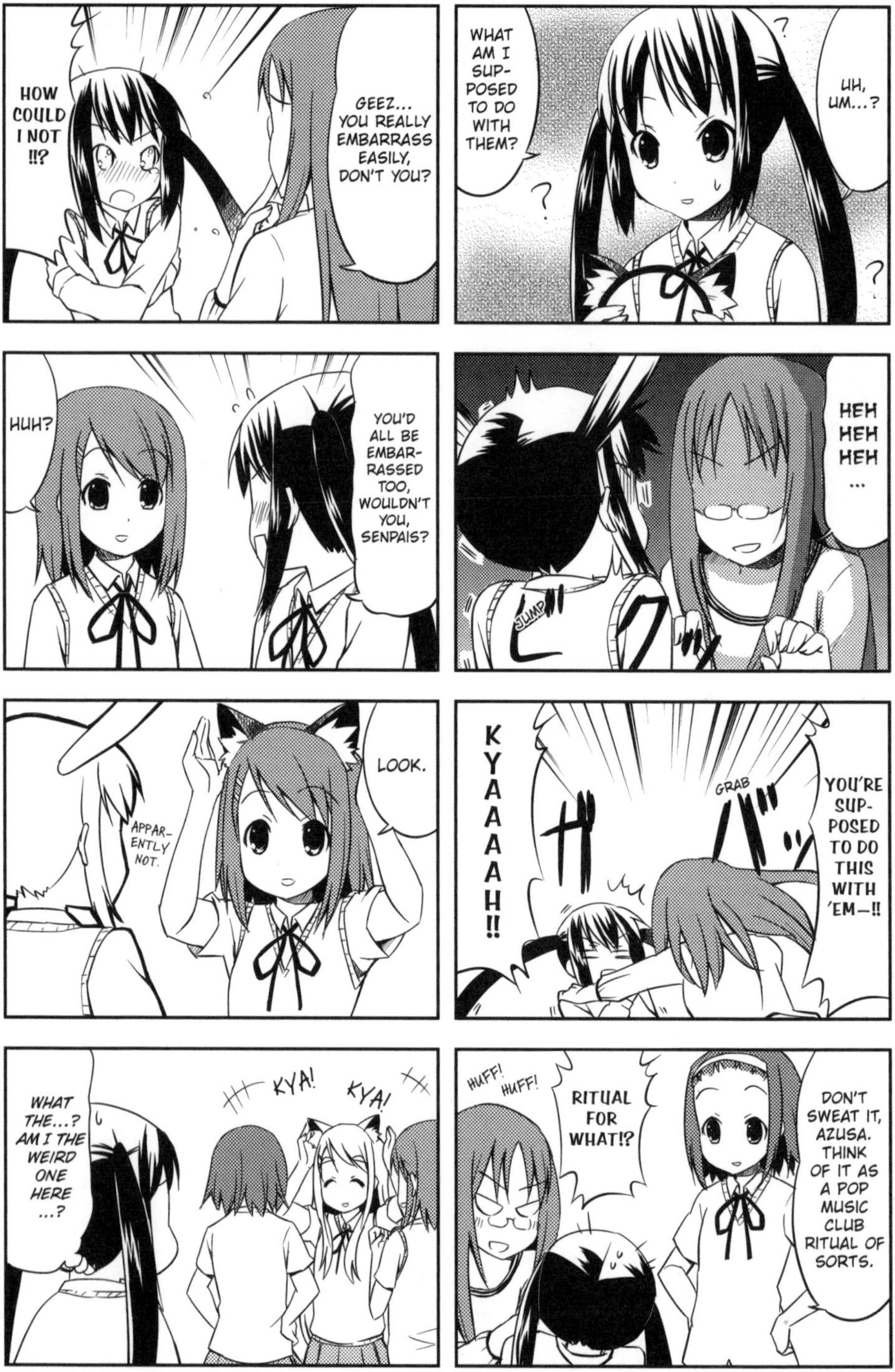

UH, UM...?
WHAT AM I SUPPOSED TO DO WITH THEM?
HEH HEH HEH ...
JUMP
YOU'RE SUPPOSED TO DO THIS WITH 'EM—!!
GRAB
KYAAAAAH!!
DON'T SWEAT IT, AZUSA. THINK OF IT AS A POP MUSIC CLUB RITUAL OF SORTS.
RITUAL FOR WHAT!?
HUFF! HUFF!
GEEZ... YOU REALLY EMBARRASS EASILY, DON'T YOU?
HOW COULD I NOT !!?
YOU'D ALL BE EMBARRASSED TOO, WOULDN'T YOU, SENPAIS?
HUH?
LOOK.
APPARENTLY NOT.
KYA! KYA!
WHAT THE...? AM I THE WEIRD ONE HERE ...?

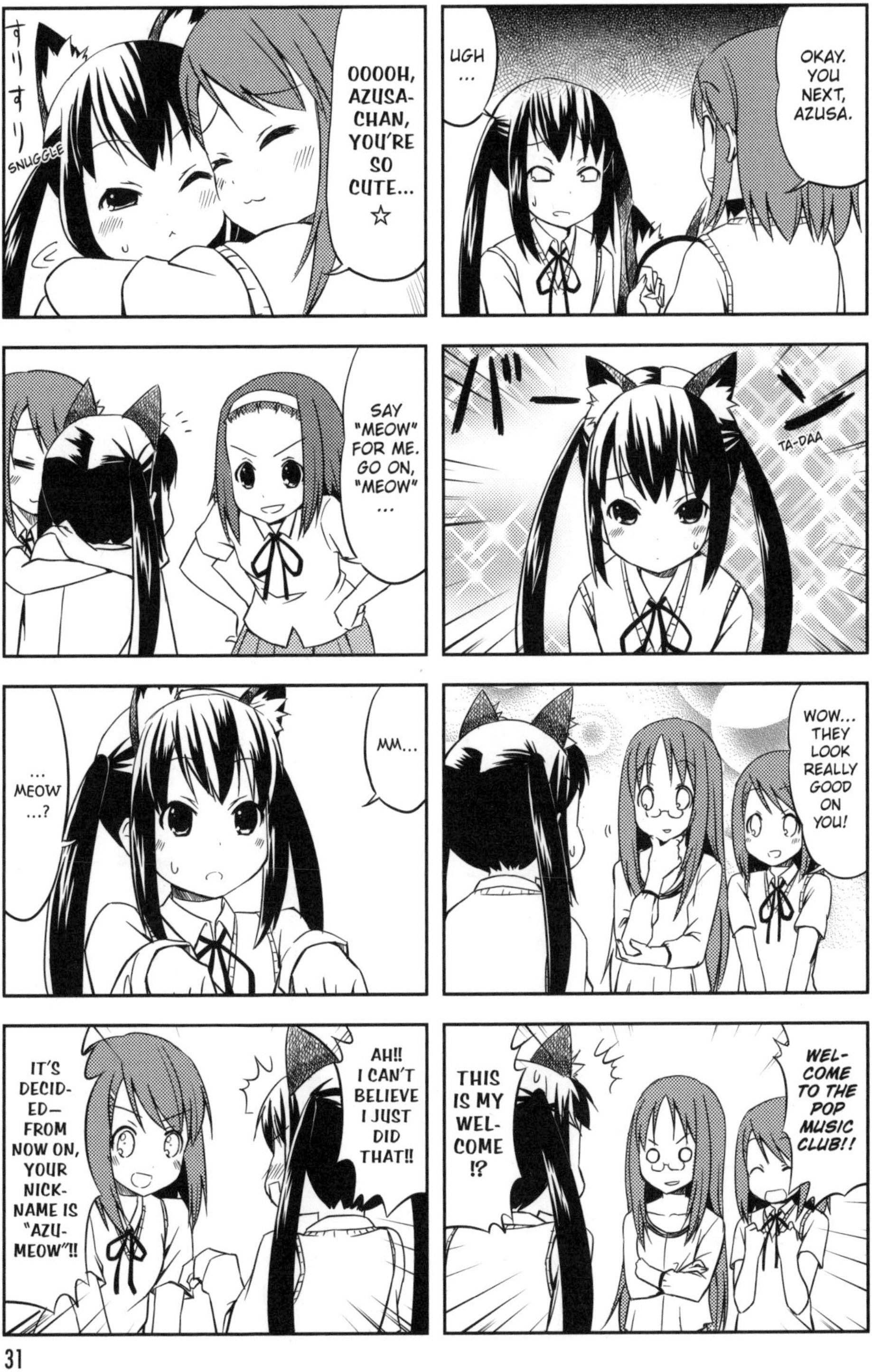
OKAY. YOU NEXT, AZUSA.
UGH ...
OOOOH, AZUSA-CHAN, YOU'RE SO CUTE... ☆
すりすり
SNUGGLE
バー
TA-DAA
SAY "MEOW" FOR ME. GO ON, "MEOW" ...
WOW... THEY LOOK REALLY GOOD ON YOU!
MM...
... MEOW ...?
WEL-COME TO THE POP MUSIC CLUB!!
THIS IS MY WEL-COME !?
AH!! I CAN'T BELIEVE I JUST DID THAT!!
IT'S DECID-ED— FROM NOW ON, YOUR NICK-NAME IS "AZU-MEOW"!!

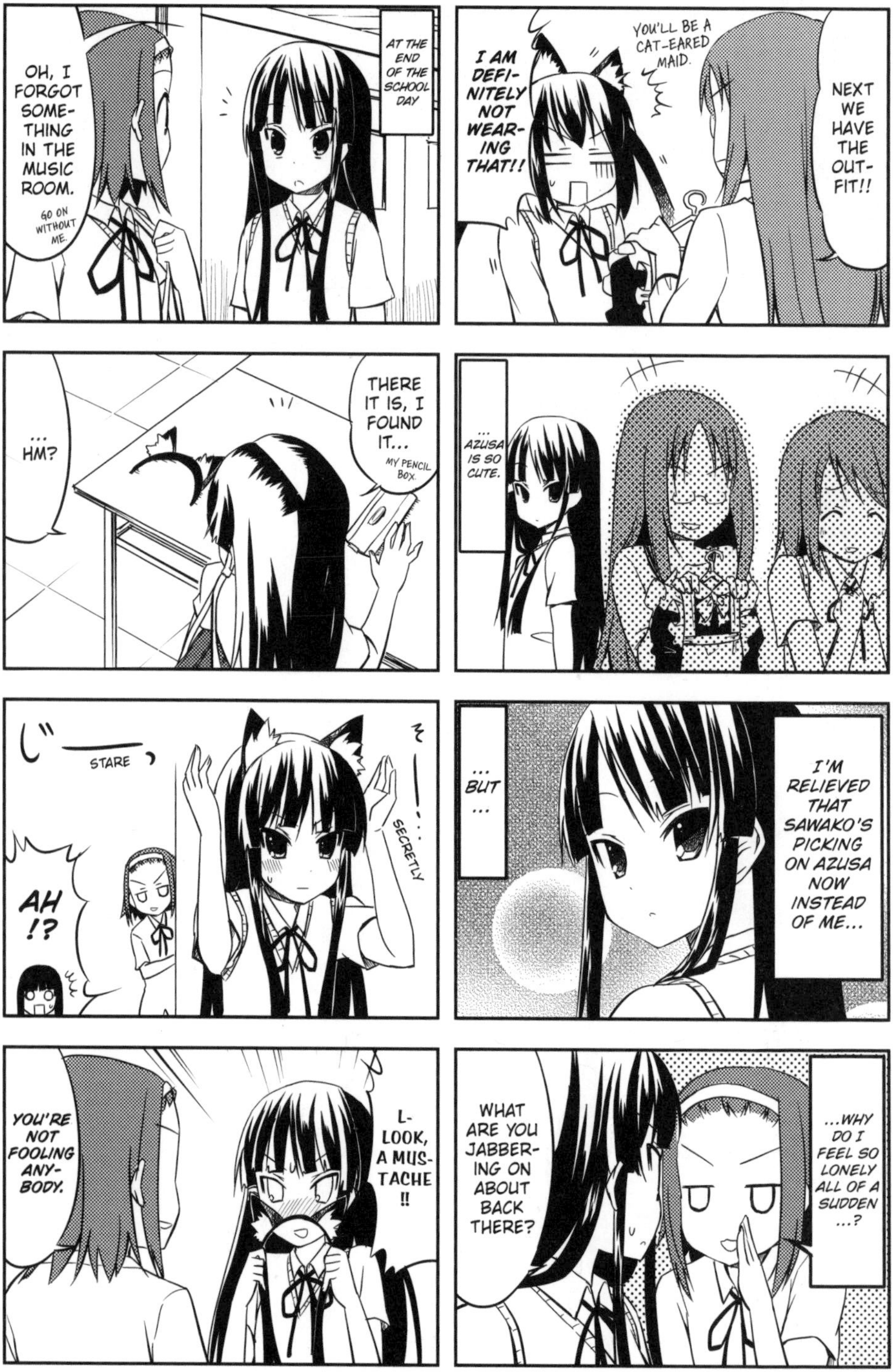
NEXT WE HAVE THE OUTFIT!!
YOU'LL BE A CAT-EARED MAID.
I AM DEFINITELY NOT WEARING THAT!!
...AZUSA IS SO CUTE.
...BUT...
I'M RELIEVED THAT SAWAKO'S PICKING ON AZUSA NOW INSTEAD OF ME...
...WHY DO I FEEL SO LONELY ALL OF A SUDDEN...?
WHAT ARE YOU JABBERING ON ABOUT BACK THERE?
AT THE END OF THE SCHOOL DAY
OH, I FORGOT SOMETHING IN THE MUSIC ROOM.
GO ON WITHOUT ME.
THERE IT IS, I FOUND IT...
MY PENCIL BOX.
...HM?
SECRETLY
STARE
AH!?
L-LOOK, A MUSTACHE!!
YOU'RE NOT FOOLING ANYBODY.

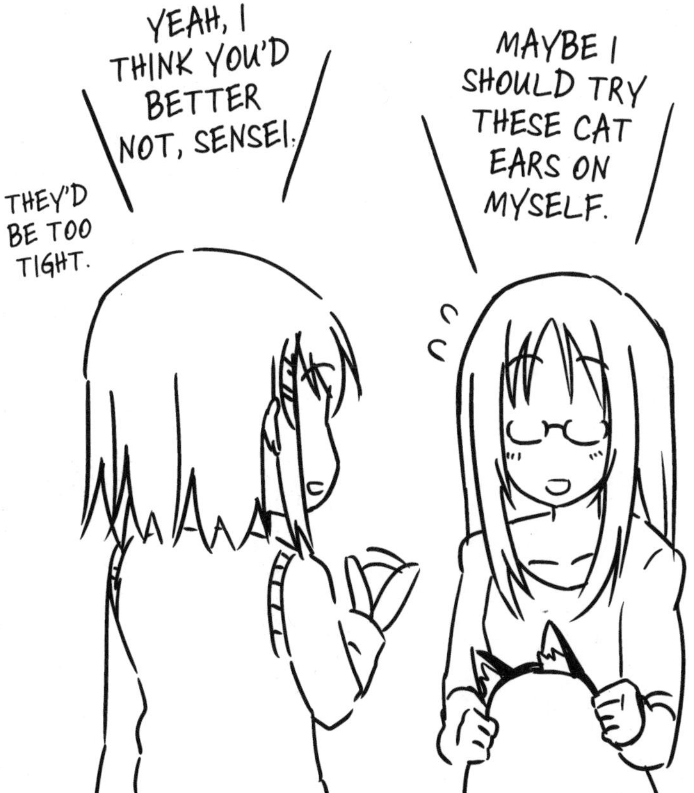
MAYBE I SHOULD TRY THESE CAT EARS ON MYSELF.
YEAH, I THINK YOU'D BETTER NOT, SENSEI.
THEY'D BE TOO TIGHT.

ポン…
PAT

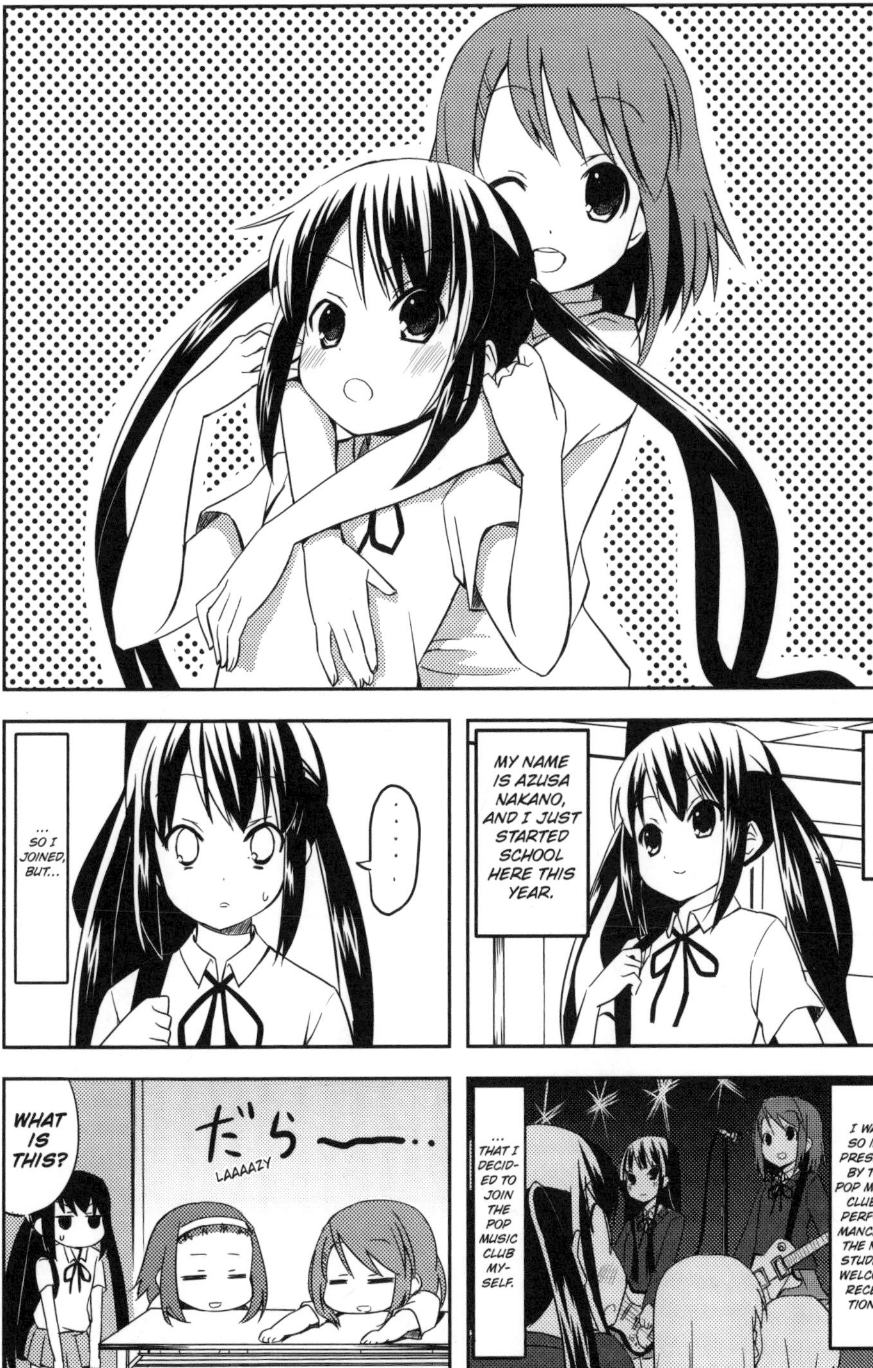
HELLO.
MY NAME IS AZUSA NAKANO, AND I JUST STARTED SCHOOL HERE THIS YEAR.
... SO I JOINED, BUT...
......
I WAS SO IMPRESSED BY THE POP MUSIC CLUB'S PERFORMANCE AT THE NEW STUDENT WELCOME RECEPTION...
... THAT I DECIDED TO JOIN THE POP MUSIC CLUB MYSELF.
WHAT IS THIS?
だら〜〜‥
LAAAAZY

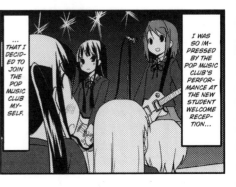

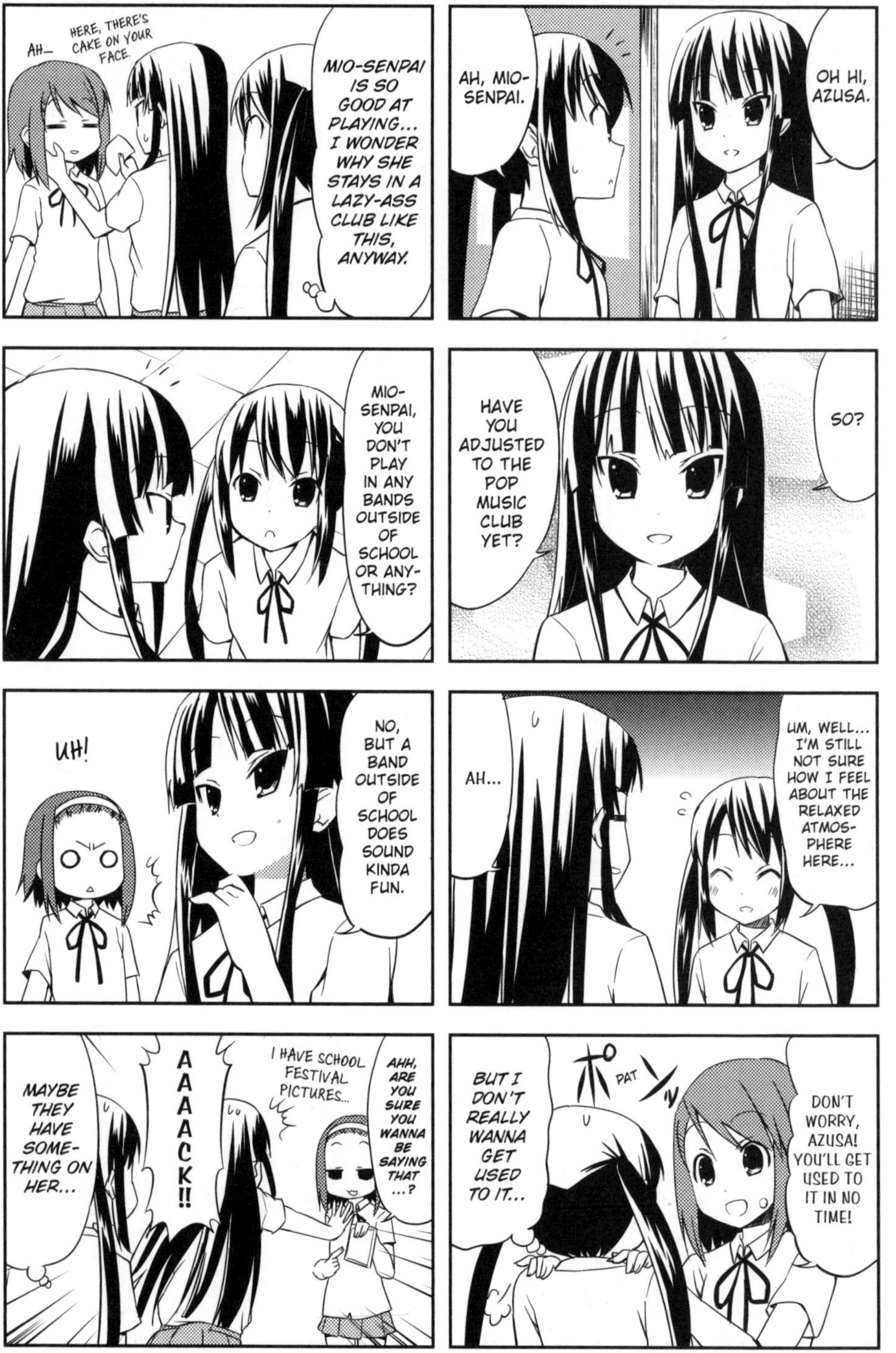
OH HI, AZUSA.
AH, MIO-SENPAI.
MIO-SENPAI IS SO GOOD AT PLAYING... I WONDER WHY SHE STAYS IN A LAZY-ASS CLUB LIKE THIS, ANYWAY.
HERE, THERE'S CAKE ON YOUR FACE.
AH_
SO?
HAVE YOU ADJUSTED TO THE POP MUSIC CLUB YET?
MIO-SENPAI, YOU DON'T PLAY IN ANY BANDS OUTSIDE OF SCHOOL OR ANYTHING?
UM, WELL... I'M STILL NOT SURE HOW I FEEL ABOUT THE RELAXED ATMOSPHERE HERE...
AH...
NO, BUT A BAND OUTSIDE OF SCHOOL DOES SOUND KINDA FUN.
UH!
DON'T WORRY, AZUSA! YOU'LL GET USED TO IT IN NO TIME!
ポン
PAT
BUT I DON'T REALLY WANNA GET USED TO IT...
AHH, ARE YOU SURE YOU WANNA BE SAYING THAT ...?
I HAVE SCHOOL FESTIVAL PICTURES...
AAAAACK!!
MAYBE THEY HAVE SOMETHING ON HER...

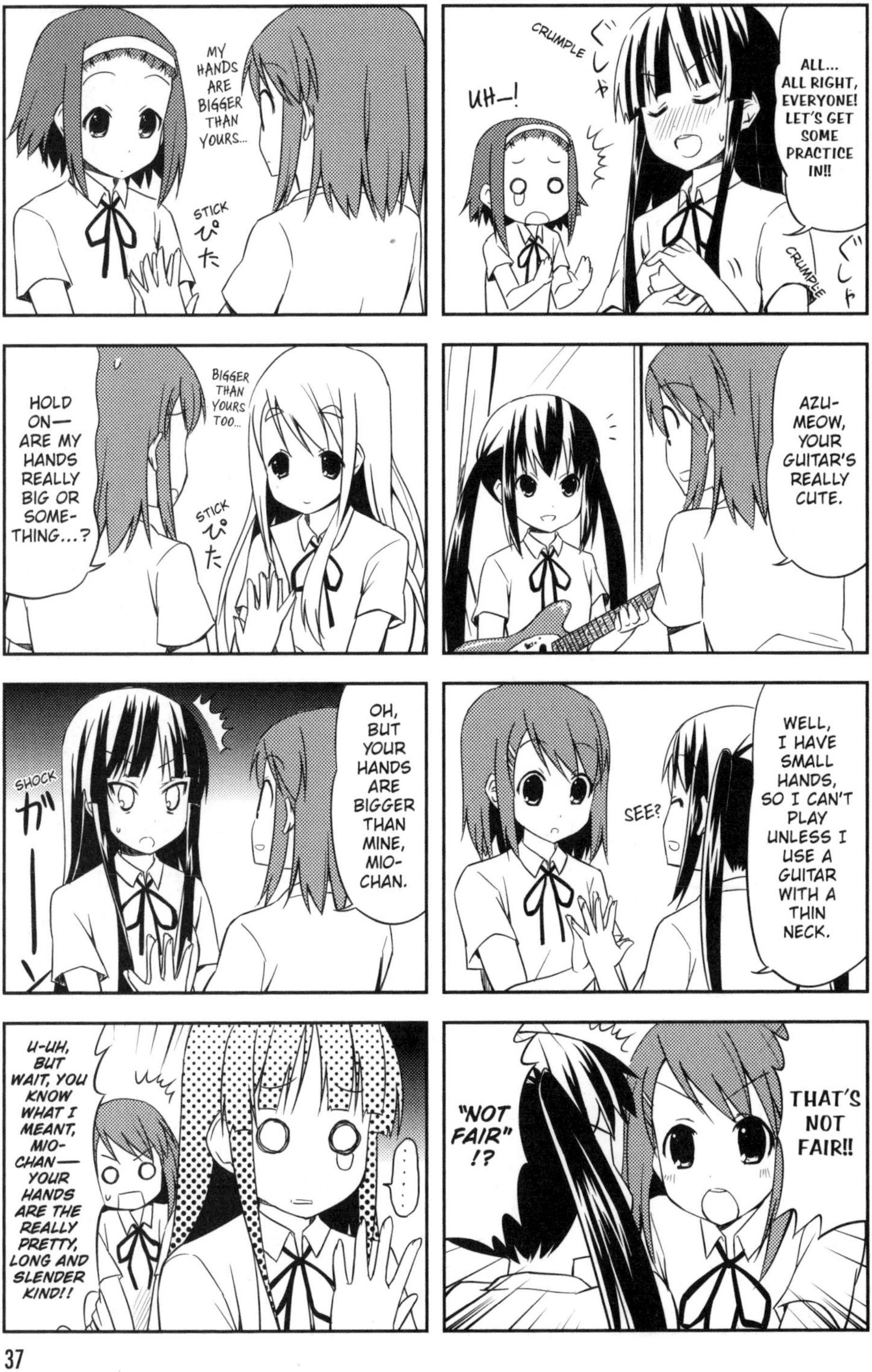
CRUMPLE
UH—!
ALL... ALL RIGHT, EVERYONE! LET'S GET SOME PRACTICE IN!!
CRUMPLE
AZU-MEOW, YOUR GUITAR'S REALLY CUTE.
WELL, I HAVE SMALL HANDS, SO I CAN'T PLAY UNLESS I USE A GUITAR WITH A THIN NECK.
SEE?
THAT'S NOT FAIR!!
"NOT FAIR" !?
MY HANDS ARE BIGGER THAN YOURS...
STICK
BIGGER THAN YOURS TOO...
HOLD ON— ARE MY HANDS REALLY BIG OR SOMETHING...?
STICK
OH, BUT YOUR HANDS ARE BIGGER THAN MINE, MIO-CHAN.
SHOCK
U-UH, BUT WAIT, YOU KNOW WHAT I MEANT, MIO-CHAN— YOUR HANDS ARE THE REALLY PRETTY, LONG AND SLENDER KIND!!
......

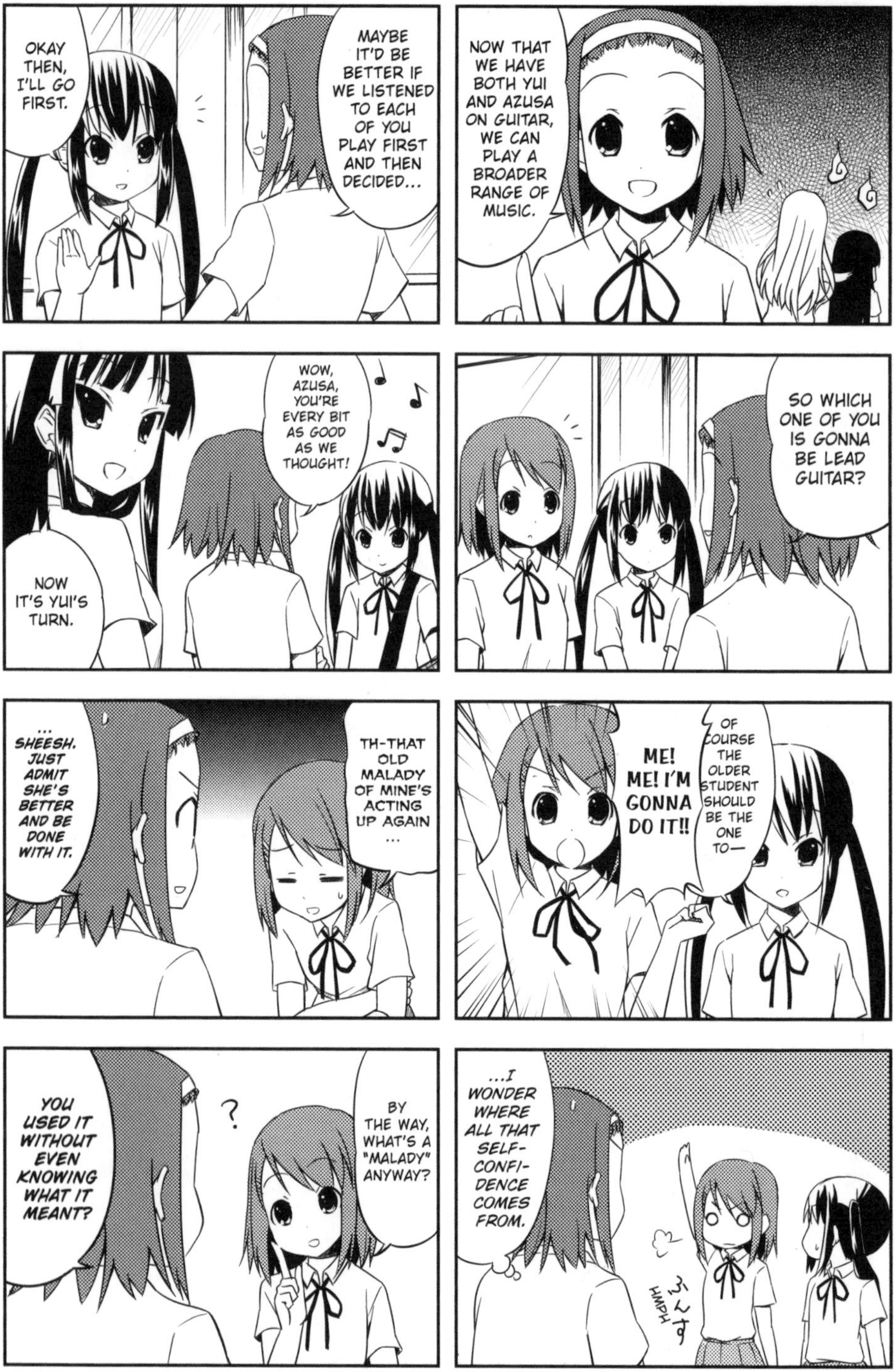
NOW THAT WE HAVE BOTH YUI AND AZUSA ON GUITAR, WE CAN PLAY A BROADER RANGE OF MUSIC.
SO WHICH ONE OF YOU IS GONNA BE LEAD GUITAR?
OF COURSE THE OLDER STUDENT SHOULD BE THE ONE TO—
ME! ME! I'M GONNA DO IT!!
...I WONDER WHERE ALL THAT SELF-CONFI-DENCE COMES FROM.
ふんす
HMPH
MAYBE IT'D BE BETTER IF WE LISTENED TO EACH OF YOU PLAY FIRST AND THEN DECIDED...
OKAY THEN, I'LL GO FIRST.
WOW, AZUSA, YOU'RE EVERY BIT AS GOOD AS WE THOUGHT!
NOW IT'S YUI'S TURN.
TH-THAT OLD MALADY OF MINE'S ACTING UP AGAIN ...
...SHEESH. JUST ADMIT SHE'S BETTER AND BE DONE WITH IT.
BY THE WAY, WHAT'S A "MALADY" ANYWAY?
?
YOU USED IT WITHOUT EVEN KNOWING WHAT IT MEANT?

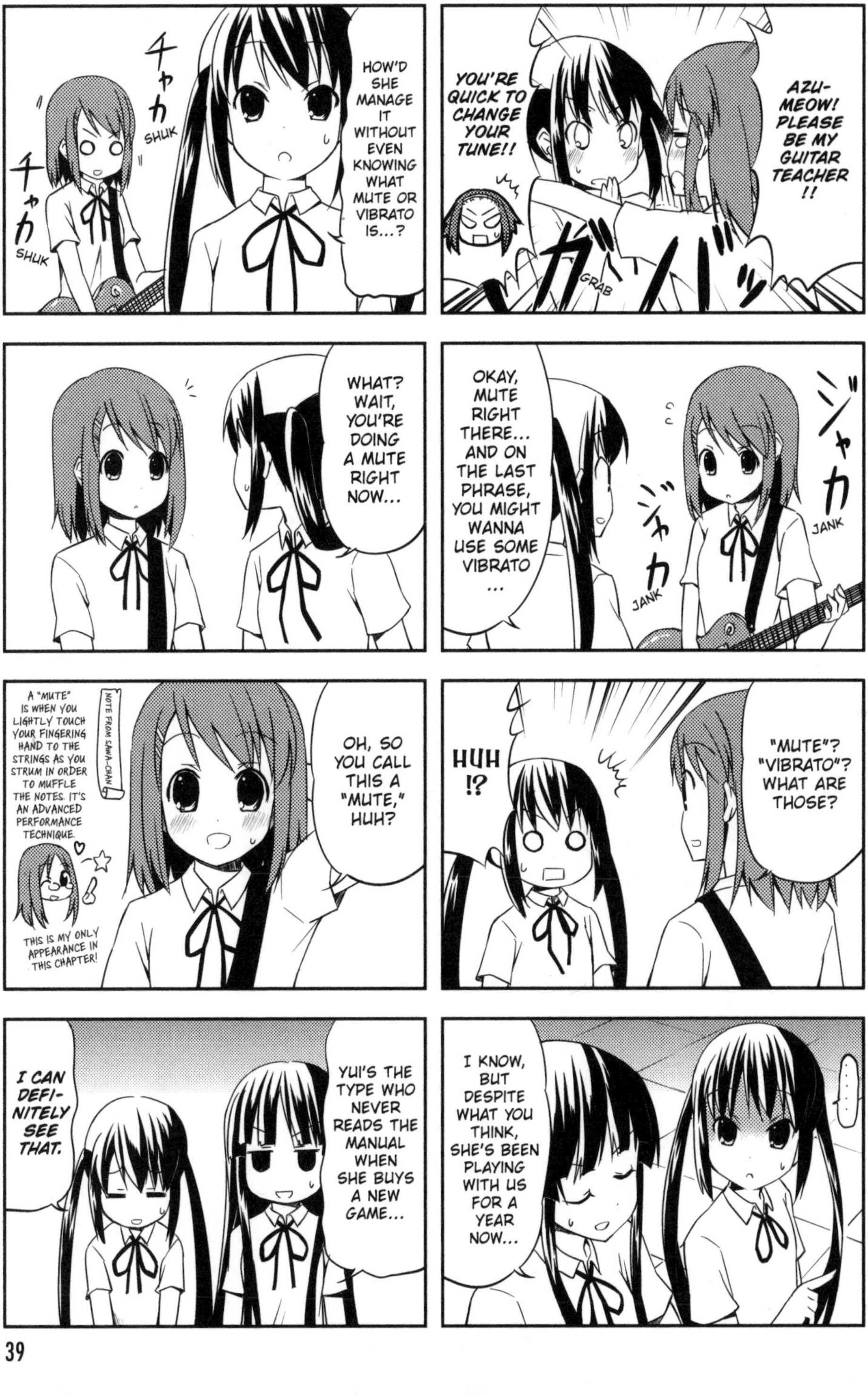
AZU-MEOW! PLEASE BE MY GUITAR TEACHER!!
YOU'RE QUICK TO CHANGE YOUR TUNE!!
ガバッ
GRAB
ジャカ
JANK
OKAY, MUTE RIGHT THERE... AND ON THE LAST PHRASE, YOU MIGHT WANNA USE SOME VIBRATO...
ジャカ
JANK
"MUTE"? "VIBRATO"? WHAT ARE THOSE?
HUH!?
...
I KNOW, BUT DESPITE WHAT YOU THINK, SHE'S BEEN PLAYING WITH US FOR A YEAR NOW...
HOW'D SHE MANAGE IT WITHOUT EVEN KNOWING WHAT MUTE OR VIBRATO IS...?
チャカ
SHUK
チャカ
SHUK
WHAT? WAIT, YOU'RE DOING A MUTE RIGHT NOW...
OH, SO YOU CALL THIS A "MUTE," HUH?
NOTE FROM SAWA-CHAN
A "MUTE" IS WHEN YOU LIGHTLY TOUCH YOUR FINGERING HAND TO THE STRINGS AS YOU STRUM IN ORDER TO MUFFLE THE NOTES. IT'S AN ADVANCED PERFORMANCE TECHNIQUE.
THIS IS MY ONLY APPEARANCE IN THIS CHAPTER!
YUI'S THE TYPE WHO NEVER READS THE MANUAL WHEN SHE BUYS A NEW GAME...
I CAN DEFINITELY SEE THAT.

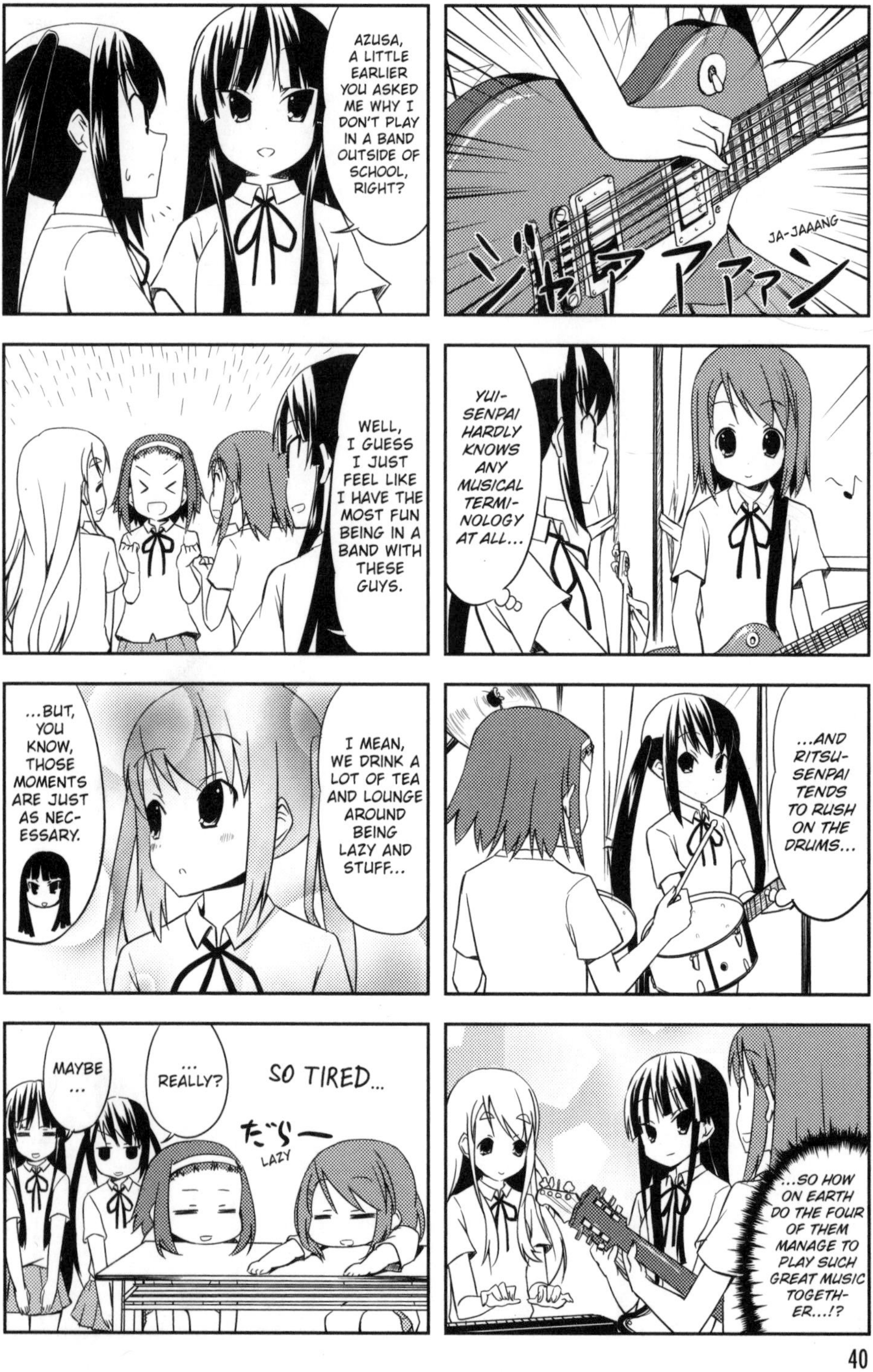

ジャアアァン
JA-JAAANG
AZUSA, A LITTLE EARLIER YOU ASKED ME WHY I DON'T PLAY IN A BAND OUTSIDE OF SCHOOL, RIGHT?
YUI-SENPAI HARDLY KNOWS ANY MUSICAL TERMI-NOLOGY AT ALL...
WELL, I GUESS I JUST FEEL LIKE I HAVE THE MOST FUN BEING IN A BAND WITH THESE GUYS.
...AND RITSU-SENPAI TENDS TO RUSH ON THE DRUMS...
I MEAN, WE DRINK A LOT OF TEA AND LOUNGE AROUND BEING LAZY AND STUFF...
...BUT, YOU KNOW, THOSE MOMENTS ARE JUST AS NEC-ESSARY.
...SO HOW ON EARTH DO THE FOUR OF THEM MANAGE TO PLAY SUCH GREAT MUSIC TOGETH-ER...!?
MAYBE ...
... REALLY?
SO TIRED...
だらー
LAZY

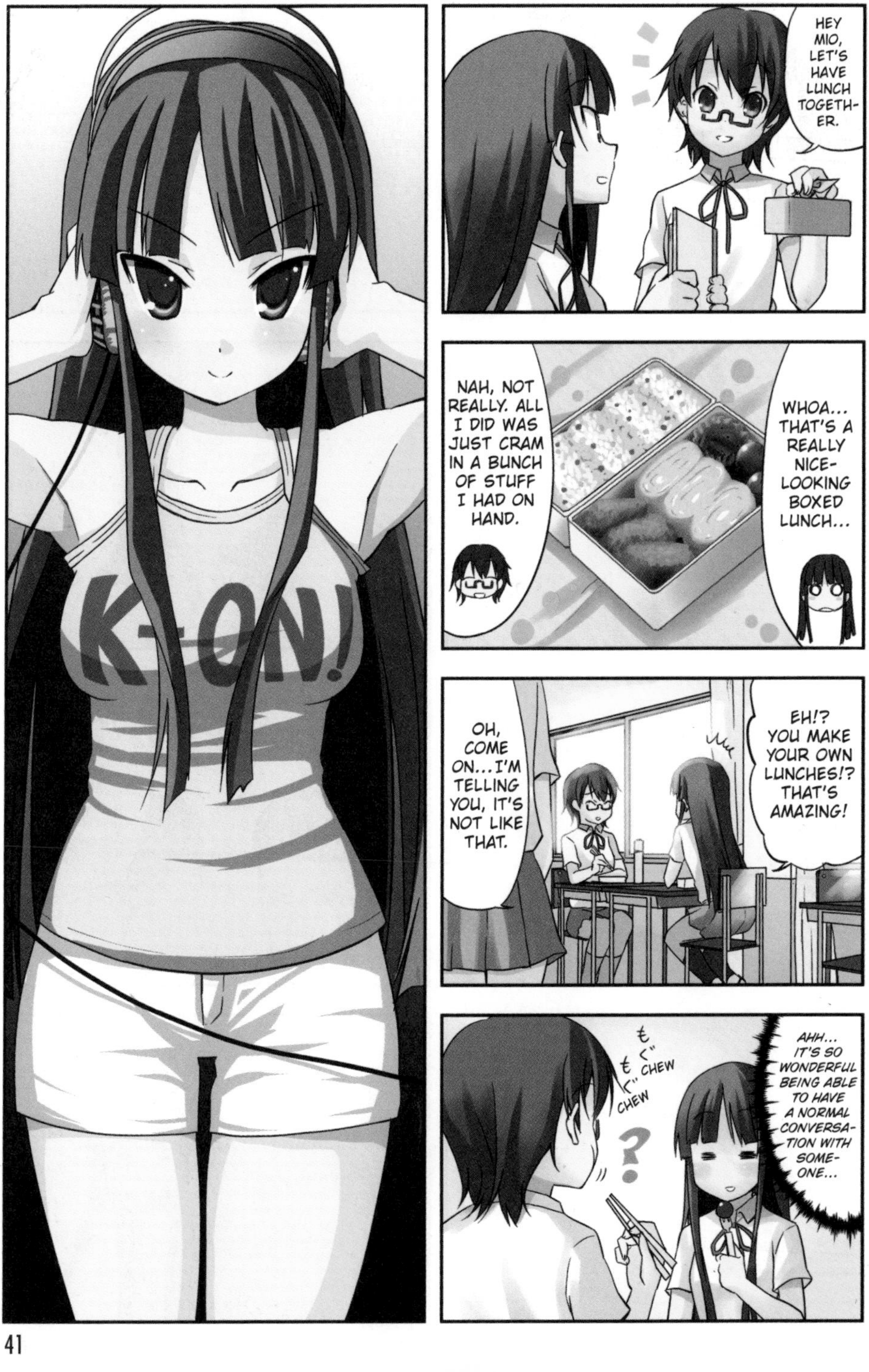
HEY MIO, LET'S HAVE LUNCH TOGETH-ER.
WHOA... THAT'S A REALLY NICE-LOOKING BOXED LUNCH...
NAH, NOT REALLY. ALL I DID WAS JUST CRAM IN A BUNCH OF STUFF I HAD ON HAND.
EH!? YOU MAKE YOUR OWN LUNCHES!? THAT'S AMAZING!
OH, COME ON... I'M TELLING YOU, IT'S NOT LIKE THAT.
AHH... IT'S SO WONDERFUL BEING ABLE TO HAVE A NORMAL CONVERSA-TION WITH SOME-ONE...
もぐ CHEW
もぐ CHEW
K-ON!

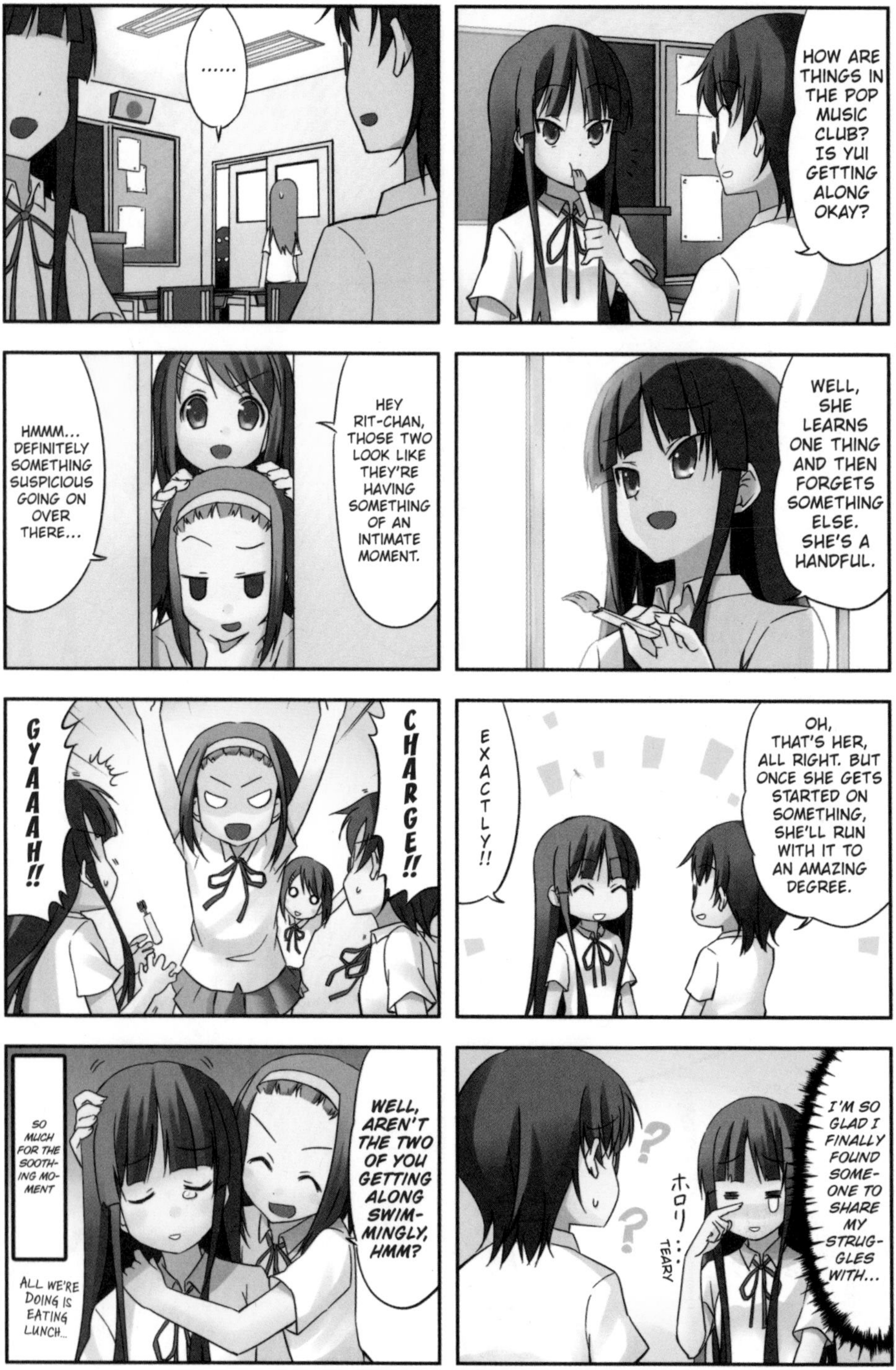
HOW ARE THINGS IN THE POP MUSIC CLUB? IS YUI GETTING ALONG OKAY?
......
WELL, SHE LEARNS ONE THING AND THEN FORGETS SOMETHING ELSE. SHE'S A HANDFUL.
HEY RIT-CHAN, THOSE TWO LOOK LIKE THEY'RE HAVING SOMETHING OF AN INTIMATE MOMENT.
HMMM... DEFINITELY SOMETHING SUSPICIOUS GOING ON OVER THERE...
OH, THAT'S HER, ALL RIGHT. BUT ONCE SHE GETS STARTED ON SOMETHING, SHE'LL RUN WITH IT TO AN AMAZING DEGREE.
EXACTLY!!
CHARGE!!
GYAAAAH!!
I'M SO GLAD I FINALLY FOUND SOME-ONE TO SHARE MY STRUG-GLES WITH...
ホロリ… TEARY
WELL, AREN'T THE TWO OF YOU GETTING ALONG SWIM-MINGLY, HMM?
SO MUCH FOR THE SOOTH-ING MO-MENT
ALL WE'RE DOING IS EATING LUNCH...

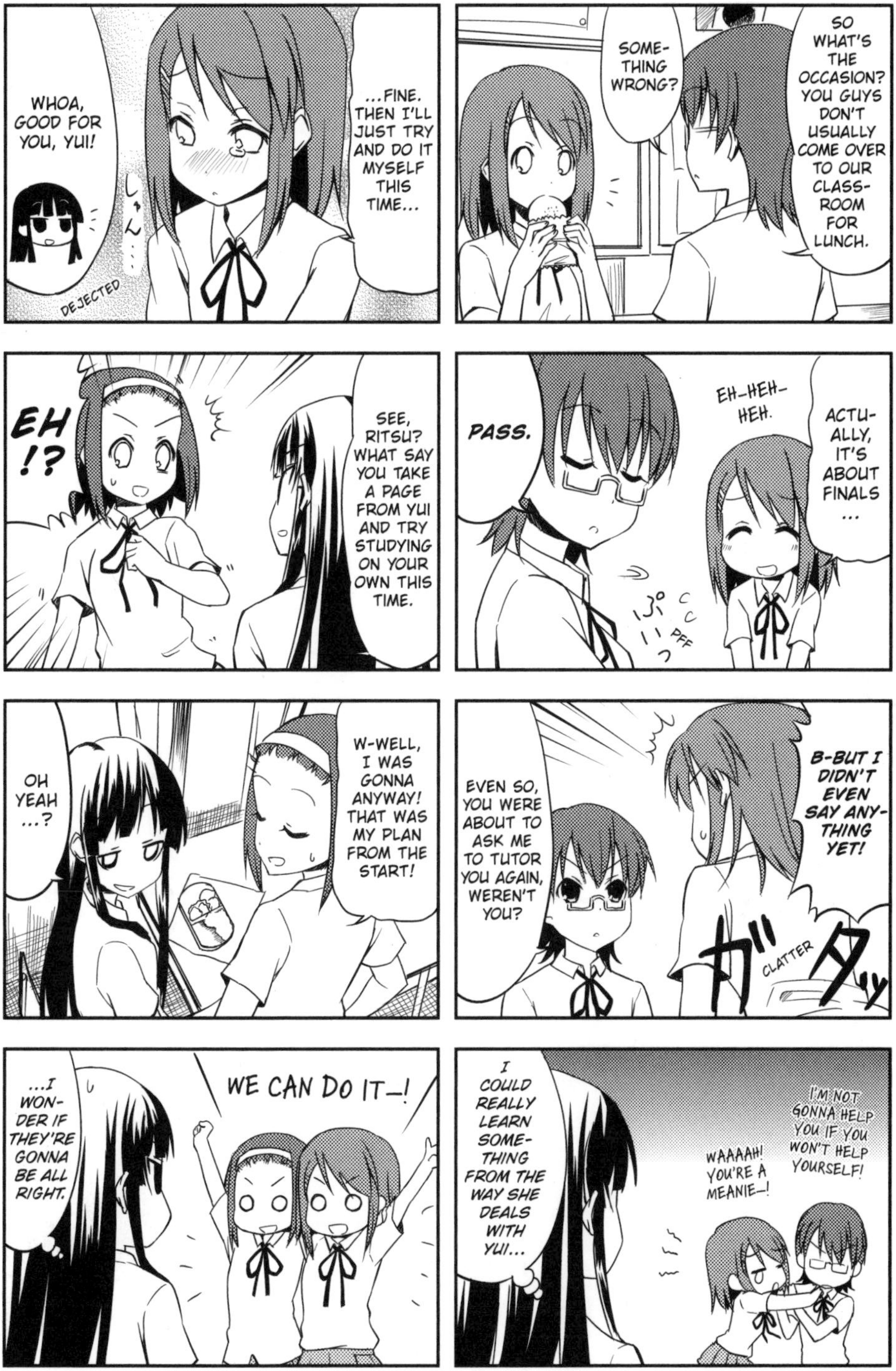
SO WHAT'S THE OCCASION? YOU GUYS DON'T USUALLY COME OVER TO OUR CLASSROOM FOR LUNCH.
SOMETHING WRONG?
ACTUALLY, IT'S ABOUT FINALS...
EH-HEH-HEH.
PASS.
ぷっ
PFF
B-BUT I DIDN'T EVEN SAY ANYTHING YET!
EVEN SO, YOU WERE ABOUT TO ASK ME TO TUTOR YOU AGAIN, WEREN'T YOU?
ガタッ
CLATTER
I'M NOT GONNA HELP YOU IF YOU WON'T HELP YOURSELF!
WAAAAH! YOU'RE A MEANIE—!
I COULD REALLY LEARN SOMETHING FROM THE WAY SHE DEALS WITH YUI...
...FINE. THEN I'LL JUST TRY AND DO IT MYSELF THIS TIME...
しょん...
DEJECTED
WHOA, GOOD FOR YOU, YUI!
SEE, RITSU? WHAT SAY YOU TAKE A PAGE FROM YUI AND TRY STUDYING ON YOUR OWN THIS TIME.
EH!?
W-WELL, I WAS GONNA ANYWAY! THAT WAS MY PLAN FROM THE START!
OH YEAH...?
WE CAN DO IT—!
...I WONDER IF THEY'RE GONNA BE ALL RIGHT.

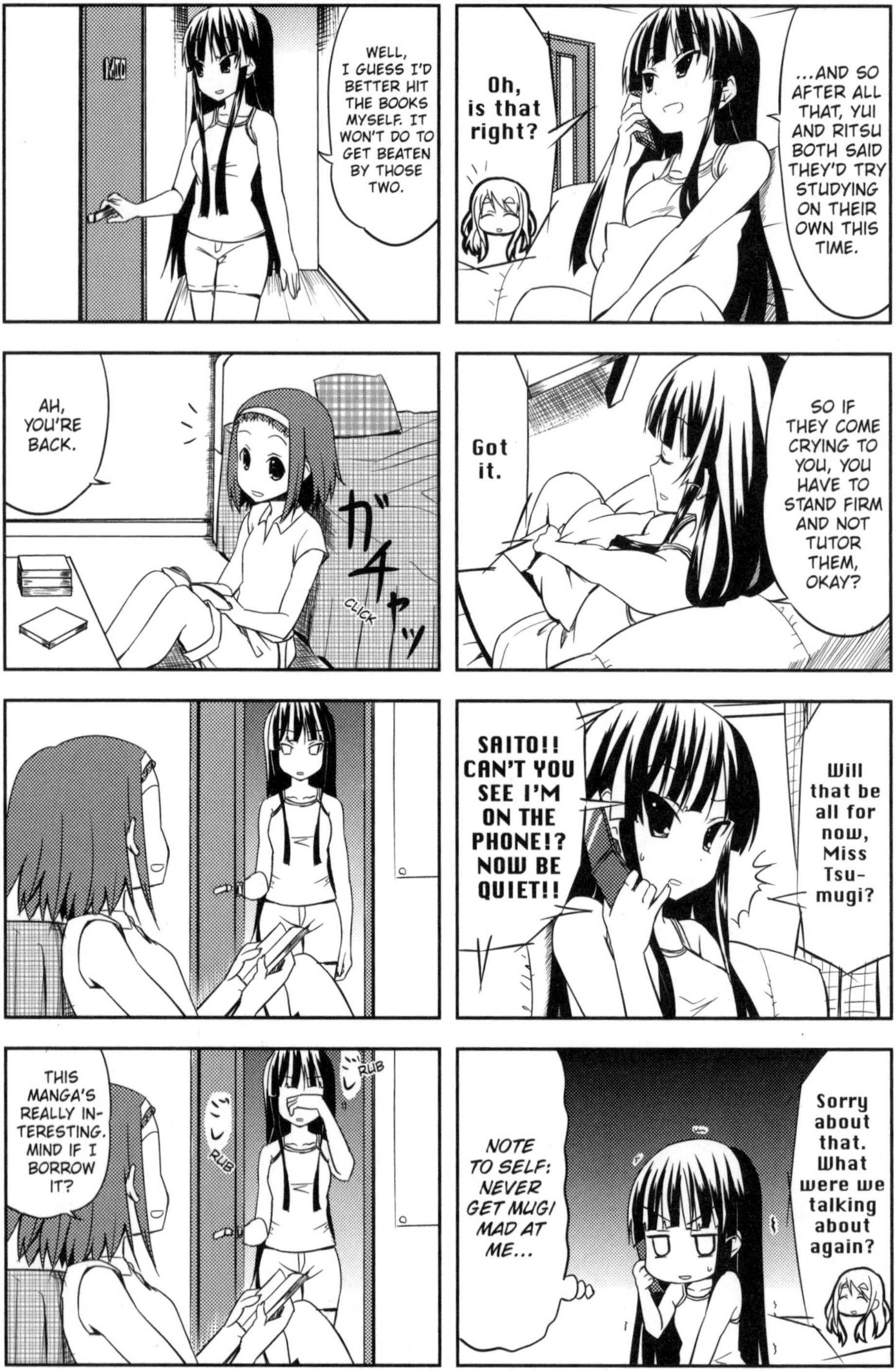

...AND SO AFTER ALL THAT, YUI AND RITSU BOTH SAID THEY'D TRY STUDYING ON THEIR OWN THIS TIME.
Oh, is that right?
WELL, I GUESS I'D BETTER HIT THE BOOKS MYSELF. IT WON'T DO TO GET BEATEN BY THOSE TWO.
SO IF THEY COME CRYING TO YOU, YOU HAVE TO STAND FIRM AND NOT TUTOR THEM, OKAY?
Got it.
AH, YOU'RE BACK.
ガチャッ
CLICK
Will that be all for now, Miss Tsu-mugi?
SAITO!! CAN'T YOU SEE I'M ON THE PHONE!? NOW BE QUIET!!
Sorry about that. What were we talking about again?
NOTE TO SELF: NEVER GET MUGI MAD AT ME...
RUB
RUB
THIS MANGA'S REALLY IN-TERESTING. MIND IF I BORROW IT?

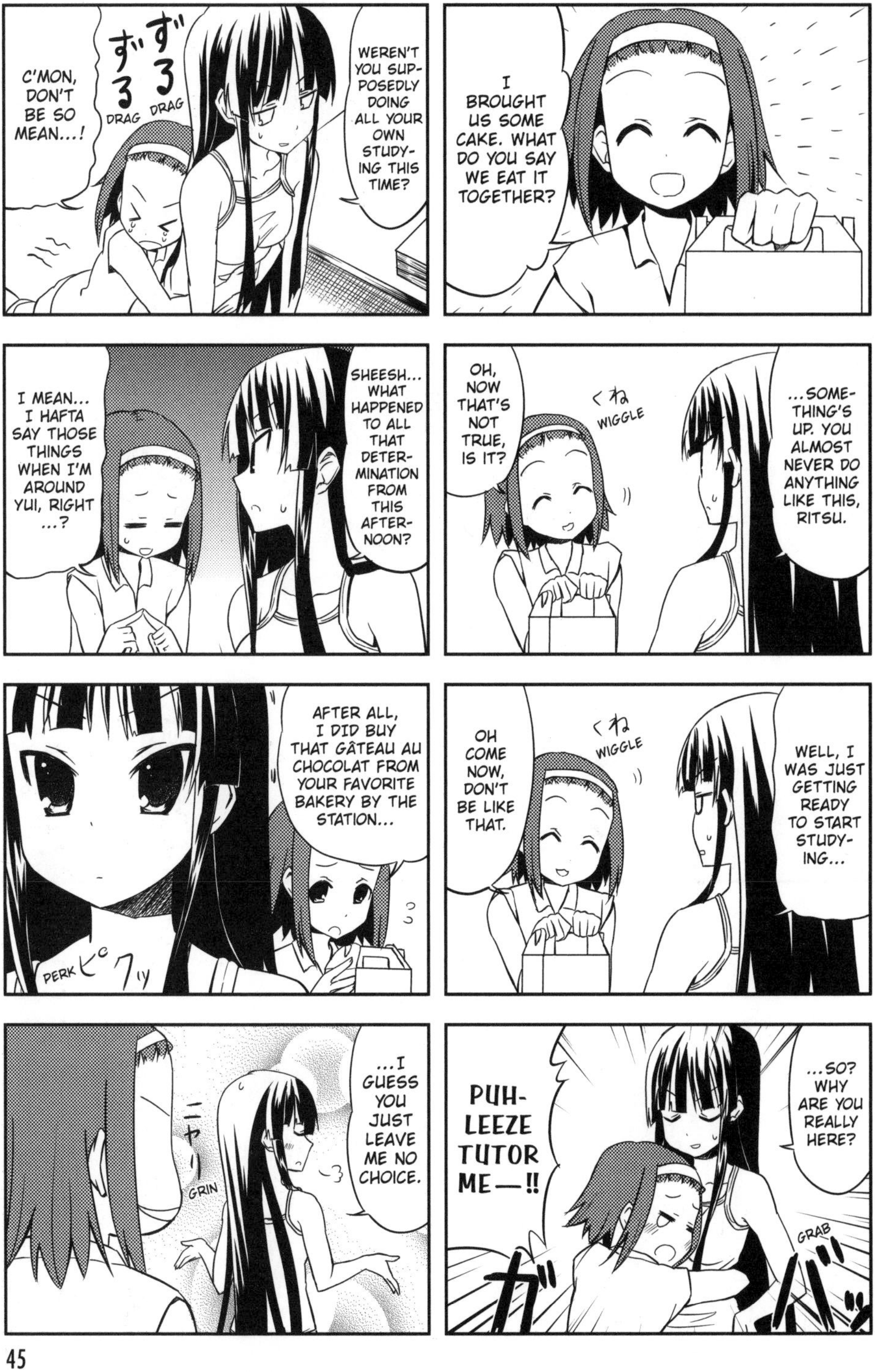
I BROUGHT US SOME CAKE. WHAT DO YOU SAY WE EAT IT TOGETHER?
WEREN'T YOU SUPPOSEDLY DOING ALL YOUR OWN STUDYING THIS TIME?
ずるずる DRAG DRAG
C'MON, DON'T BE SO MEAN...!
...SOMETHING'S UP. YOU ALMOST NEVER DO ANYTHING LIKE THIS, RITSU.
くね WIGGLE
OH, NOW THAT'S NOT TRUE, IS IT?
SHEESH... WHAT HAPPENED TO ALL THAT DETERMINATION FROM THIS AFTERNOON?
I MEAN... I HAFTA SAY THOSE THINGS WHEN I'M AROUND YUI, RIGHT...?
WELL, I WAS JUST GETTING READY TO START STUDYING...
くね WIGGLE
OH COME NOW, DON'T BE LIKE THAT.
AFTER ALL, I DID BUY THAT GÂTEAU AU CHOCOLAT FROM YOUR FAVORITE BAKERY BY THE STATION...
PERK ピクッ
...SO? WHY ARE YOU REALLY HERE?
PUH-LEEZE TUTOR ME—!!
GRAB ガバッ
...I GUESS YOU JUST LEAVE ME NO CHOICE.
ニヤリ GRIN

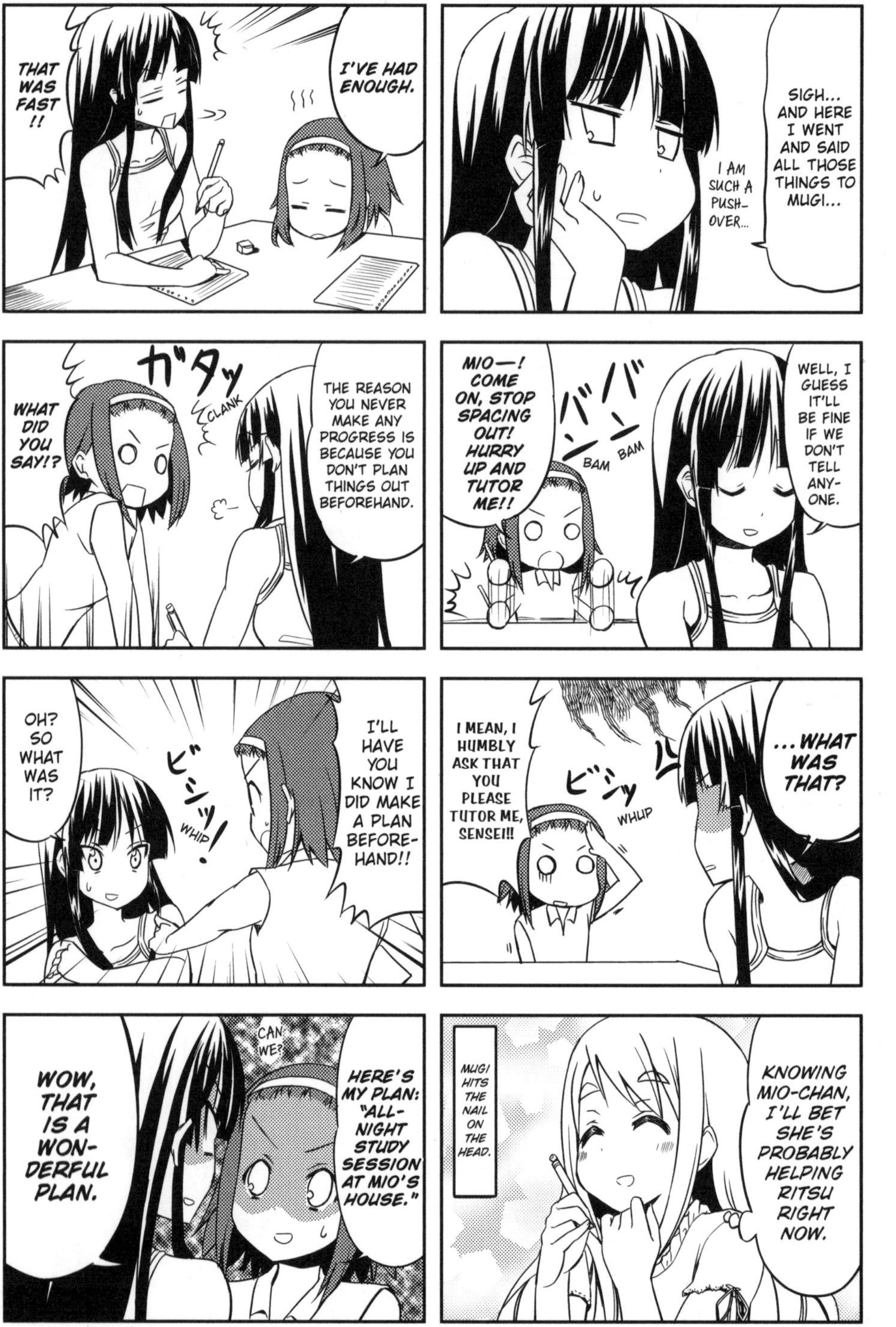
SIGH... AND HERE I WENT AND SAID ALL THOSE THINGS TO MUGI...
I AM SUCH A PUSH-OVER...
WELL, I GUESS IT'LL BE FINE IF WE DON'T TELL ANY-ONE.
バンバン
BAM BAM
MIO—! COME ON, STOP SPACING OUT! HURRY UP AND TUTOR ME!!
...WHAT WAS THAT?
ビシッ
WHUP
I MEAN, I HUMBLY ASK THAT YOU PLEASE TUTOR ME, SENSEI!!
KNOWING MIO-CHAN, I'LL BET SHE'S PROBABLY HELPING RITSU RIGHT NOW.
MUGI HITS THE NAIL ON THE HEAD.
I'VE HAD ENOUGH.
THAT WAS FAST!!
THE REASON YOU NEVER MAKE ANY PROGRESS IS BECAUSE YOU DON'T PLAN THINGS OUT BEFOREHAND.
ガタッ
CLANK
WHAT DID YOU SAY!?
I'LL HAVE YOU KNOW I DID MAKE A PLAN BEFORE-HAND!!
ビシッ!
WHIP
OH? SO WHAT WAS IT?
HERE'S MY PLAN: "ALL-NIGHT STUDY SESSION AT MIO'S HOUSE."
CAN WE?
WOW, THAT IS A WON-DERFUL PLAN.

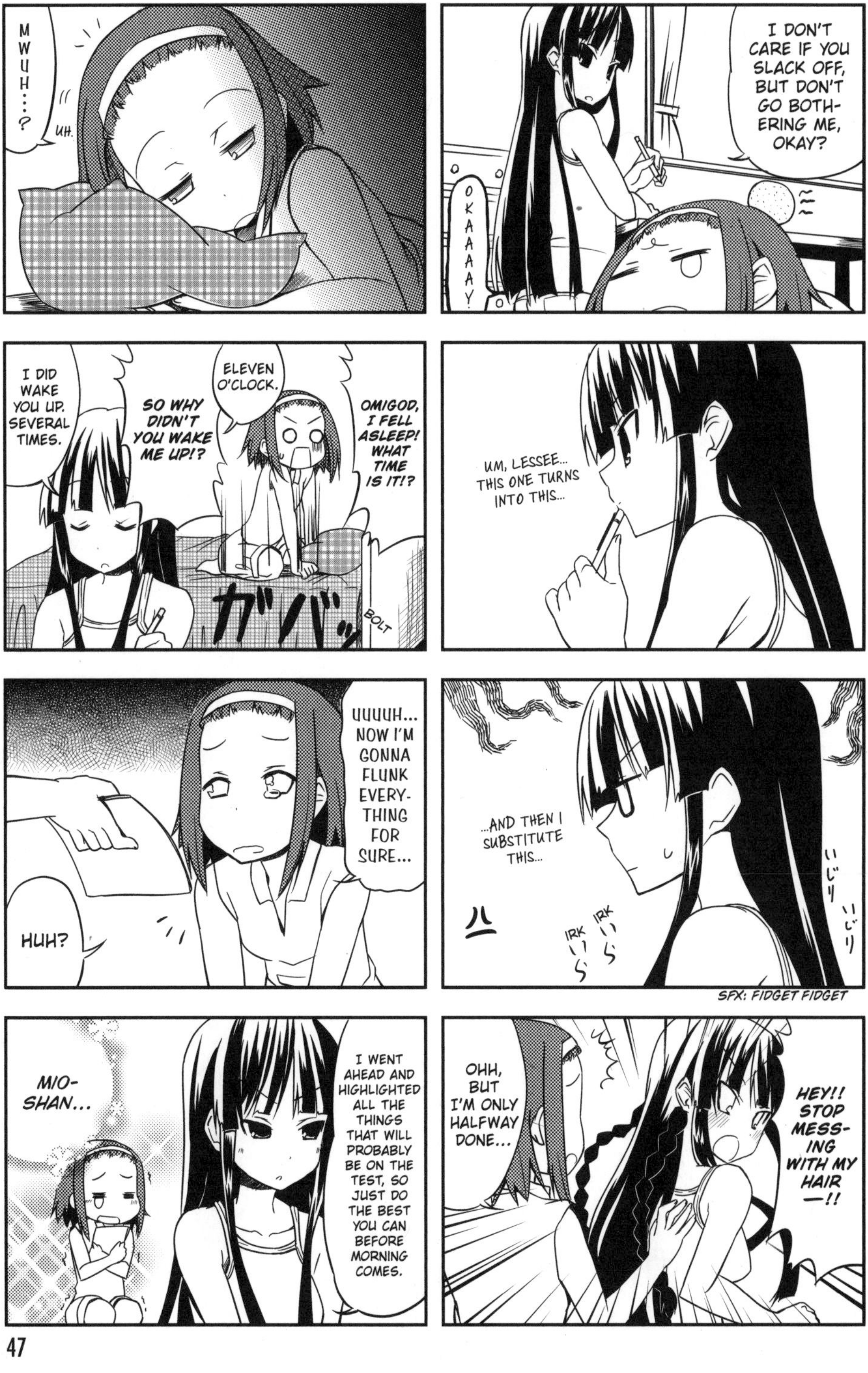
I DON'T CARE IF YOU SLACK OFF, BUT DON'T GO BOTHERING ME, OKAY?
OKAAAAAY!
UM, LESSEE... THIS ONE TURNS INTO THIS...
...AND THEN I SUBSTITUTE THIS...
IRK いら
IRK いら
いじり
いじり
HEY!! STOP MESSING WITH MY HAIR—!!
OHH, BUT I'M ONLY HALFWAY DONE...
MWUH...?
UH.
OMIGOD, I FELL ASLEEP! WHAT TIME IS IT!?
ELEVEN O'CLOCK.
SO WHY DIDN'T YOU WAKE ME UP!?
I DID WAKE YOU UP. SEVERAL TIMES.
ガバッ
BOLT
UUUUH... NOW I'M GONNA FLUNK EVERYTHING FOR SURE...
HUH?
I WENT AHEAD AND HIGHLIGHTED ALL THE THINGS THAT WILL PROBABLY BE ON THE TEST, SO JUST DO THE BEST YOU CAN BEFORE MORNING COMES.
MIO-SHAN...
SFX: FIDGET FIDGET

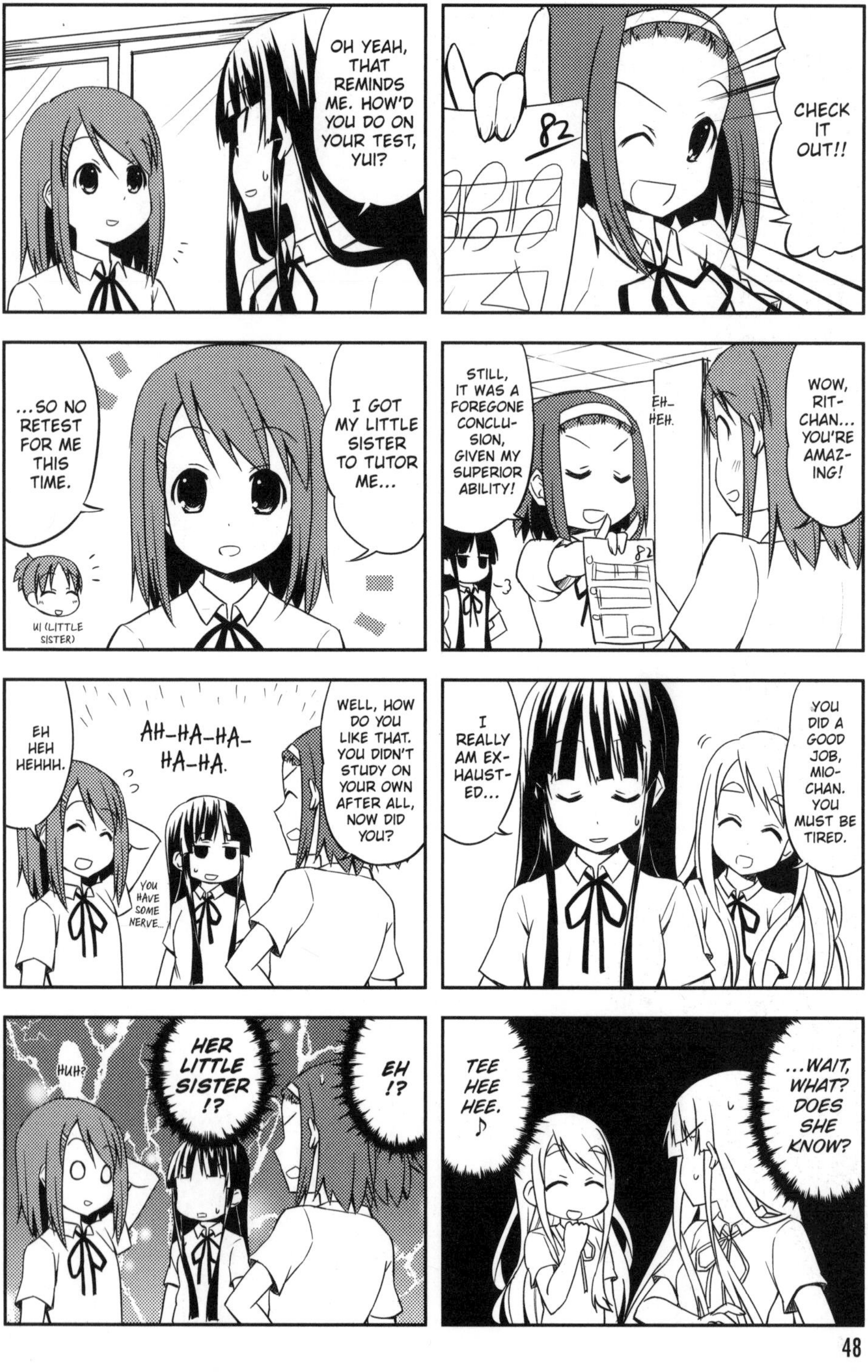
CHECK IT OUT!!
WOW, RIT-CHAN... YOU'RE AMAZING!
EH-HEH.
STILL, IT WAS A FOREGONE CONCLUSION, GIVEN MY SUPERIOR ABILITY!
YOU DID A GOOD JOB, MIO-CHAN. YOU MUST BE TIRED.
I REALLY AM EXHAUSTED...
...WAIT, WHAT? DOES SHE KNOW?
TEE HEE HEE. ♪
OH YEAH, THAT REMINDS ME. HOW'D YOU DO ON YOUR TEST, YUI?
I GOT MY LITTLE SISTER TO TUTOR ME...
...SO NO RETEST FOR ME THIS TIME.
UI (LITTLE SISTER)
WELL, HOW DO YOU LIKE THAT. YOU DIDN'T STUDY ON YOUR OWN AFTER ALL, NOW DID YOU?
AH-HA-HA-HA-HA.
EH HEH HEHHH.
YOU HAVE SOME NERVE...
EH!?
HER LITTLE SISTER!?
HUH?

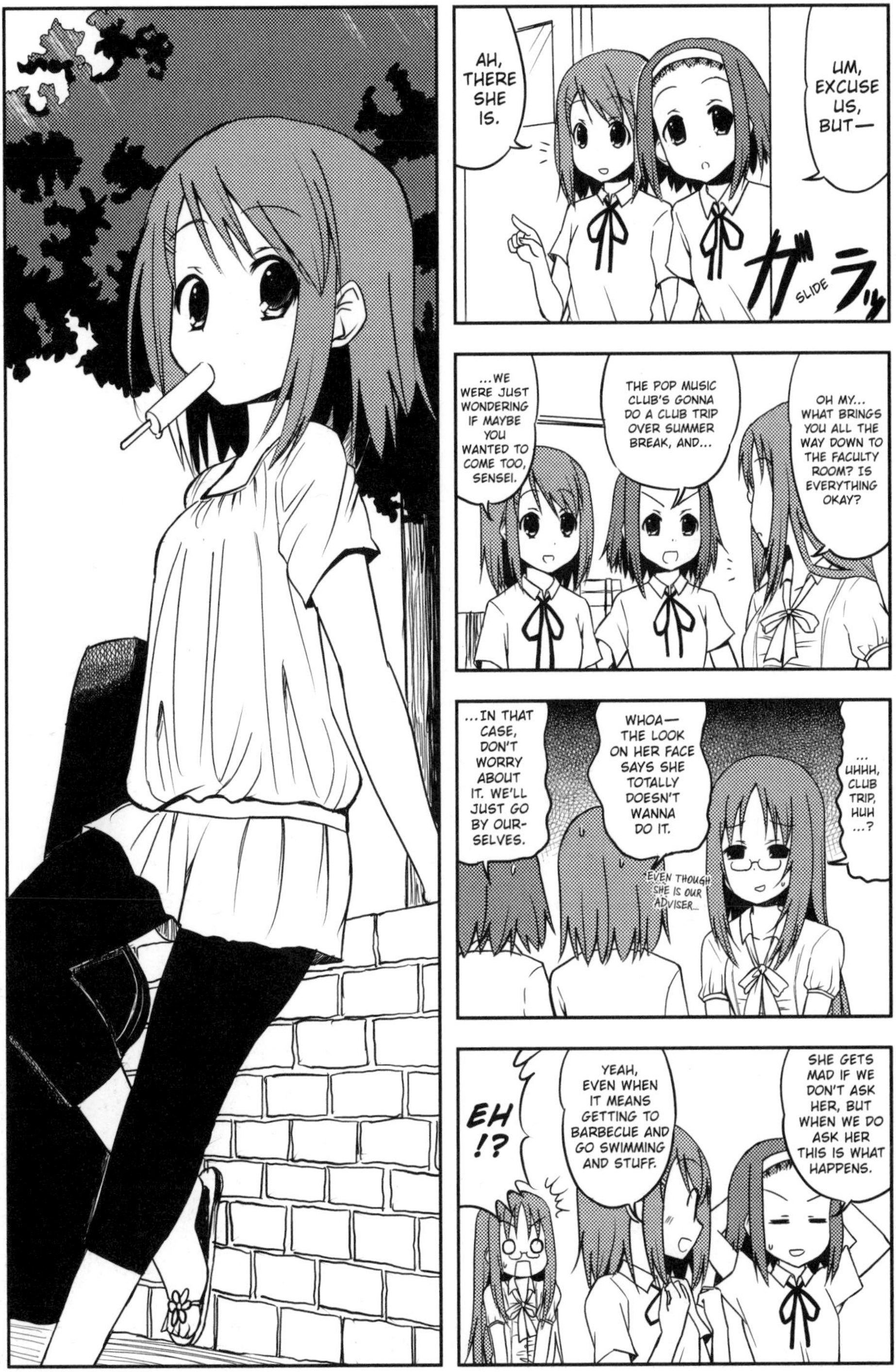
UM, EXCUSE US, BUT—
AH, THERE SHE IS.
ガラッ
SLIDE
OH MY... WHAT BRINGS YOU ALL THE WAY DOWN TO THE FACULTY ROOM? IS EVERYTHING OKAY?
THE POP MUSIC CLUB'S GONNA DO A CLUB TRIP OVER SUMMER BREAK, AND...
...WE WERE JUST WONDERING IF MAYBE YOU WANTED TO COME TOO, SENSEI.
... UHHH, CLUB TRIP, HUH ...?
WHOA— THE LOOK ON HER FACE SAYS SHE TOTALLY DOESN'T WANNA DO IT.
EVEN THOUGH SHE IS OUR ADVISER...
...IN THAT CASE, DON'T WORRY ABOUT IT. WE'LL JUST GO BY OUR-SELVES.
SHE GETS MAD IF WE DON'T ASK HER, BUT WHEN WE DO ASK HER THIS IS WHAT HAPPENS.
YEAH, EVEN WHEN IT MEANS GETTING TO BARBECUE AND GO SWIMMING AND STUFF.
EH !?

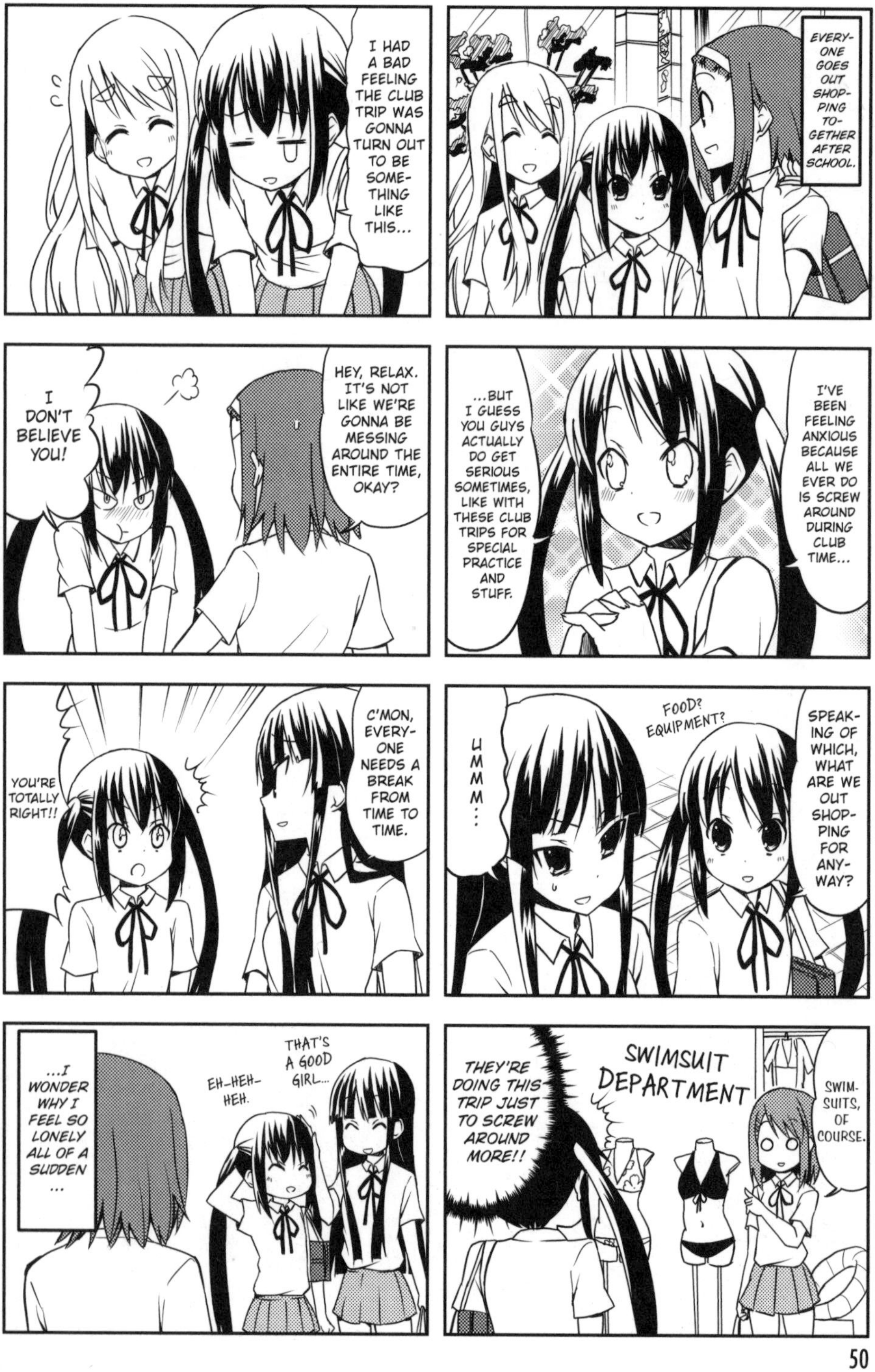
EVERY-ONE GOES OUT SHOP-PING TO-GETHER AFTER SCHOOL.
I HAD A BAD FEELING THE CLUB TRIP WAS GONNA TURN OUT TO BE SOME-THING LIKE THIS...
I'VE BEEN FEELING ANXIOUS BECAUSE ALL WE EVER DO IS SCREW AROUND DURING CLUB TIME...
...BUT I GUESS YOU GUYS ACTUALLY DO GET SERIOUS SOMETIMES, LIKE WITH THESE CLUB TRIPS FOR SPECIAL PRACTICE AND STUFF.
HEY, RELAX. IT'S NOT LIKE WE'RE GONNA BE MESSING AROUND THE ENTIRE TIME, OKAY?
I DON'T BELIEVE YOU!
SPEAK-ING OF WHICH, WHAT ARE WE OUT SHOP-PING FOR ANY-WAY?
FOOD? EQUIPMENT?
UMMM...
C'MON, EVERY-ONE NEEDS A BREAK FROM TIME TO TIME.
YOU'RE TOTALLY RIGHT!!
SWIM-SUITS, OF COURSE.
SWIMSUIT DEPARTMENT
THEY'RE DOING THIS TRIP JUST TO SCREW AROUND MORE!!
THAT'S A GOOD GIRL...
EH-HEH-HEH.
...I WONDER WHY I FEEL SO LONELY ALL OF A SUDDEN...

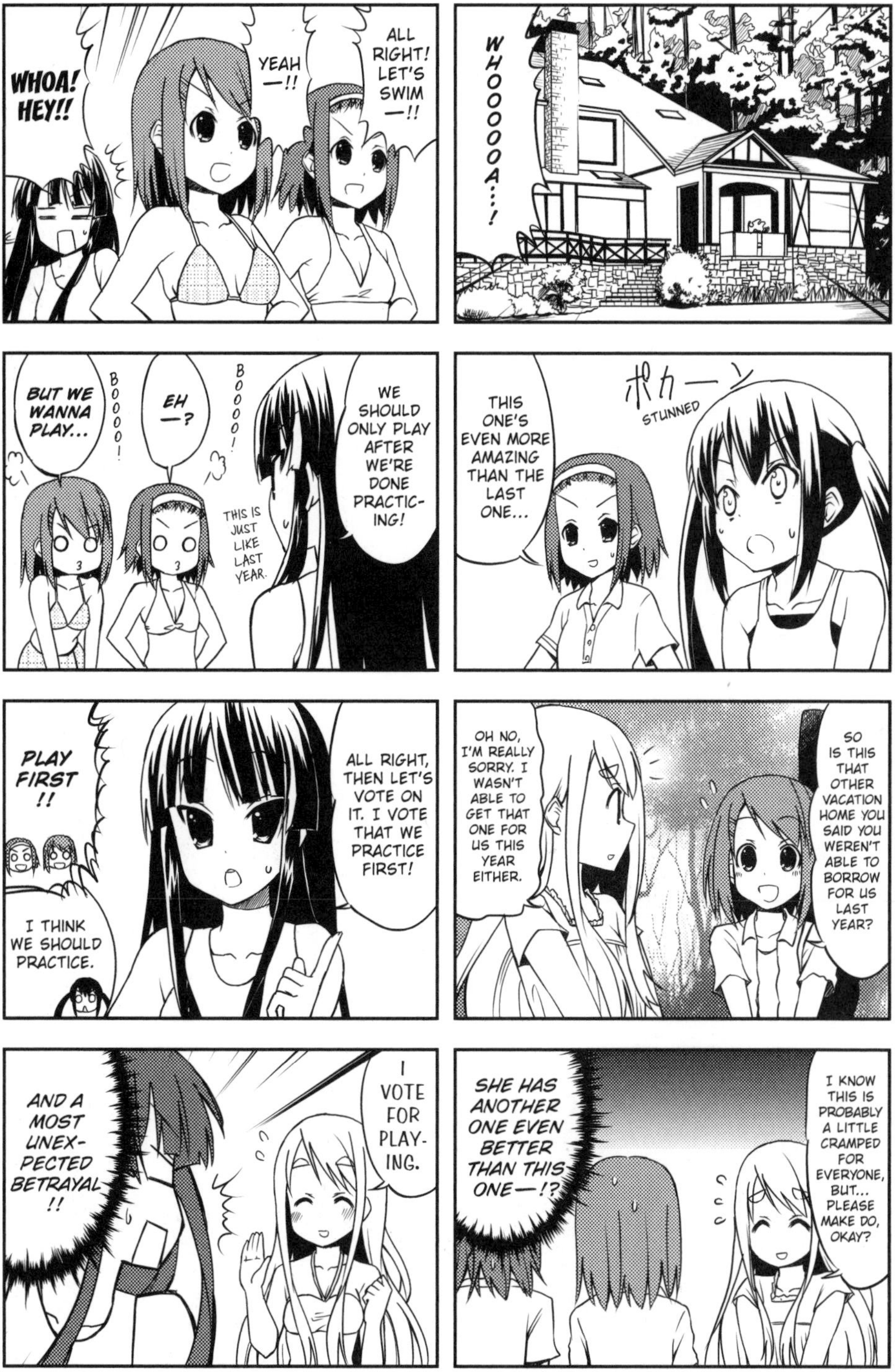
WHOOOOOOA...!
ポカーン
STUNNED
THIS ONE'S EVEN MORE AMAZING THAN THE LAST ONE...
SO IS THIS THAT OTHER VACATION HOME YOU SAID YOU WEREN'T ABLE TO BORROW FOR US LAST YEAR?
OH NO, I'M REALLY SORRY. I WASN'T ABLE TO GET THAT ONE FOR US THIS YEAR EITHER.
I KNOW THIS IS PROBABLY A LITTLE CRAMPED FOR EVERYONE, BUT... PLEASE MAKE DO, OKAY?
SHE HAS ANOTHER ONE EVEN BETTER THAN THIS ONE—!?
ALL RIGHT! LET'S SWIM—!!
YEAH—!!
WHOA! HEY!!
WE SHOULD ONLY PLAY AFTER WE'RE DONE PRACTIC-ING!
BOOOOO!
THIS IS JUST LIKE LAST YEAR.
EH—?
BOOOOO!
BUT WE WANNA PLAY...
ALL RIGHT, THEN LET'S VOTE ON IT. I VOTE THAT WE PRACTICE FIRST!
PLAY FIRST!!
I THINK WE SHOULD PRACTICE.
I VOTE FOR PLAY-ING.
AND A MOST UNEX-PECTED BETRAYAL!!

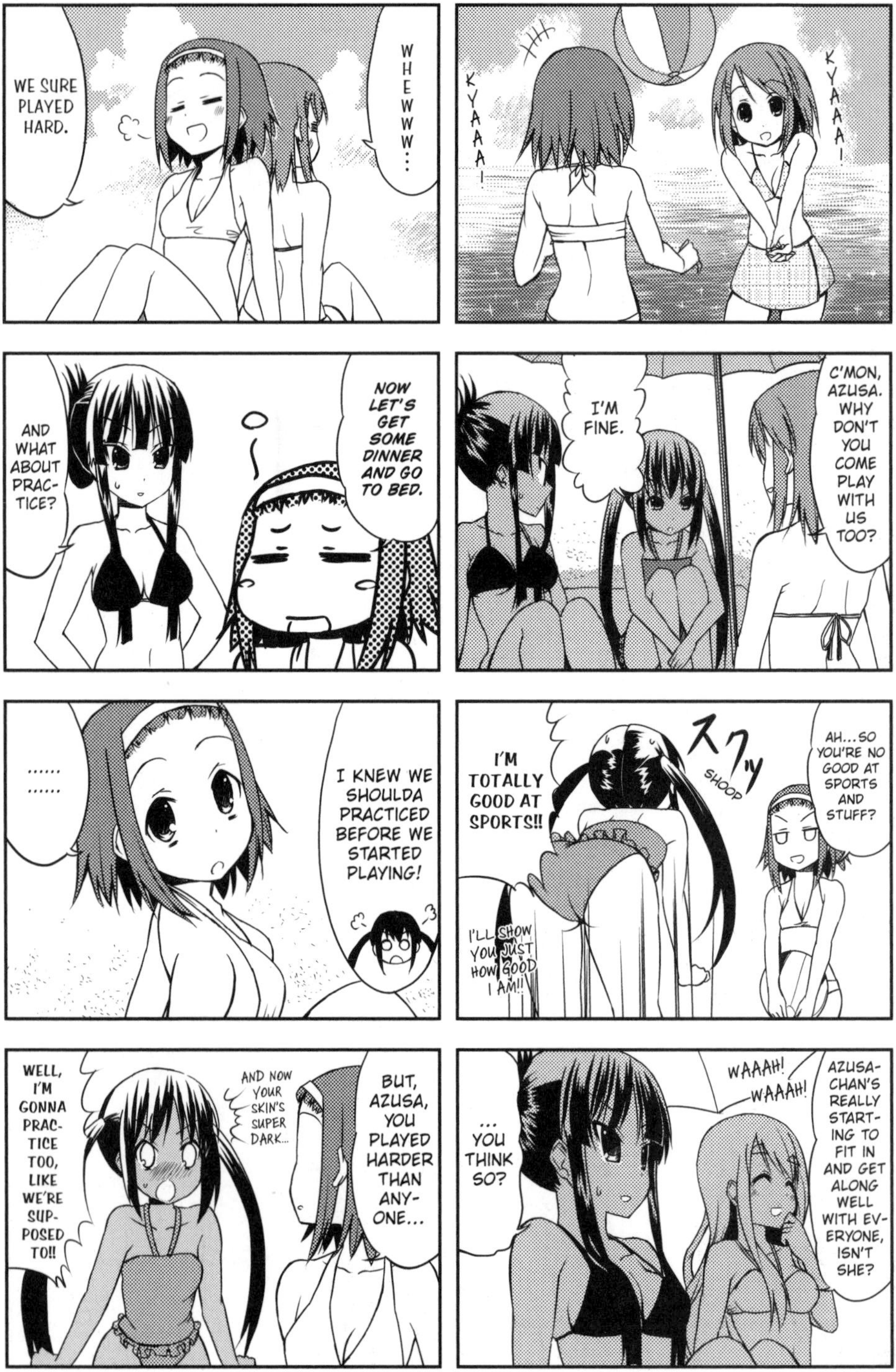
KYAAAI
KYAAAI
WHEWWWW...
WE SURE PLAYED HARD.
C'MON, AZUSA. WHY DON'T YOU COME PLAY WITH US TOO?
I'M FINE.
NOW LET'S GET SOME DINNER AND GO TO BED.
AND WHAT ABOUT PRAC-TICE?
AH...SO YOU'RE NO GOOD AT SPORTS AND STUFF?
スクッ
SHOOP
I'M TOTALLY GOOD AT SPORTS!!
I'LL SHOW YOU JUST HOW GOOD I AM!!
I KNEW WE SHOULDA PRACTICED BEFORE WE STARTED PLAYING!
......
......
AZUSA-CHAN'S REALLY START-ING TO FIT IN AND GET ALONG WELL WITH EV-ERYONE, ISN'T SHE?
WAAAH!
WAAAH!
... YOU THINK SO?
BUT, AZUSA, YOU PLAYED HARDER THAN ANY-ONE...
AND NOW YOUR SKIN'S SUPER DARK...
WELL, I'M GONNA PRAC-TICE TOO, LIKE WE'RE SUP-POSED TO!!

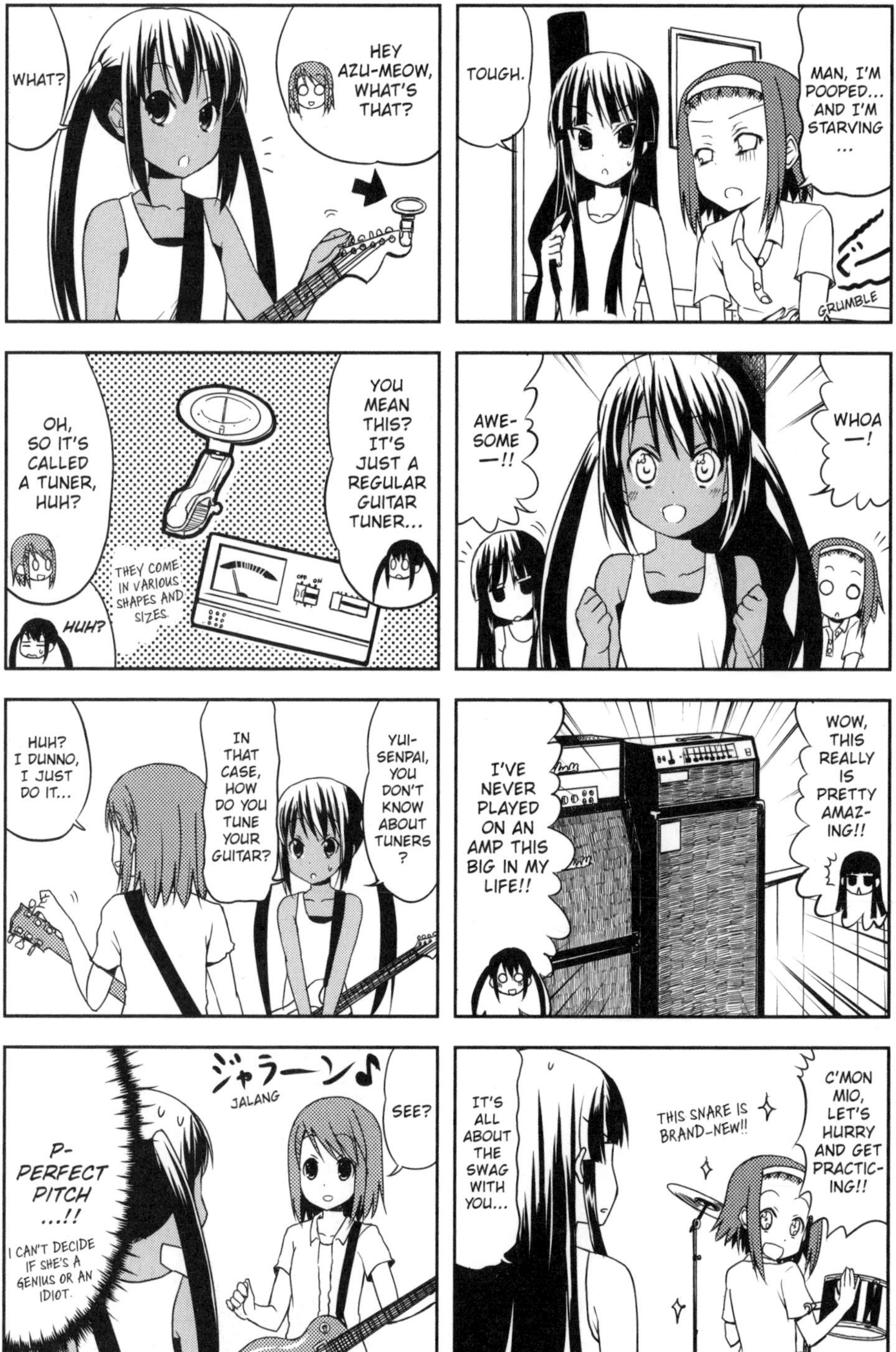
MAN, I'M POOPED... AND I'M STARVING ...
TOUGH.
GRUMBLE
WHOA —!
AWESOME —!!
WOW, THIS REALLY IS PRETTY AMAZING!!
I'VE NEVER PLAYED ON AN AMP THIS BIG IN MY LIFE!!
C'MON MIO, LET'S HURRY AND GET PRACTICING!!
THIS SNARE IS BRAND-NEW!!
IT'S ALL ABOUT THE SWAG WITH YOU...
HEY AZU-MEOW, WHAT'S THAT?
WHAT?
YOU MEAN THIS? IT'S JUST A REGULAR GUITAR TUNER...
OH, SO IT'S CALLED A TUNER, HUH?
THEY COME IN VARIOUS SHAPES AND SIZES.
HUH?
YUI-SENPAI, YOU DON'T KNOW ABOUT TUNERS ?
IN THAT CASE, HOW DO YOU TUNE YOUR GUITAR?
HUH? I DUNNO, I JUST DO IT...
SEE?
ジャラーン♪
JALANG
P-PERFECT PITCH ...!!
I CAN'T DECIDE IF SHE'S A GENIUS OR AN IDIOT.

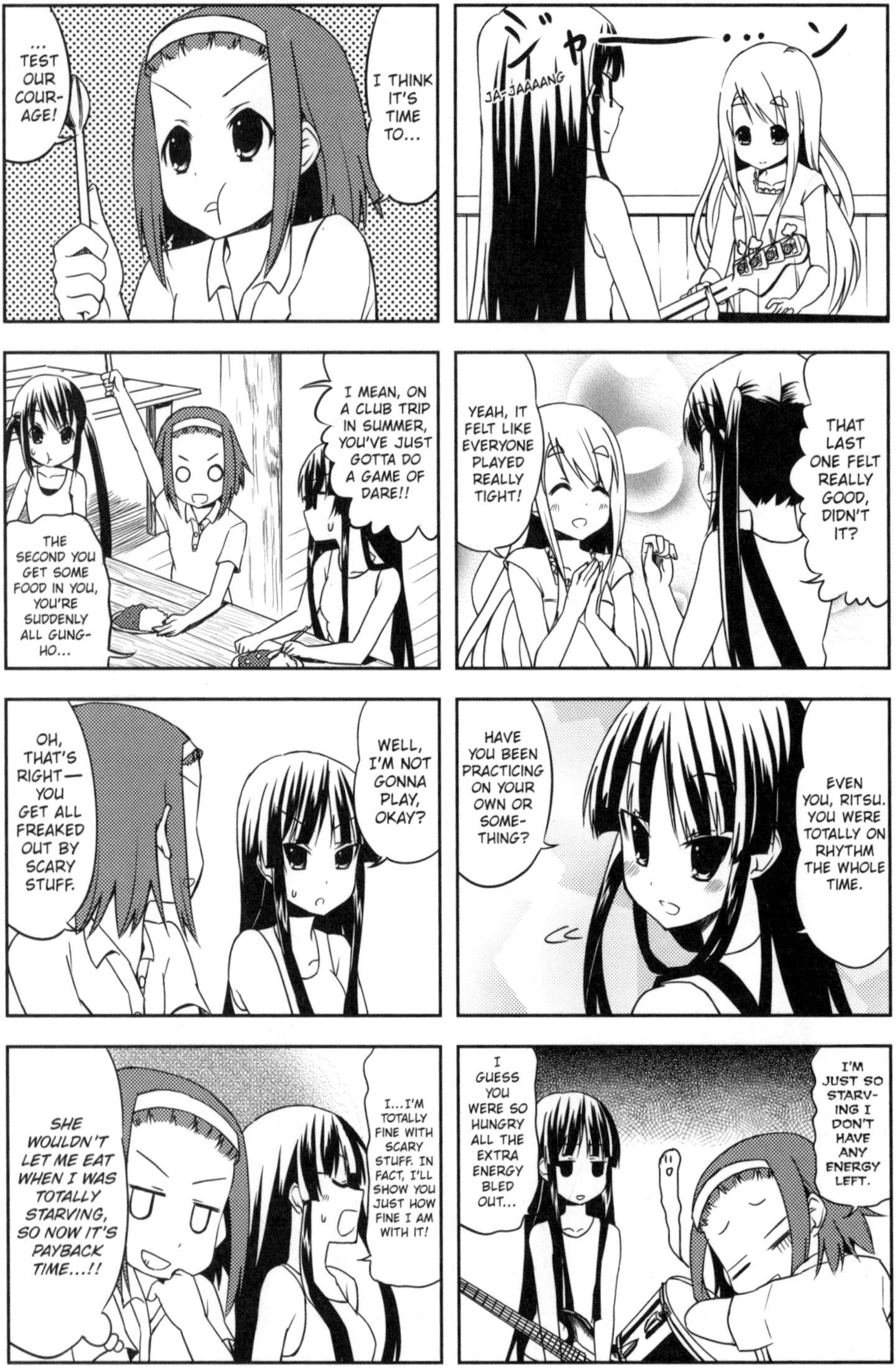
ジャーー…ン
JA-JAAAANG
THAT LAST ONE FELT REALLY GOOD, DIDN'T IT?
YEAH, IT FELT LIKE EVERYONE PLAYED REALLY TIGHT!
EVEN YOU, RITSU. YOU WERE TOTALLY ON RHYTHM THE WHOLE TIME.
HAVE YOU BEEN PRACTICING ON YOUR OWN OR SOMETHING?
I'M JUST SO STARVING I DON'T HAVE ANY ENERGY LEFT.
I GUESS YOU WERE SO HUNGRY ALL THE EXTRA ENERGY BLED OUT...
I THINK IT'S TIME TO...
...TEST OUR COURAGE!
I MEAN, ON A CLUB TRIP IN SUMMER, YOU'VE JUST GOTTA DO A GAME OF DARE!!
THE SECOND YOU GET SOME FOOD IN YOU, YOU'RE SUDDENLY ALL GUNG-HO...
WELL, I'M NOT GONNA PLAY, OKAY?
OH, THAT'S RIGHT—YOU GET ALL FREAKED OUT BY SCARY STUFF.
I...I'M TOTALLY FINE WITH SCARY STUFF. IN FACT, I'LL SHOW YOU JUST HOW FINE I AM WITH IT!
SHE WOULDN'T LET ME EAT WHEN I WAS TOTALLY STARVING, SO NOW IT'S PAYBACK TIME...!!

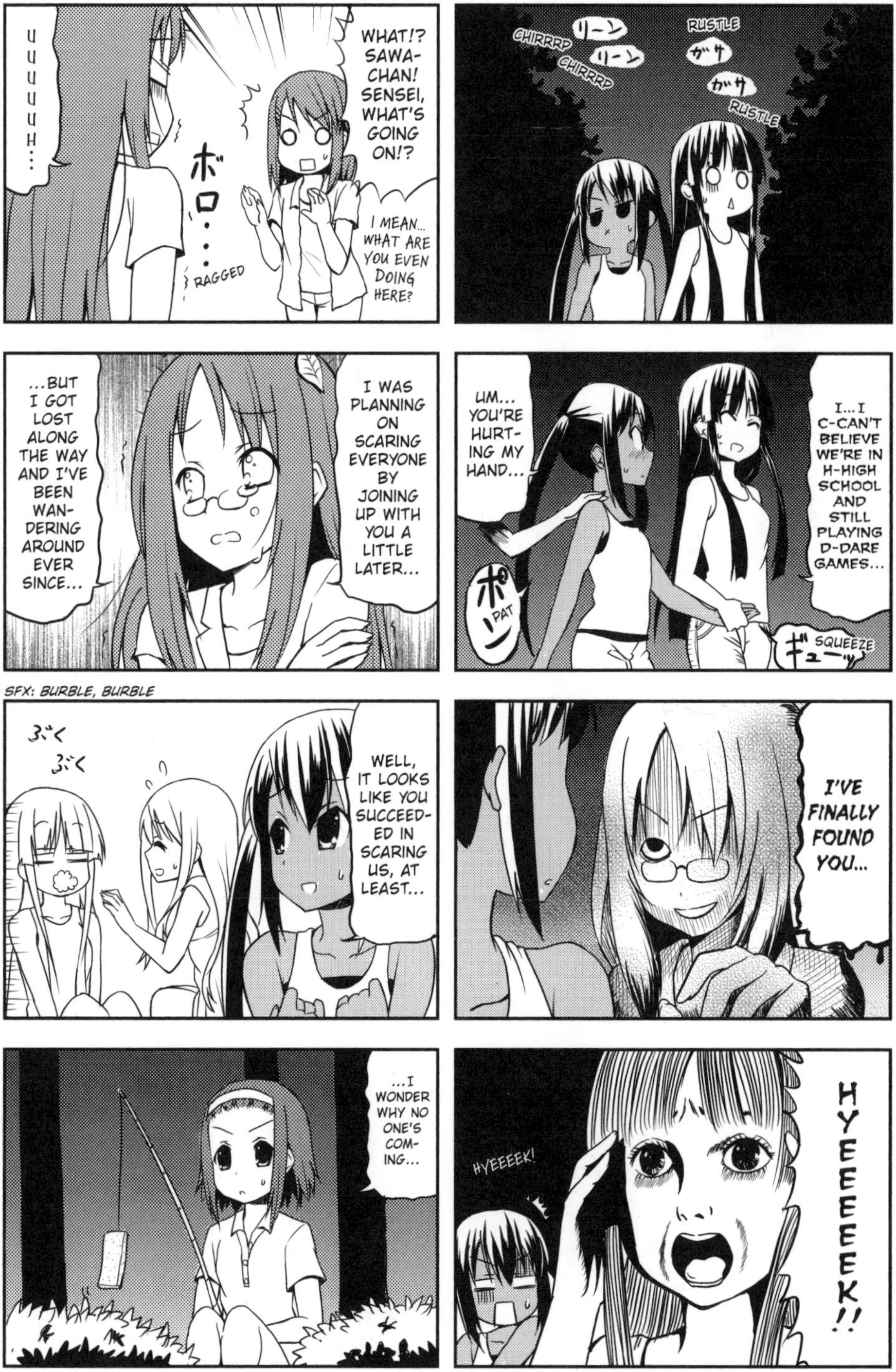
CHIRRRP
リーン
CHIRRRP
リーン
RUSTLE
ガサ
ガサ
RUSTLE
I...I C-CAN'T BELIEVE WE'RE IN H-HIGH SCHOOL AND STILL PLAYING D-DARE GAMES...
UM... YOU'RE HURT-ING MY HAND...
ポン PAT
ギューッ SQUEEZE
I'VE FINALLY FOUND YOU...
HYEEEEEK!!
HYEEEEK!
WHAT!? SAWA-CHAN! SENSEI, WHAT'S GOING ON!?
I MEAN... WHAT ARE YOU EVEN DOING HERE?
UUUUUUUH...
ボロ・・・ RAGGED
I WAS PLANNING ON SCARING EVERYONE BY JOINING UP WITH YOU A LITTLE LATER...
...BUT I GOT LOST ALONG THE WAY AND I'VE BEEN WAN-DERING AROUND EVER SINCE...
SFX: BURBLE, BURBLE
WELL, IT LOOKS LIKE YOU SUCCEEDED-ED IN SCARING US, AT LEAST...
ぶく
ぶく
...I WONDER WHY NO ONE'S COM-ING...

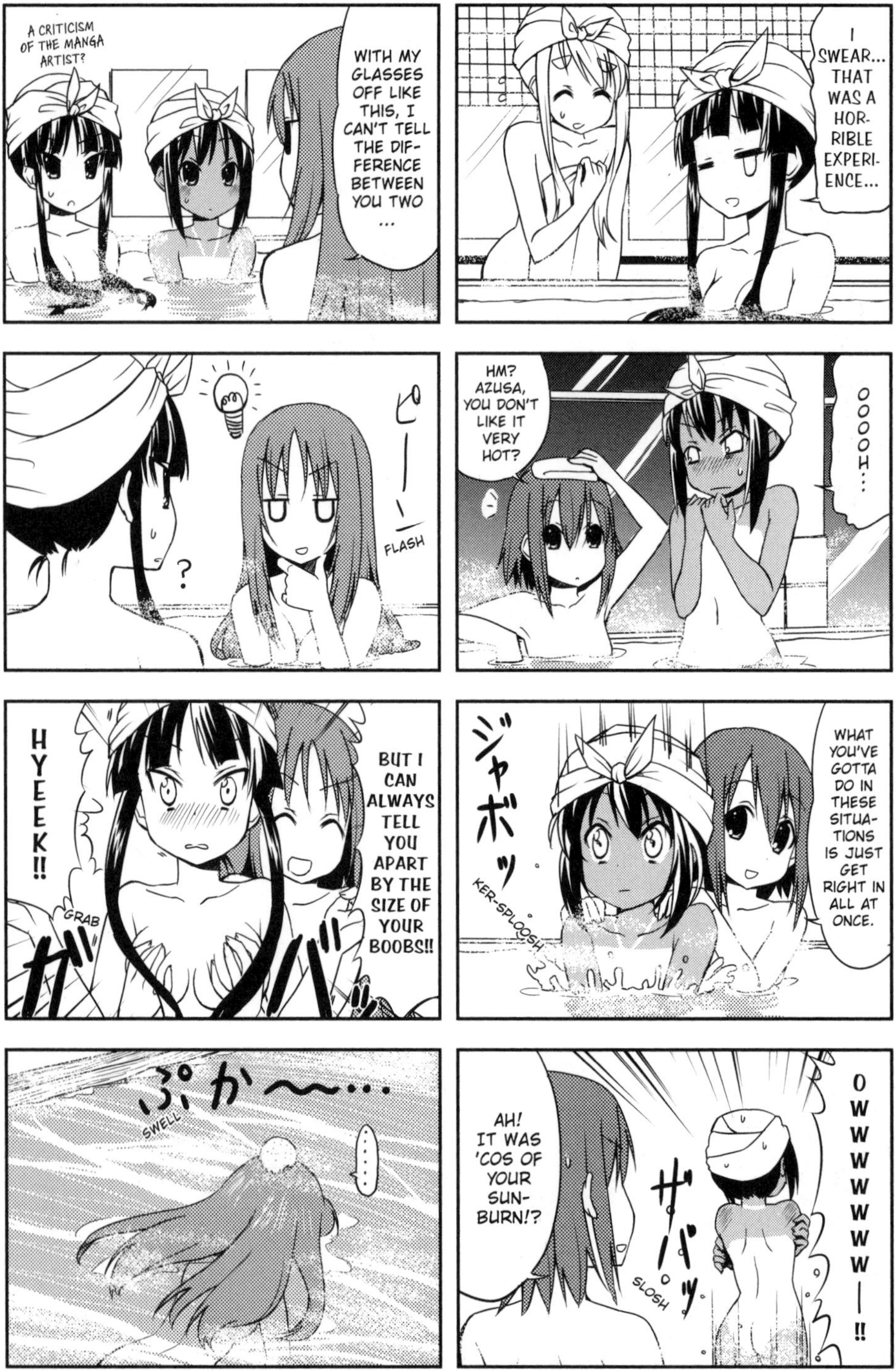
I SWEAR... THAT WAS A HORRIBLE EXPERIENCE...
HM? AZUSA, YOU DON'T LIKE IT VERY HOT?
OOOOH...
WHAT YOU'VE GOTTA DO IN THESE SITUATIONS IS JUST GET RIGHT IN ALL AT ONCE.
ジャボッ
KER-SPLOOSH
OWWWWWWWWW—!!
AH! IT WAS 'COS OF YOUR SUNBURN!?
ザバッ
SLOSH
WITH MY GLASSES OFF LIKE THIS, I CAN'T TELL THE DIFFERENCE BETWEEN YOU TWO ...
A CRITICISM OF THE MANGA ARTIST?
ピーン
FLASH
?
HYEEEK!!
BUT I CAN ALWAYS TELL YOU APART BY THE SIZE OF YOUR BOOBS!!
GRAB
ぷか～～…
SWELL
.....

MAN, YOU'RE REALLY LATE... ER, I MEAN...

SORRY! SORRY I'M LATE!

TMP

TMP

TODAY I'M GOING OUT WITH MY FRIEND AZUSA-CHAN.

HI, MY NAME IS UI HIRA-SAWA.

...WHO ARE YOU?

HER SKIN'S REALLY DARK.

SHOCK

?

AH.

HI—!

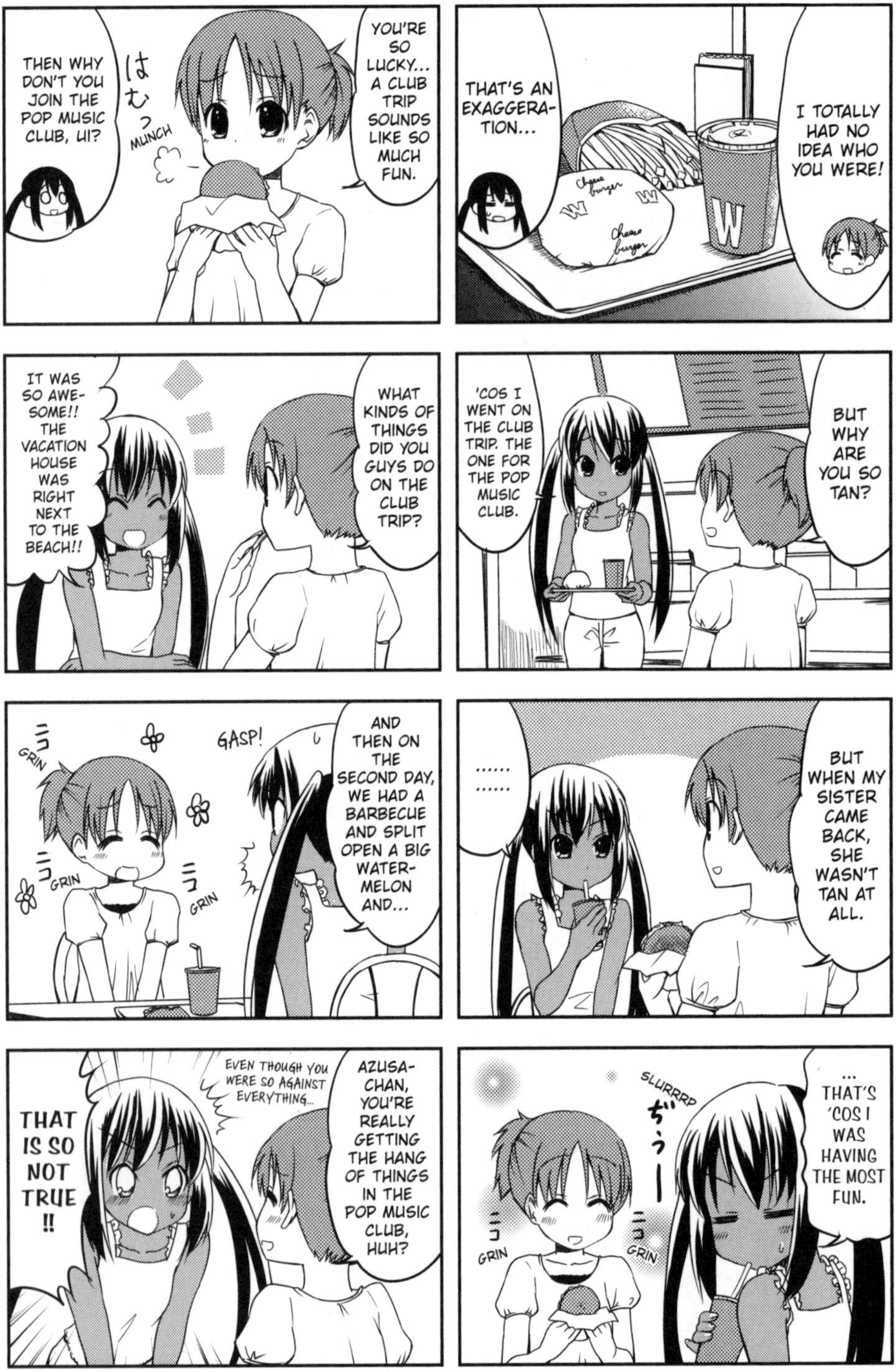
I TOTALLY HAD NO IDEA WHO YOU WERE!
THAT'S AN EXAGGERA-TION...
YOU'RE SO LUCKY... A CLUB TRIP SOUNDS LIKE SO MUCH FUN.
はむっ
MUNCH
THEN WHY DON'T YOU JOIN THE POP MUSIC CLUB, UI?
BUT WHY ARE YOU SO TAN?
'COS I WENT ON THE CLUB TRIP. THE ONE FOR THE POP MUSIC CLUB.
WHAT KINDS OF THINGS DID YOU GUYS DO ON THE CLUB TRIP?
IT WAS SO AWE-SOME!! THE VACATION HOUSE WAS RIGHT NEXT TO THE BEACH!!
BUT WHEN MY SISTER CAME BACK, SHE WASN'T TAN AT ALL.
....
AND THEN ON THE SECOND DAY, WE HAD A BARBECUE AND SPLIT OPEN A BIG WATER-MELON AND...
GASP!
ニコ GRIN
ニコ GRIN
ニコ GRIN
...THAT'S 'COS I WAS HAVING THE MOST FUN.
ぢぅー
SLURRRP
ニコ GRIN
ニコ GRIN
AZUSA-CHAN, YOU'RE REALLY GETTING THE HANG OF THINGS IN THE POP MUSIC CLUB, HUH?
EVEN THOUGH YOU WERE SO AGAINST EVERYTHING...
THAT IS SO NOT TRUE!!

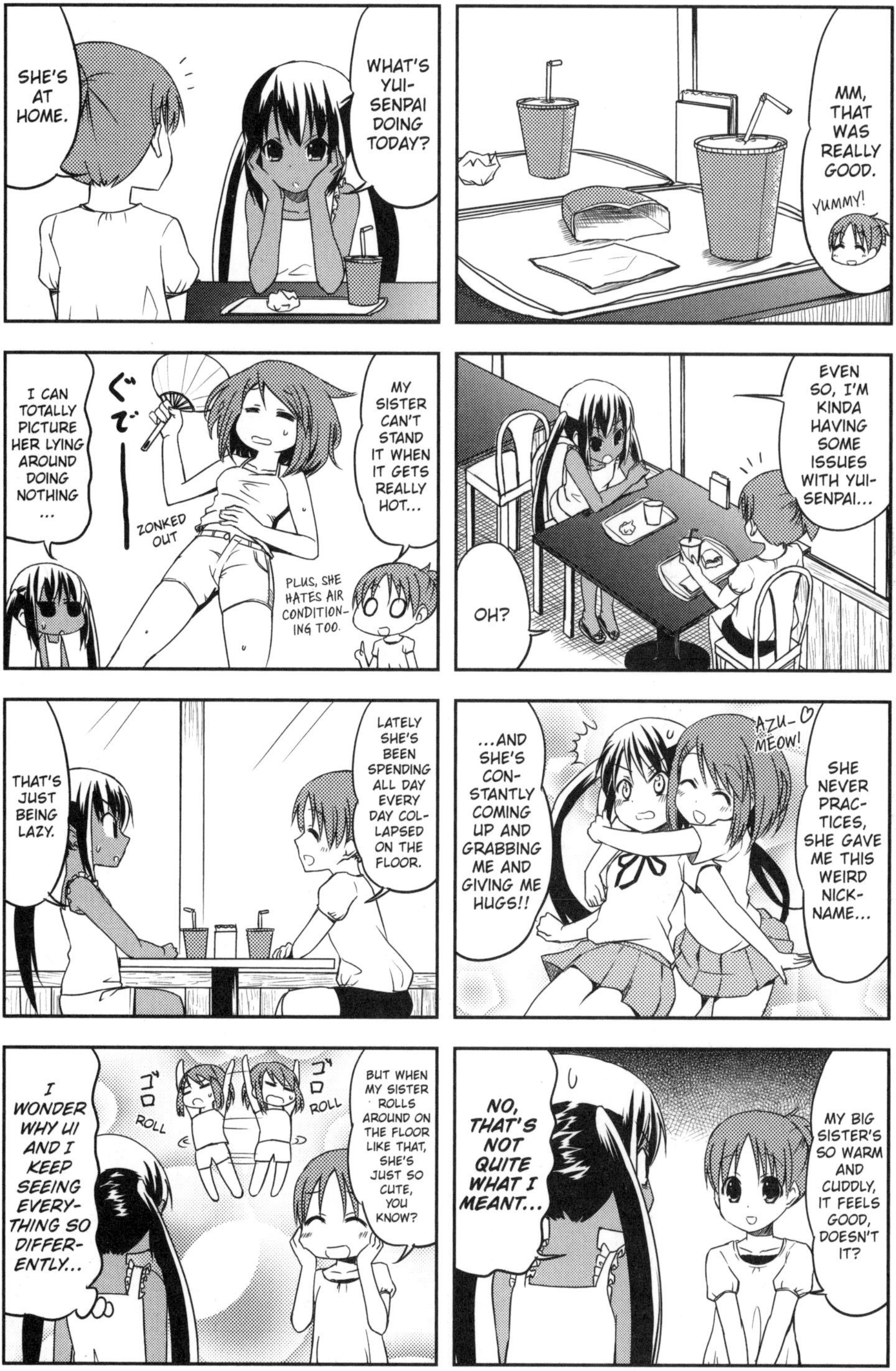
MM, THAT WAS REALLY GOOD.
YUMMY!
WHAT'S YUI-SENPAI DOING TODAY?
SHE'S AT HOME.
EVEN SO, I'M KINDA HAVING SOME ISSUES WITH YUI-SENPAI...
OH?
MY SISTER CAN'T STAND IT WHEN IT GETS REALLY HOT...
ぐでー
ZONKED OUT
I CAN TOTALLY PICTURE HER LYING AROUND DOING NOTHING...
PLUS, SHE HATES AIR CONDITIONING TOO.
SHE NEVER PRACTICES, SHE GAVE ME THIS WEIRD NICKNAME...
AZU-♡ MEOW!
...AND SHE'S CONSTANTLY COMING UP AND GRABBING ME AND GIVING ME HUGS!!
LATELY SHE'S BEEN SPENDING ALL DAY EVERY DAY COLLAPSED ON THE FLOOR.
THAT'S JUST BEING LAZY.
MY BIG SISTER'S SO WARM AND CUDDLY, IT FEELS GOOD, DOESN'T IT?
NO, THAT'S NOT QUITE WHAT I MEANT...
BUT WHEN MY SISTER ROLLS AROUND ON THE FLOOR LIKE THAT, SHE'S JUST SO CUTE, YOU KNOW?
ゴロ ROLL
ゴロ ROLL
I WONDER WHY UI AND I KEEP SEEING EVERYTHING SO DIFFERENTLY...

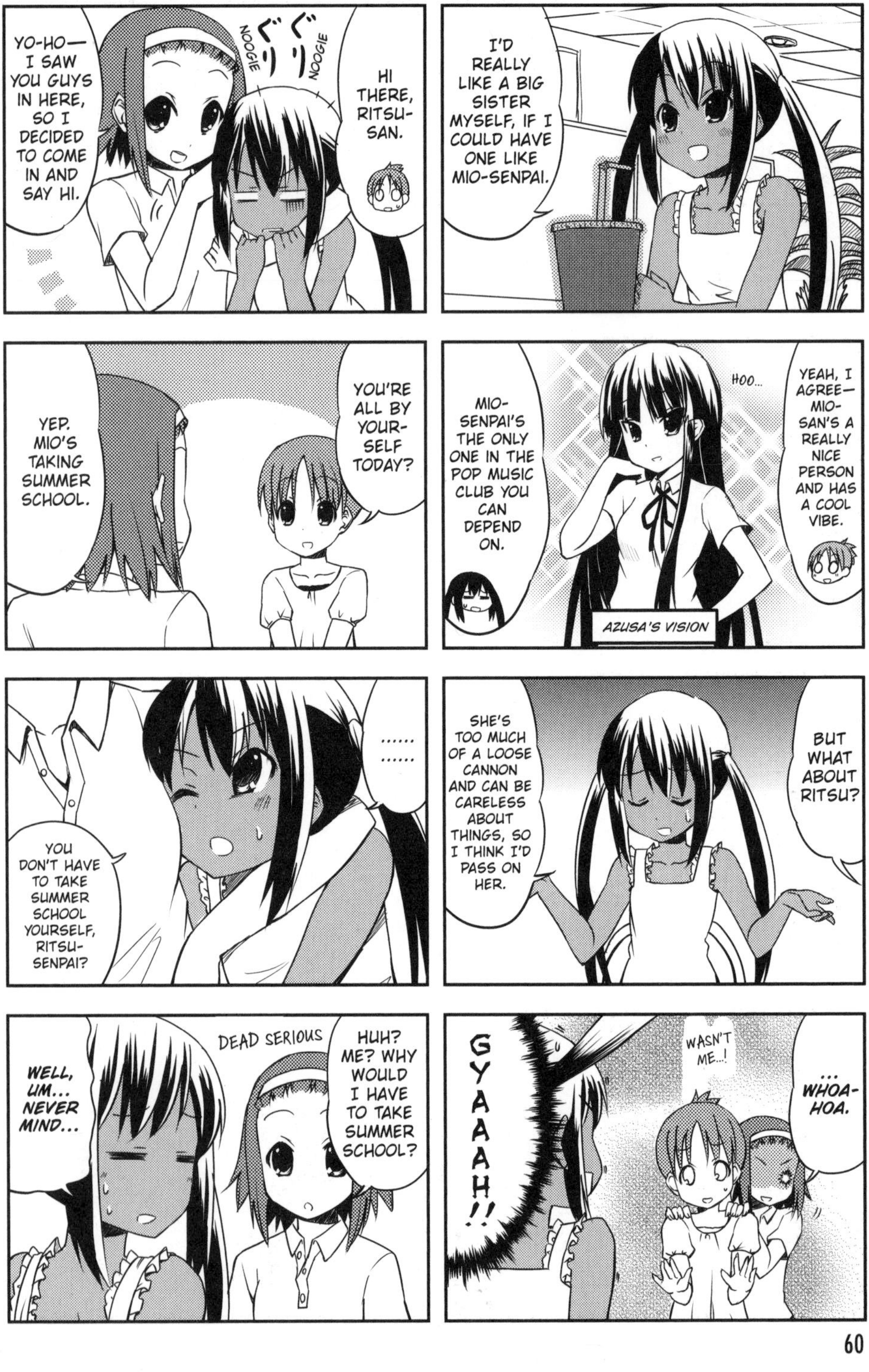

I'D REALLY LIKE A BIG SISTER MYSELF, IF I COULD HAVE ONE LIKE MIO-SENPAI.
YEAH, I AGREE—MIO-SAN'S A REALLY NICE PERSON AND HAS A COOL VIBE.
HOO...
MIO-SENPAI'S THE ONLY ONE IN THE POP MUSIC CLUB YOU CAN DEPEND ON.
AZUSA'S VISION
BUT WHAT ABOUT RITSU?
SHE'S TOO MUCH OF A LOOSE CANNON AND CAN BE CARELESS ABOUT THINGS, SO I THINK I'D PASS ON HER.
... WHOA-HOA.
WASN'T ME...!
GYAAAH!!
HI THERE, RITSU-SAN.
ぐりぐり
NOOGIE NOOGIE
YO-HO— I SAW YOU GUYS IN HERE, SO I DECIDED TO COME IN AND SAY HI.
YOU'RE ALL BY YOURSELF TODAY?
YEP. MIO'S TAKING SUMMER SCHOOL.
......
......
YOU DON'T HAVE TO TAKE SUMMER SCHOOL YOURSELF, RITSU-SENPAI?
HUH? ME? WHY WOULD I HAVE TO TAKE SUMMER SCHOOL?
DEAD SERIOUS
WELL, UM... NEVER MIND...

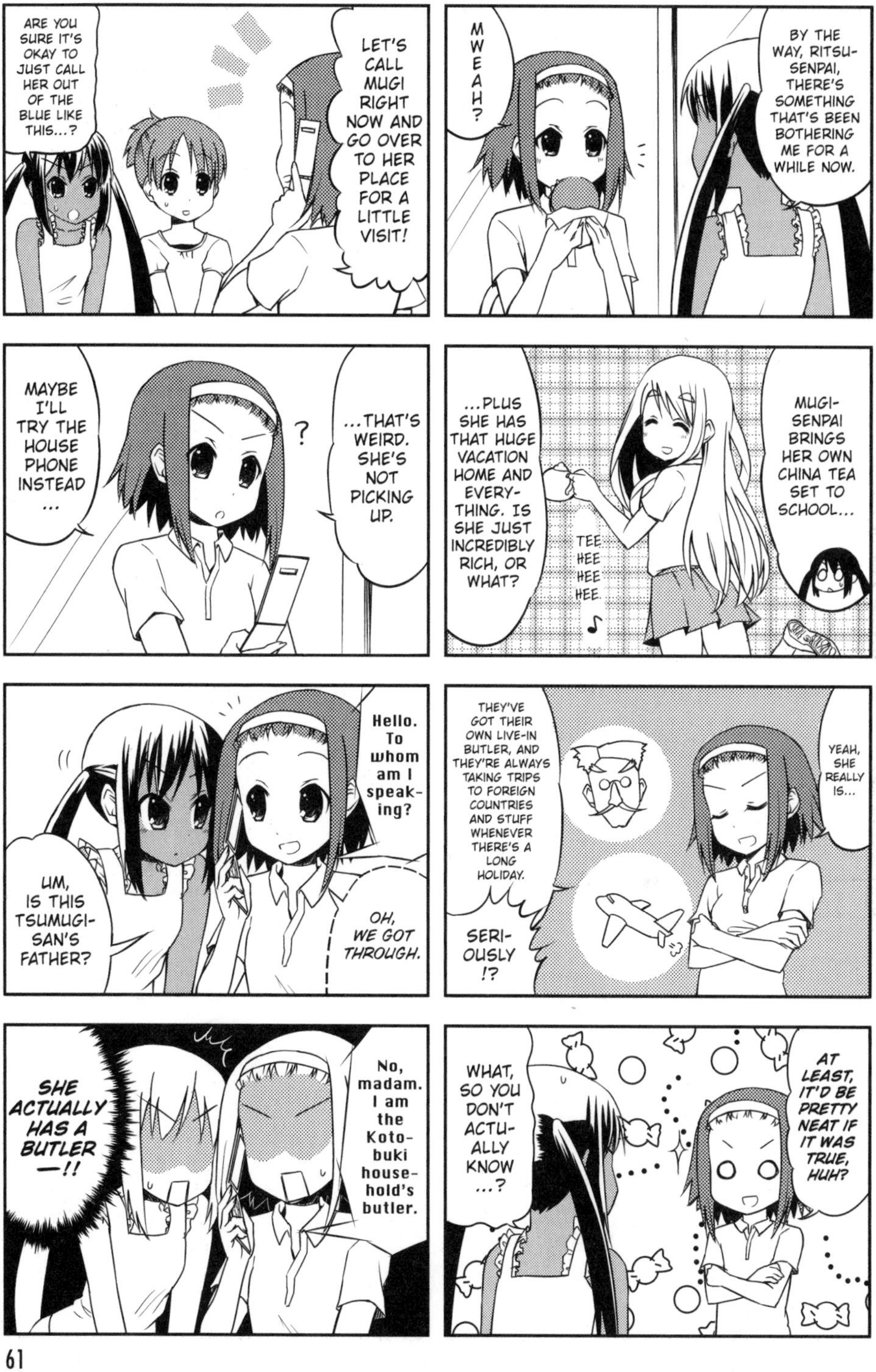
BY THE WAY, RITSU-SENPAI, THERE'S SOMETHING THAT'S BEEN BOTHERING ME FOR A WHILE NOW.
MWEAH?
MUGI-SENPAI BRINGS HER OWN CHINA TEA SET TO SCHOOL...
...PLUS SHE HAS THAT HUGE VACATION HOME AND EVERY-THING. IS SHE JUST INCREDIBLY RICH, OR WHAT?
TEE HEE HEE HEE.
YEAH, SHE REALLY IS...
THEY'VE GOT THEIR OWN LIVE-IN BUTLER, AND THEY'RE ALWAYS TAKING TRIPS TO FOREIGN COUNTRIES AND STUFF WHENEVER THERE'S A LONG HOLIDAY.
SERI-OUSLY !?
AT LEAST, IT'D BE PRETTY NEAT IF IT WAS TRUE, HUH?
WHAT, SO YOU DON'T ACTU-ALLY KNOW ...?
LET'S CALL MUGI RIGHT NOW AND GO OVER TO HER PLACE FOR A LITTLE VISIT!
ARE YOU SURE IT'S OKAY TO JUST CALL HER OUT OF THE BLUE LIKE THIS...?
...THAT'S WEIRD. SHE'S NOT PICKING UP.
MAYBE I'LL TRY THE HOUSE PHONE INSTEAD ...
Hello. To whom am I speak-ing?
OH, WE GOT THROUGH.
UM, IS THIS TSUMUGI-SAN'S FATHER?
No, madam. I am the Koto-buki house-hold's butler.
SHE ACTUALLY HAS A BUTLER —!!

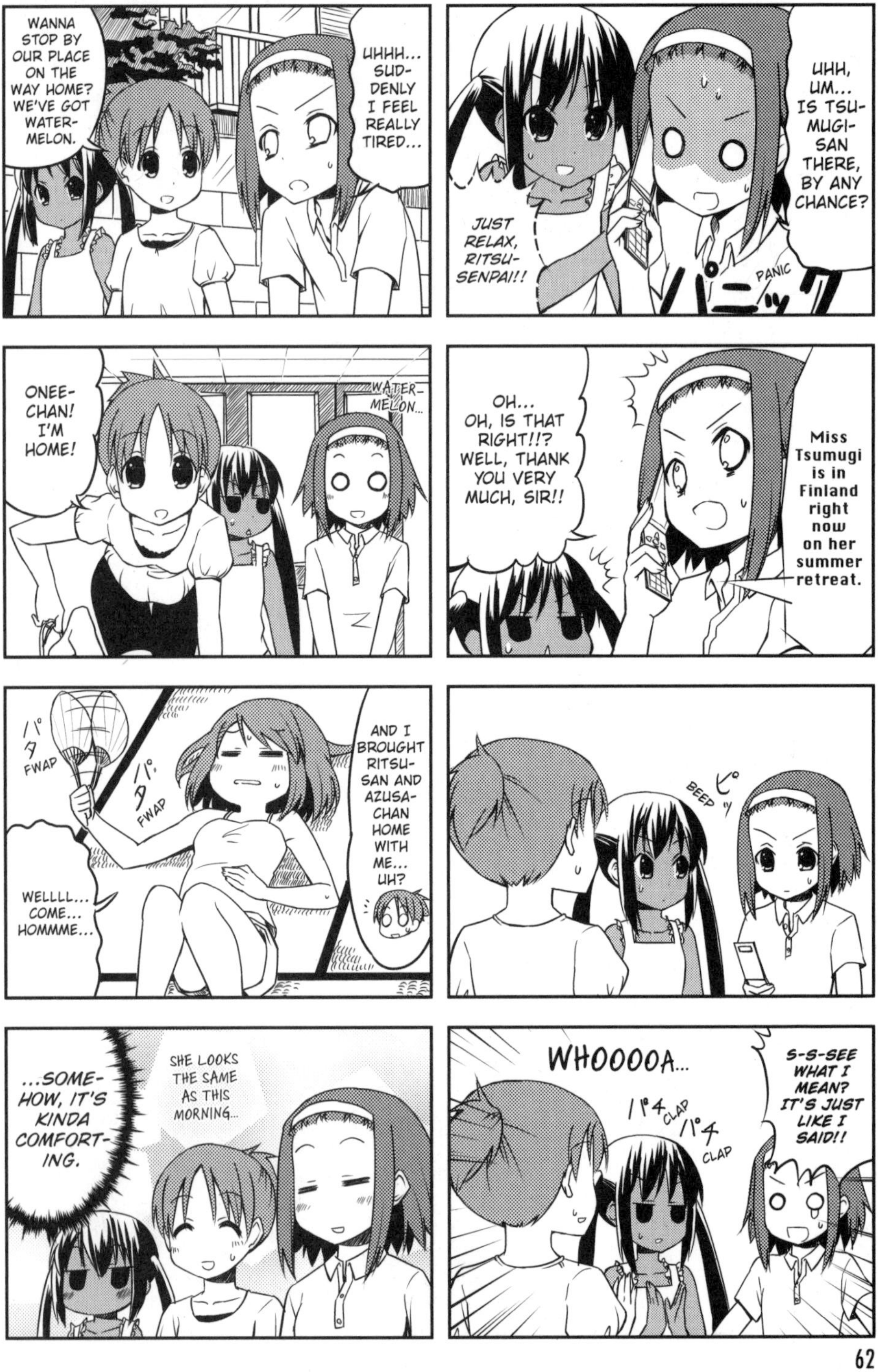
UHH, UM... IS TSUMUGI-SAN THERE, BY ANY CHANCE?
JUST RELAX, RITSU-SENPAI!!
PANIC
UHHH... SUDDENLY I FEEL REALLY TIRED...
WANNA STOP BY OUR PLACE ON THE WAY HOME? WE'VE GOT WATER-MELON.
Miss Tsumugi is in Finland right now on her summer retreat.
OH... OH, IS THAT RIGHT!!? WELL, THANK YOU VERY MUCH, SIR!!
WATER-MELON...
ONEE-CHAN! I'M HOME!
BEEP
AND I BROUGHT RITSU-SAN AND AZUSA-CHAN HOME WITH ME... UH?
FWAP
FWAP
WELLLL... COME... HOMMME...
S-S-SEE WHAT I MEAN? IT'S JUST LIKE I SAID!!
CLAP
CLAP
WHOOOOA...
SHE LOOKS THE SAME AS THIS MORNING...
...SOME-HOW, IT'S KINDA COMFORT-ING.

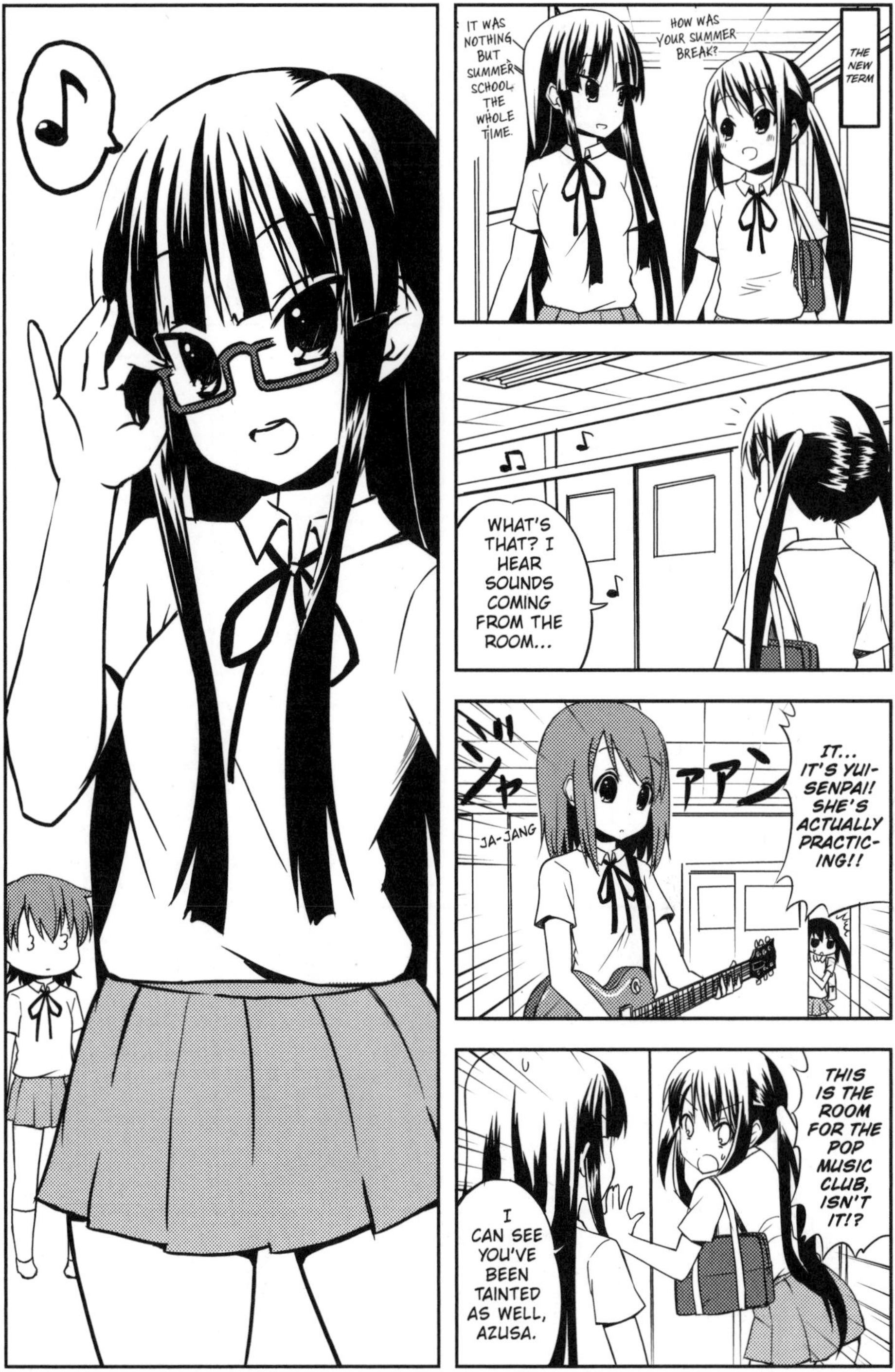
THE NEW TERM
HOW WAS YOUR SUMMER BREAK?
IT WAS NOTHING BUT SUMMER SCHOOL THE WHOLE TIME.
WHAT'S THAT? I HEAR SOUNDS COMING FROM THE ROOM...
IT... IT'S YUI-SENPAI! SHE'S ACTUALLY PRACTIC-ING!!
ジャアアン
JA-JANG
THIS IS THE ROOM FOR THE POP MUSIC CLUB, ISN'T IT!?
I CAN SEE YOU'VE BEEN TAINTED AS WELL, AZUSA.
♪

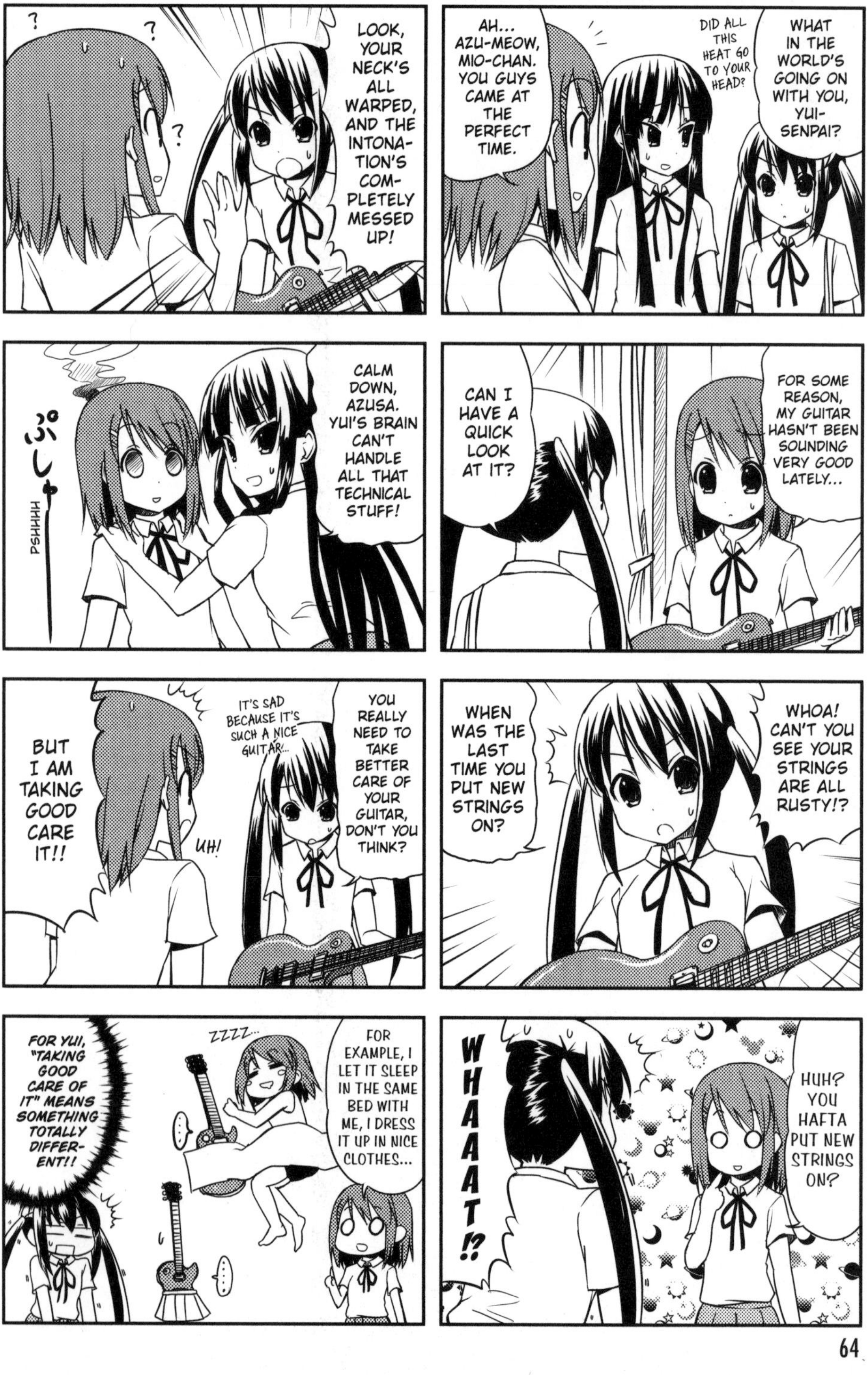
WHAT IN THE WORLD'S GOING ON WITH YOU, YUI-SENPAI?
DID ALL THIS HEAT GO TO YOUR HEAD?
AH... AZU-MEOW, MIO-CHAN. YOU GUYS CAME AT THE PERFECT TIME.
FOR SOME REASON, MY GUITAR HASN'T BEEN SOUNDING VERY GOOD LATELY...
CAN I HAVE A QUICK LOOK AT IT?
WHOA! CAN'T YOU SEE YOUR STRINGS ARE ALL RUSTY!?
WHEN WAS THE LAST TIME YOU PUT NEW STRINGS ON?
HUH? YOU HAFTA PUT NEW STRINGS ON?
WHAAAAT!?
LOOK, YOUR NECK'S ALL WARPED, AND THE INTONATION'S COMPLETELY MESSED UP!
?
?
?
CALM DOWN, AZUSA. YUI'S BRAIN CAN'T HANDLE ALL THAT TECHNICAL STUFF!
ぷしゃ
PSHHHH
YOU REALLY NEED TO TAKE BETTER CARE OF YOUR GUITAR, DON'T YOU THINK?
IT'S SAD BECAUSE IT'S SUCH A NICE GUITAR...
UH!
BUT I AM TAKING GOOD CARE IT!!
FOR EXAMPLE, I LET IT SLEEP IN THE SAME BED WITH ME, I DRESS IT UP IN NICE CLOTHES...
ZZZZ...
FOR YUI, "TAKING GOOD CARE OF IT" MEANS SOMETHING TOTALLY DIFFERENT!!

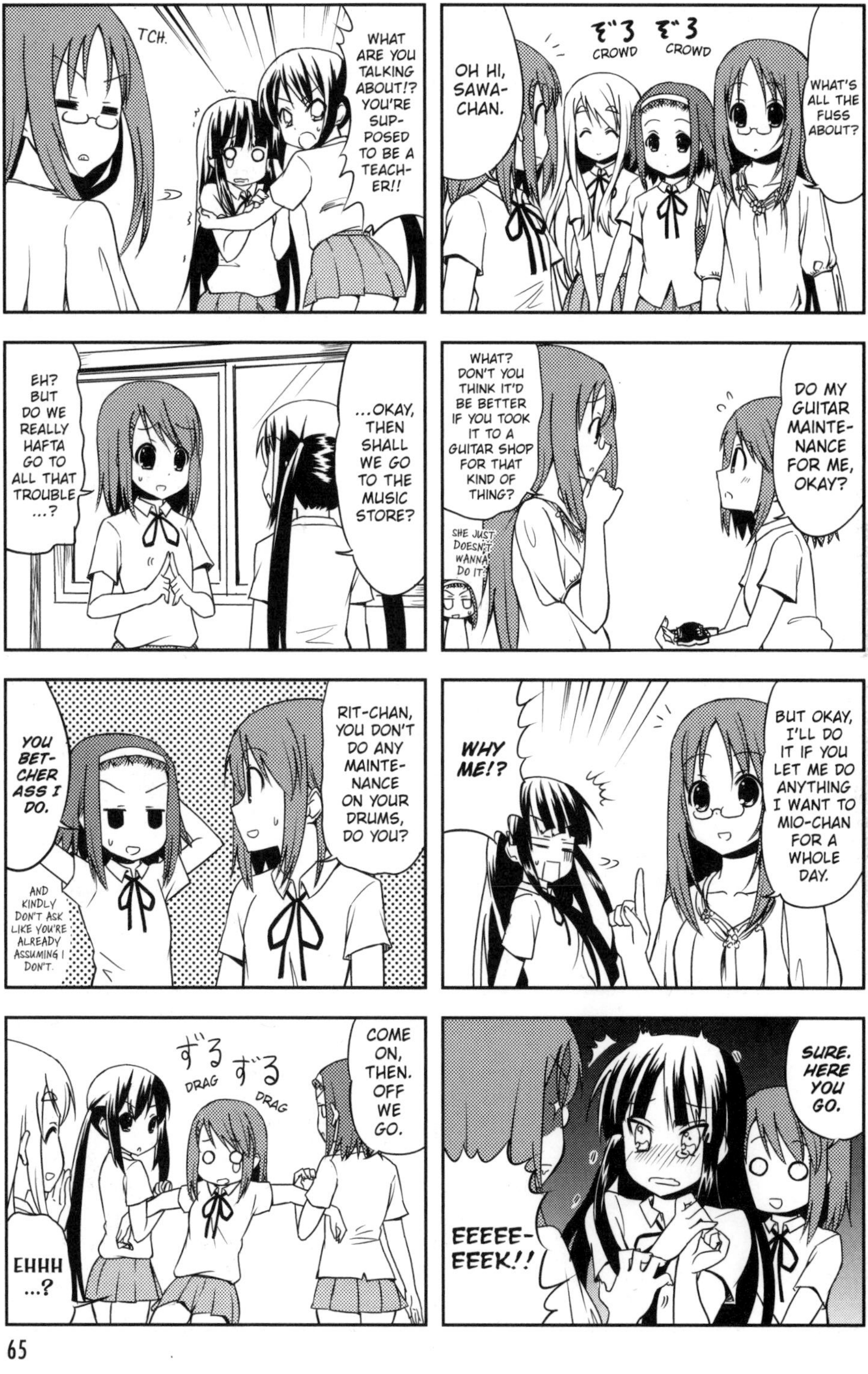
WHAT'S ALL THE FUSS ABOUT?
ぞろ ぞろ
CROWD CROWD
OH HI, SAWA-CHAN.
DO MY GUITAR MAINTENANCE FOR ME, OKAY?
WHAT? DON'T YOU THINK IT'D BE BETTER IF YOU TOOK IT TO A GUITAR SHOP FOR THAT KIND OF THING?
SHE JUST DOESN'T WANNA DO IT.
BUT OKAY, I'LL DO IT IF YOU LET ME DO ANYTHING I WANT TO MIO-CHAN FOR A WHOLE DAY.
WHY ME!?
SURE. HERE YOU GO.
EEEEE-EEEK!!
WHAT ARE YOU TALKING ABOUT!? YOU'RE SUPPOSED TO BE A TEACHER!!
TCH.
...OKAY, THEN SHALL WE GO TO THE MUSIC STORE?
EH? BUT DO WE REALLY HAFTA GO TO ALL THAT TROUBLE...?
RIT-CHAN, YOU DON'T DO ANY MAINTENANCE ON YOUR DRUMS, DO YOU?
YOU BETCHER ASS I DO.
AND KINDLY DON'T ASK LIKE YOU'RE ALREADY ASSUMING I DON'T.
COME ON, THEN. OFF WE GO.
ずる ずる
DRAG DRAG
EHHH...?

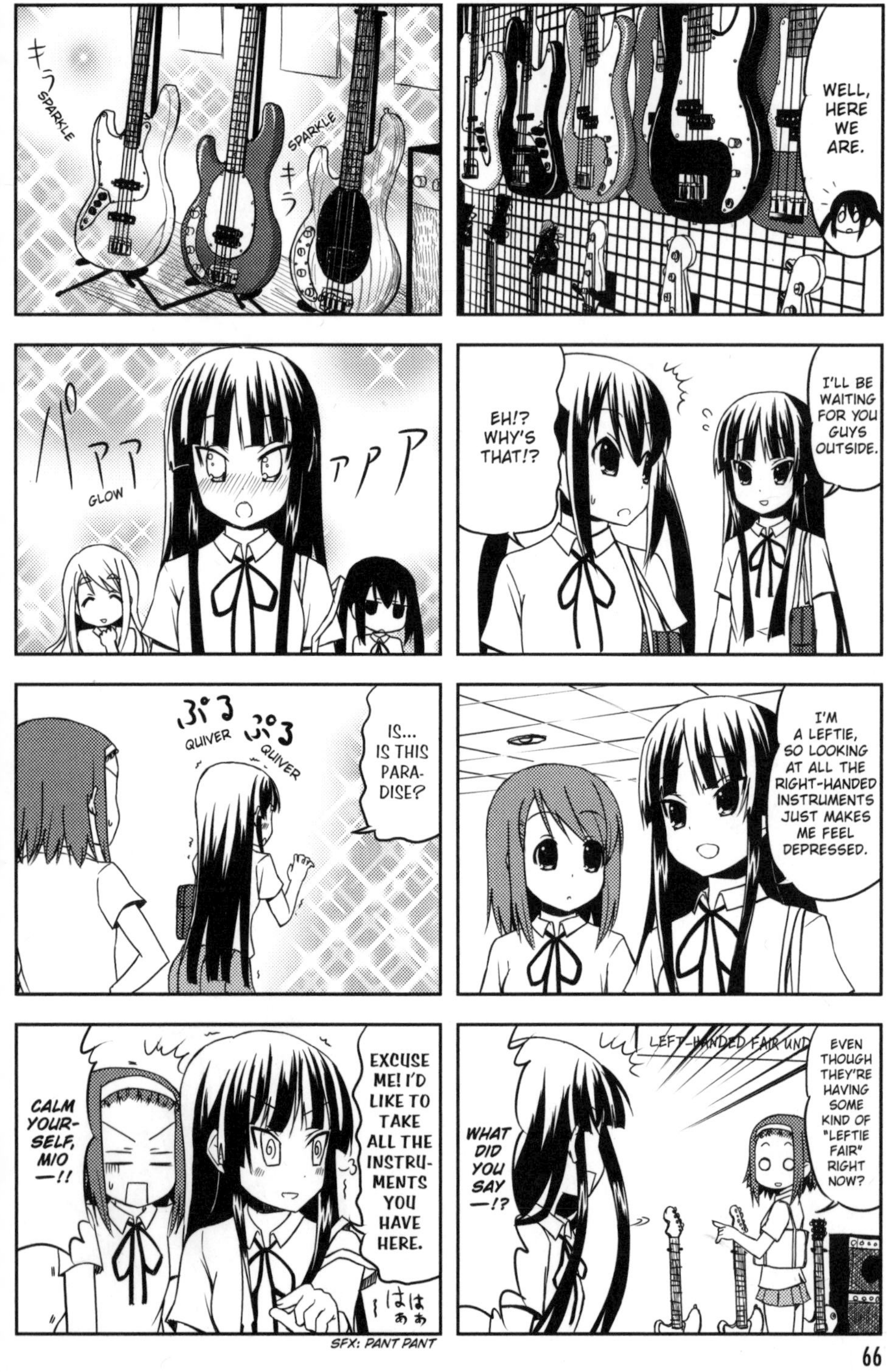
WELL, HERE WE ARE.
キラ
SPARKLE
SPARKLE
キラ
I'LL BE WAITING FOR YOU GUYS OUTSIDE.
EH!? WHY'S THAT!?
パァァァ
GLOW
I'M A LEFTIE, SO LOOKING AT ALL THE RIGHT-HANDED INSTRUMENTS JUST MAKES ME FEEL DEPRESSED.
ぷる
QUIVER
ぷる
QUIVER
IS... IS THIS PARA-DISE?
LEFT-HANDED FAIR UND
EVEN THOUGH THEY'RE HAVING SOME KIND OF "LEFTIE FAIR" RIGHT NOW?
WHAT DID YOU SAY—!?
EXCUSE ME! I'D LIKE TO TAKE ALL THE INSTRU-MENTS YOU HAVE HERE.
はぁはぁ
CALM YOUR-SELF, MIO—!!
SFX: PANT PANT

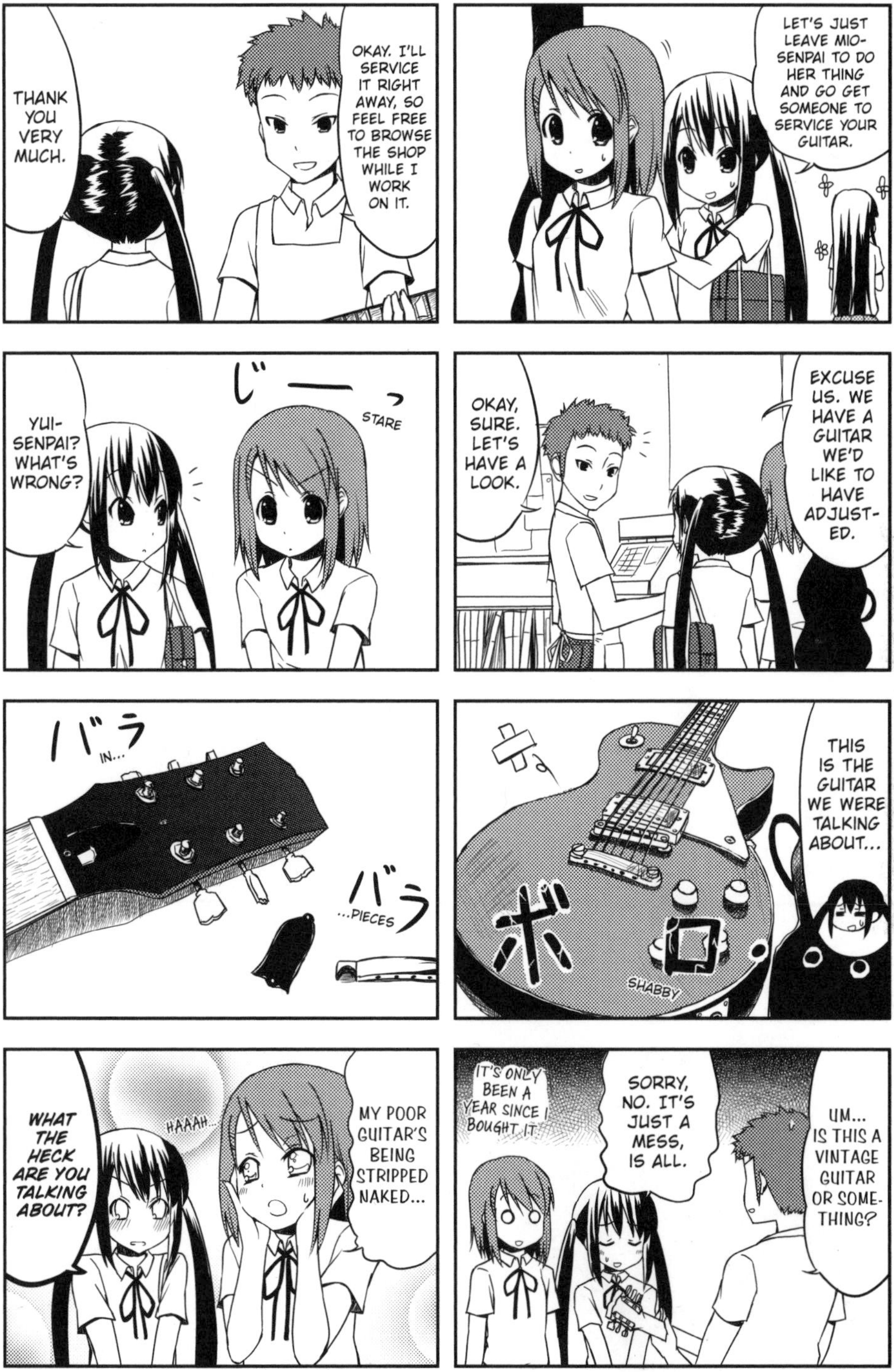
LET'S JUST LEAVE MIO-SENPAI TO DO HER THING AND GO GET SOMEONE TO SERVICE YOUR GUITAR.
OKAY. I'LL SERVICE IT RIGHT AWAY, SO FEEL FREE TO BROWSE THE SHOP WHILE I WORK ON IT.
THANK YOU VERY MUCH.
EXCUSE US. WE HAVE A GUITAR WE'D LIKE TO HAVE ADJUST-ED.
OKAY, SURE. LET'S HAVE A LOOK.
じーっ
STARE
YUI-SENPAI? WHAT'S WRONG?
THIS IS THE GUITAR WE WERE TALKING ABOUT...
ボロ
SHABBY
バラ
IN...
バラ
...PIECES
UM... IS THIS A VINTAGE GUITAR OR SOME-THING?
SORRY, NO. IT'S JUST A MESS, IS ALL.
IT'S ONLY BEEN A YEAR SINCE I BOUGHT IT.
MY POOR GUITAR'S BEING STRIPPED NAKED...
HAAAH...
WHAT THE HECK ARE YOU TALKING ABOUT?

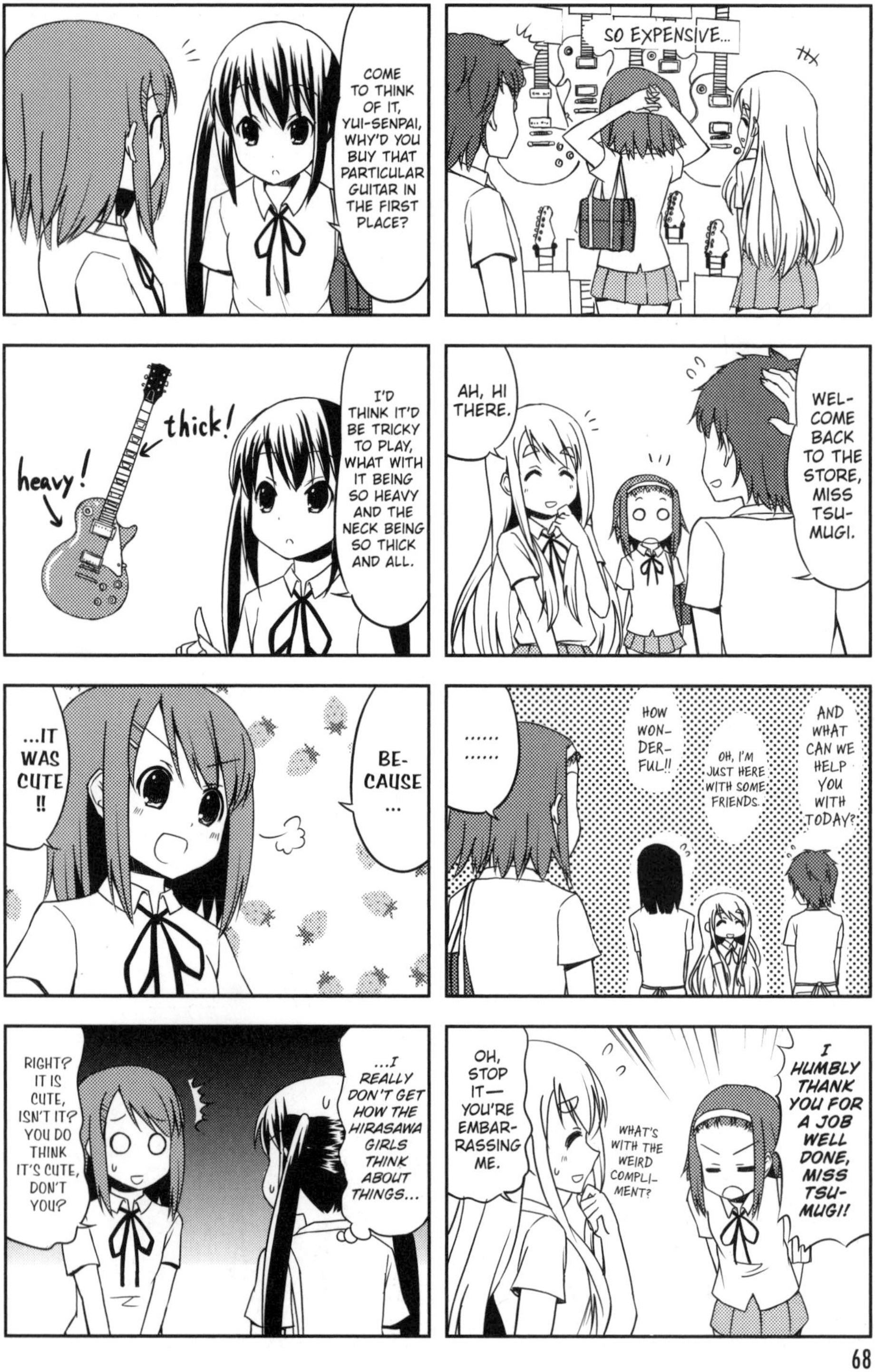
SO EXPENSIVE...
WEL-COME BACK TO THE STORE, MISS TSU-MUGI.
AH, HI THERE.
AND WHAT CAN WE HELP YOU WITH TODAY?
OH, I'M JUST HERE WITH SOME FRIENDS.
HOW WON-DER-FUL!!
......
......
I HUMBLY THANK YOU FOR A JOB WELL DONE, MISS TSU-MUGI!
WHAT'S WITH THE WEIRD COMPLI-MENT?
OH, STOP IT—YOU'RE EMBAR-RASSING ME.
COME TO THINK OF IT, YUI-SENPAI, WHY'D YOU BUY THAT PARTICULAR GUITAR IN THE FIRST PLACE?
I'D THINK IT'D BE TRICKY TO PLAY, WHAT WITH IT BEING SO HEAVY AND THE NECK BEING SO THICK AND ALL.
thick!
heavy!
BE-CAUSE ...
...IT WAS CUTE !!
...I REALLY DON'T GET HOW THE HIRASAWA GIRLS THINK ABOUT THINGS...
RIGHT? IT IS CUTE, ISN'T IT? YOU DO THINK IT'S CUTE, DON'T YOU?

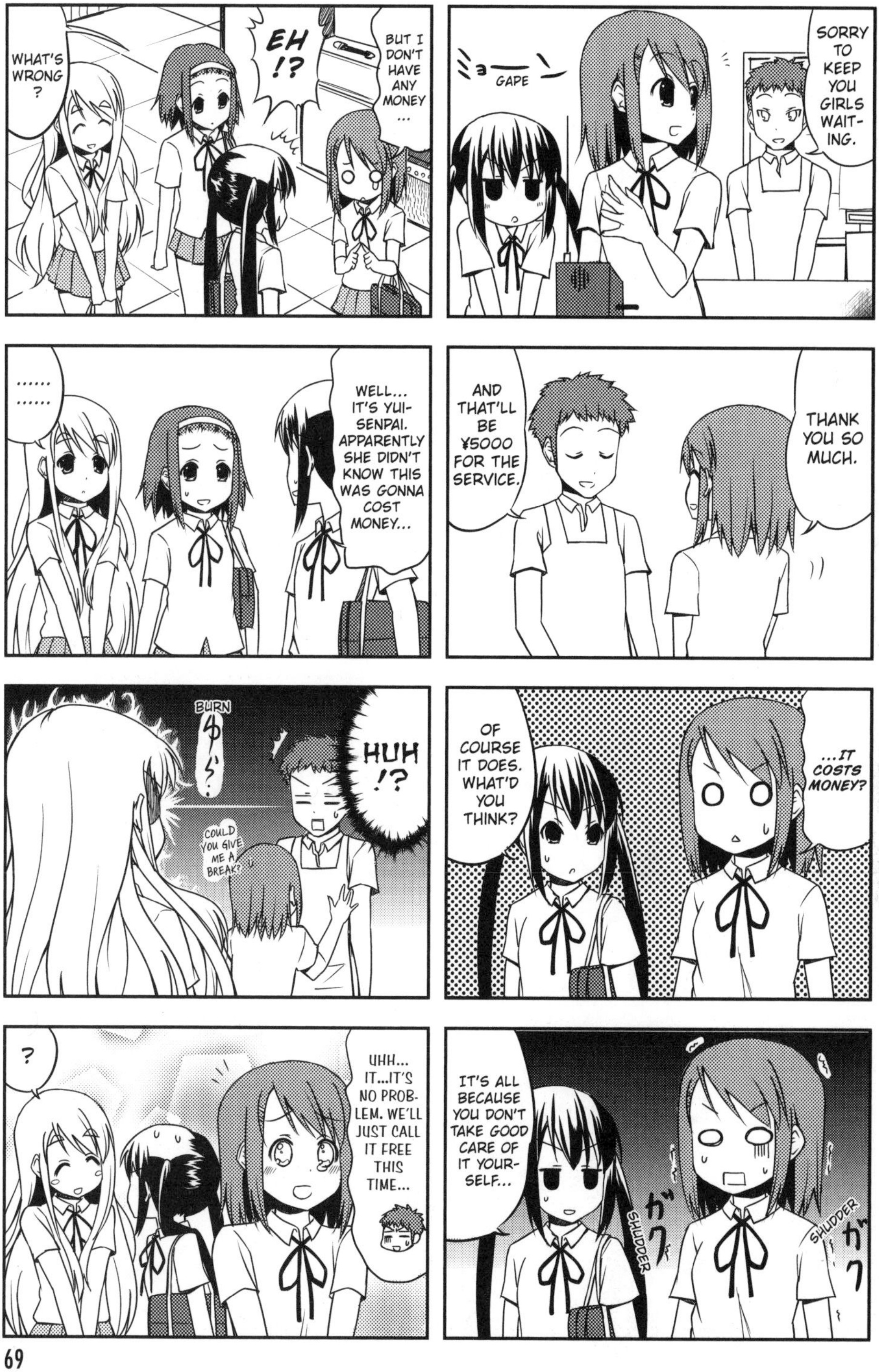

SORRY TO KEEP YOU GIRLS WAIT-ING.
GAPE
THANK YOU SO MUCH.
AND THAT'LL BE ¥5000 FOR THE SERVICE.
...IT COSTS MONEY?
OF COURSE IT DOES. WHAT'D YOU THINK?
IT'S ALL BECAUSE YOU DON'T TAKE GOOD CARE OF IT YOUR-SELF...
SHUDDER
SHUDDER
BUT I DON'T HAVE ANY MONEY...
EH!?
WHAT'S WRONG?
WELL... IT'S YUI-SENPAI. APPARENTLY SHE DIDN'T KNOW THIS WAS GONNA COST MONEY...
....
HUH!?
BURN
COULD YOU GIVE ME A BREAK?
UHH... IT...IT'S NO PROB-LEM. WE'LL JUST CALL IT FREE THIS TIME...
?

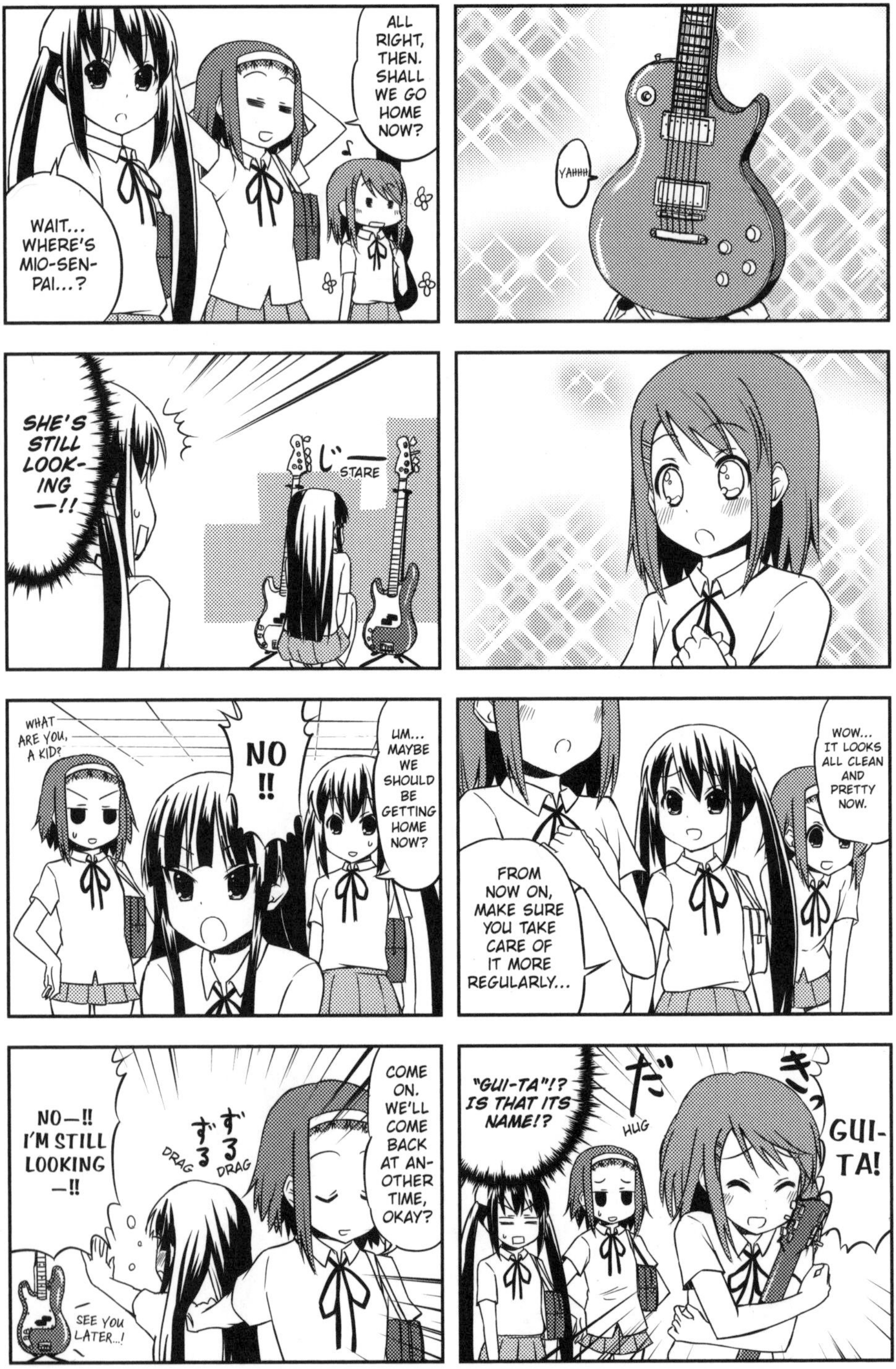
YAHHH
ALL RIGHT, THEN. SHALL WE GO HOME NOW?
WAIT... WHERE'S MIO-SENPAI...?
じー STARE
SHE'S STILL LOOKING—!!
WOW... IT LOOKS ALL CLEAN AND PRETTY NOW.
FROM NOW ON, MAKE SURE YOU TAKE CARE OF IT MORE REGULARLY...
UM... MAYBE WE SHOULD BE GETTING HOME NOW?
NO!!
WHAT ARE YOU, A KID?
きっ
GUI-TA!
だ HUG
"GUI-TA"!? IS THAT ITS NAME!?
COME ON. WE'LL COME BACK AT ANOTHER TIME, OKAY?
ずるずる DRAG DRAG
NO—!! I'M STILL LOOKING—!!
SEE YOU LATER...!

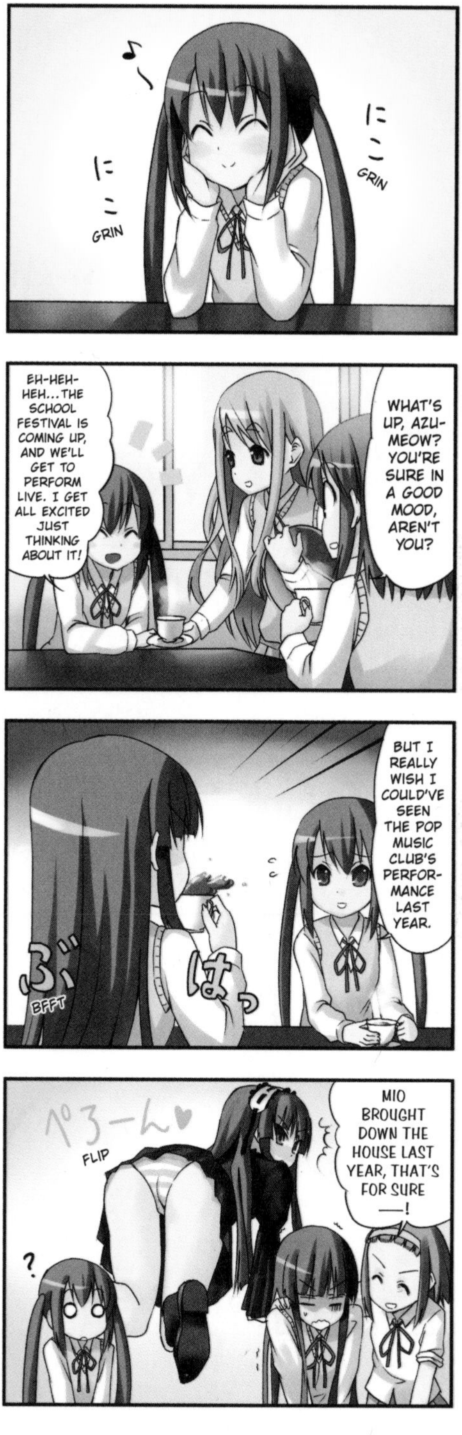
♪~
にこ
GRIN
にこ
GRIN
WHAT'S UP, AZU-MEOW? YOU'RE SURE IN A GOOD MOOD, AREN'T YOU?
EH-HEH-HEH...THE SCHOOL FESTIVAL IS COMING UP, AND WE'LL GET TO PERFORM LIVE. I GET ALL EXCITED JUST THINKING ABOUT IT!
BUT I REALLY WISH I COULD'VE SEEN THE POP MUSIC CLUB'S PERFORMANCE LAST YEAR.
ぶはっ
BFFT
MIO BROUGHT DOWN THE HOUSE LAST YEAR, THAT'S FOR SURE—!
ぺろーん♥
FLIP
?

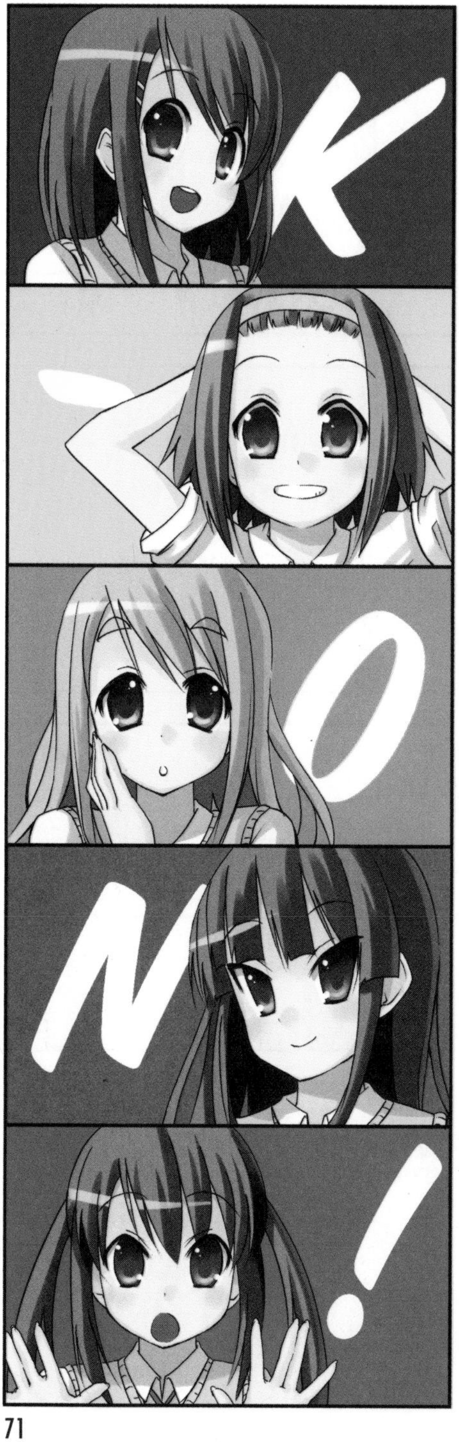
K
-
O
N
!

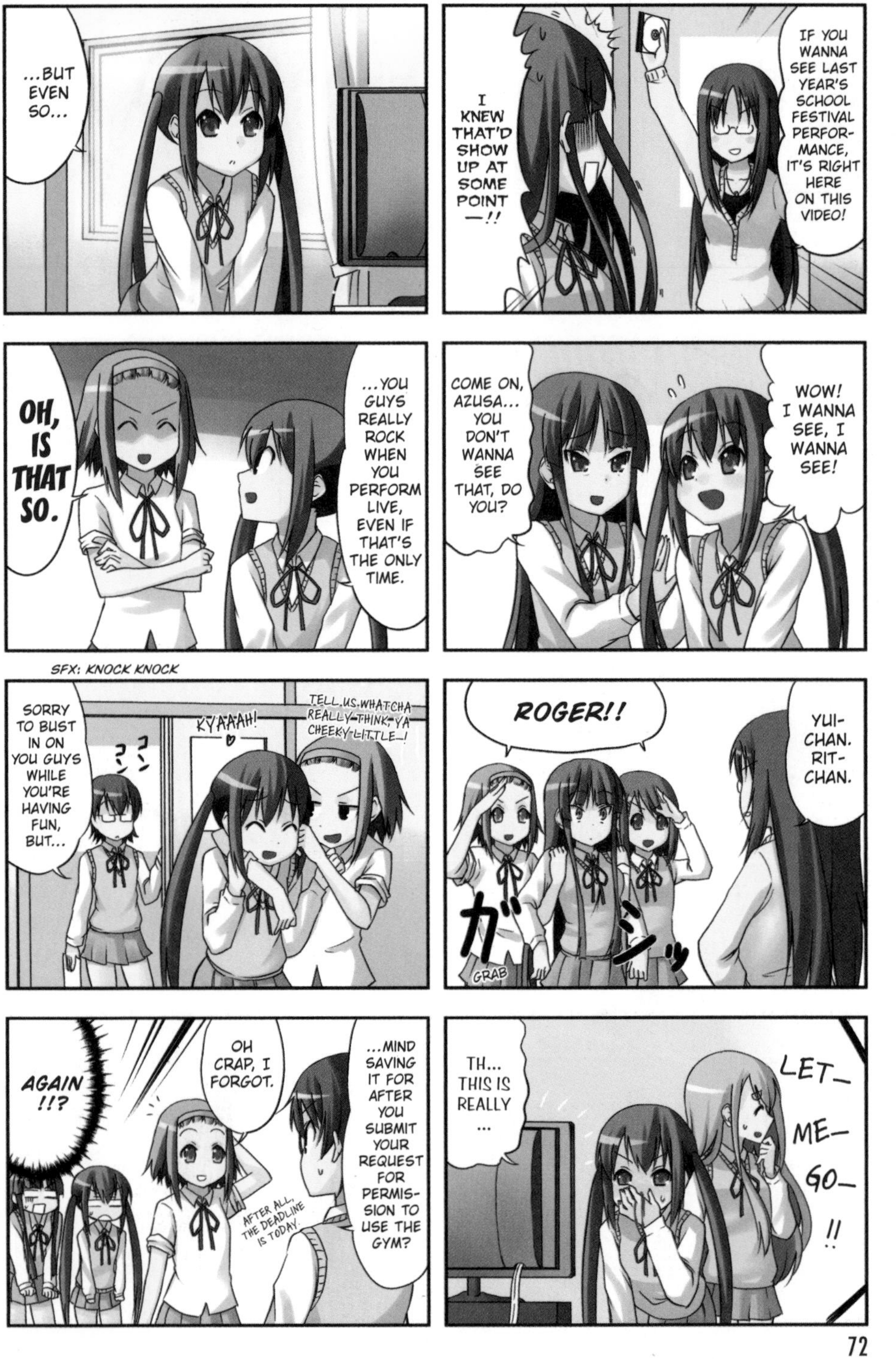
IF YOU WANNA SEE LAST YEAR'S SCHOOL FESTIVAL PERFORMANCE, IT'S RIGHT HERE ON THIS VIDEO!
I KNEW THAT'D SHOW UP AT SOME POINT—!!
WOW! I WANNA SEE, I WANNA SEE!
COME ON, AZUSA... YOU DON'T WANNA SEE THAT, DO YOU?
YUI-CHAN. RIT-CHAN.
ROGER!!
GRAB
LET— ME— GO— !!
TH... THIS IS REALLY ...
...BUT EVEN SO...
...YOU GUYS REALLY ROCK WHEN YOU PERFORM LIVE, EVEN IF THAT'S THE ONLY TIME.
OH, IS THAT SO.
SFX: KNOCK KNOCK
TELL US WHATCHA REALLY THINK, YA CHEEKY LITTLE...!
KYAAAH!
SORRY TO BUST IN ON YOU GUYS WHILE YOU'RE HAVING FUN, BUT...
...MIND SAVING IT FOR AFTER YOU SUBMIT YOUR REQUEST FOR PERMISSION TO USE THE GYM?
AFTER ALL, THE DEADLINE IS TODAY.
OH CRAP, I FORGOT.
AGAIN !!?

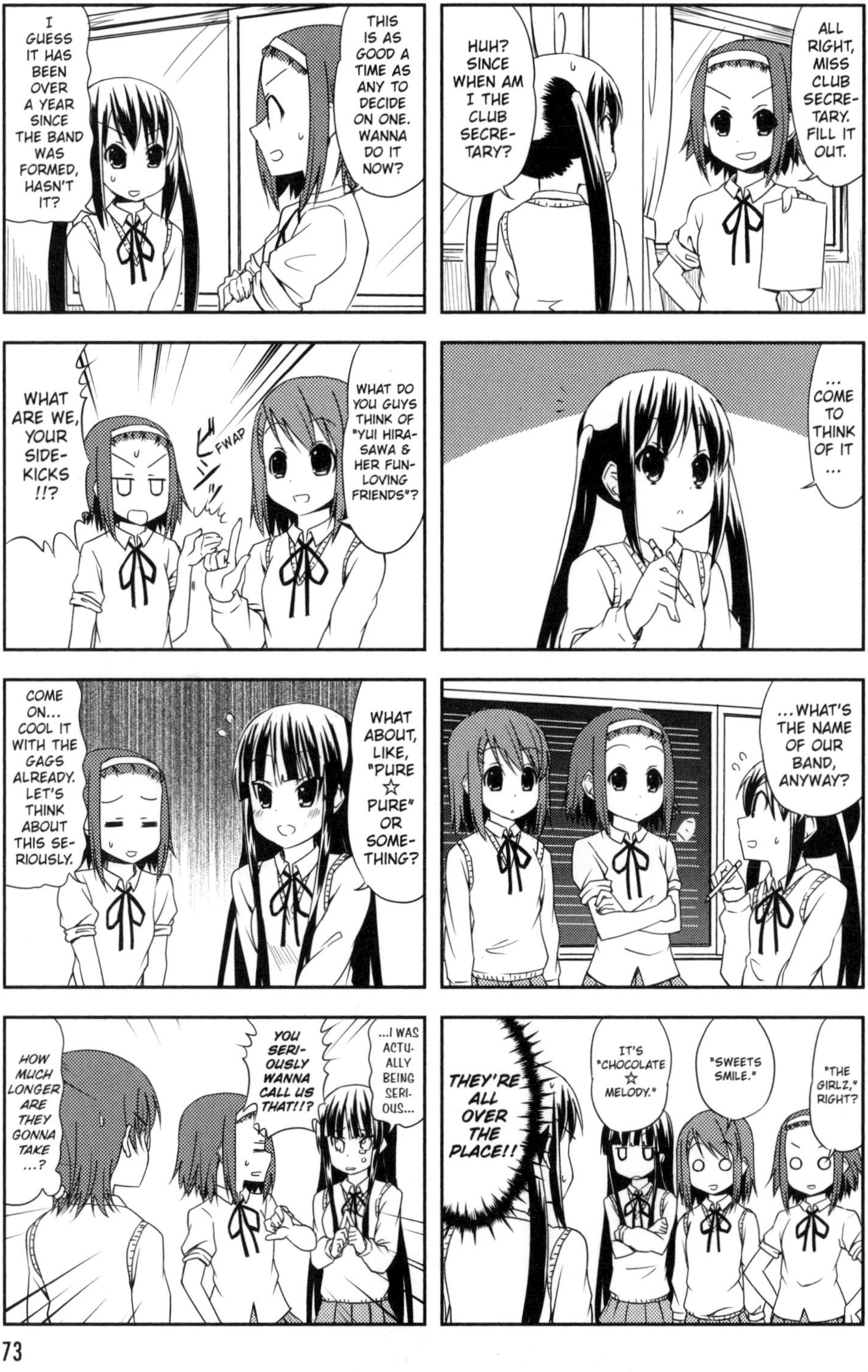
ALL RIGHT, MISS CLUB SECRETARY. FILL IT OUT.
HUH? SINCE WHEN AM I THE CLUB SECRETARY?
... COME TO THINK OF IT ...
...WHAT'S THE NAME OF OUR BAND, ANYWAY?
"THE GIRLZ," RIGHT?
"SWEETS SMILE."
IT'S "CHOCOLATE ☆ MELODY."
THEY'RE ALL OVER THE PLACE!!
THIS IS AS GOOD A TIME AS ANY TO DECIDE ON ONE. WANNA DO IT NOW?
I GUESS IT HAS BEEN OVER A YEAR SINCE THE BAND WAS FORMED, HASN'T IT?
WHAT DO YOU GUYS THINK OF "YUI HIRASAWA & HER FUN-LOVING FRIENDS"?
FWAP
WHAT ARE WE, YOUR SIDEKICKS!!?
WHAT ABOUT, LIKE, "PURE ☆ PURE" OR SOMETHING?
COME ON... COOL IT WITH THE GAGS ALREADY. LET'S THINK ABOUT THIS SERIOUSLY.
...I WAS ACTUALLY BEING SERIOUS...
YOU SERIOUSLY WANNA CALL US THAT!!?
HOW MUCH LONGER ARE THEY GONNA TAKE ...?

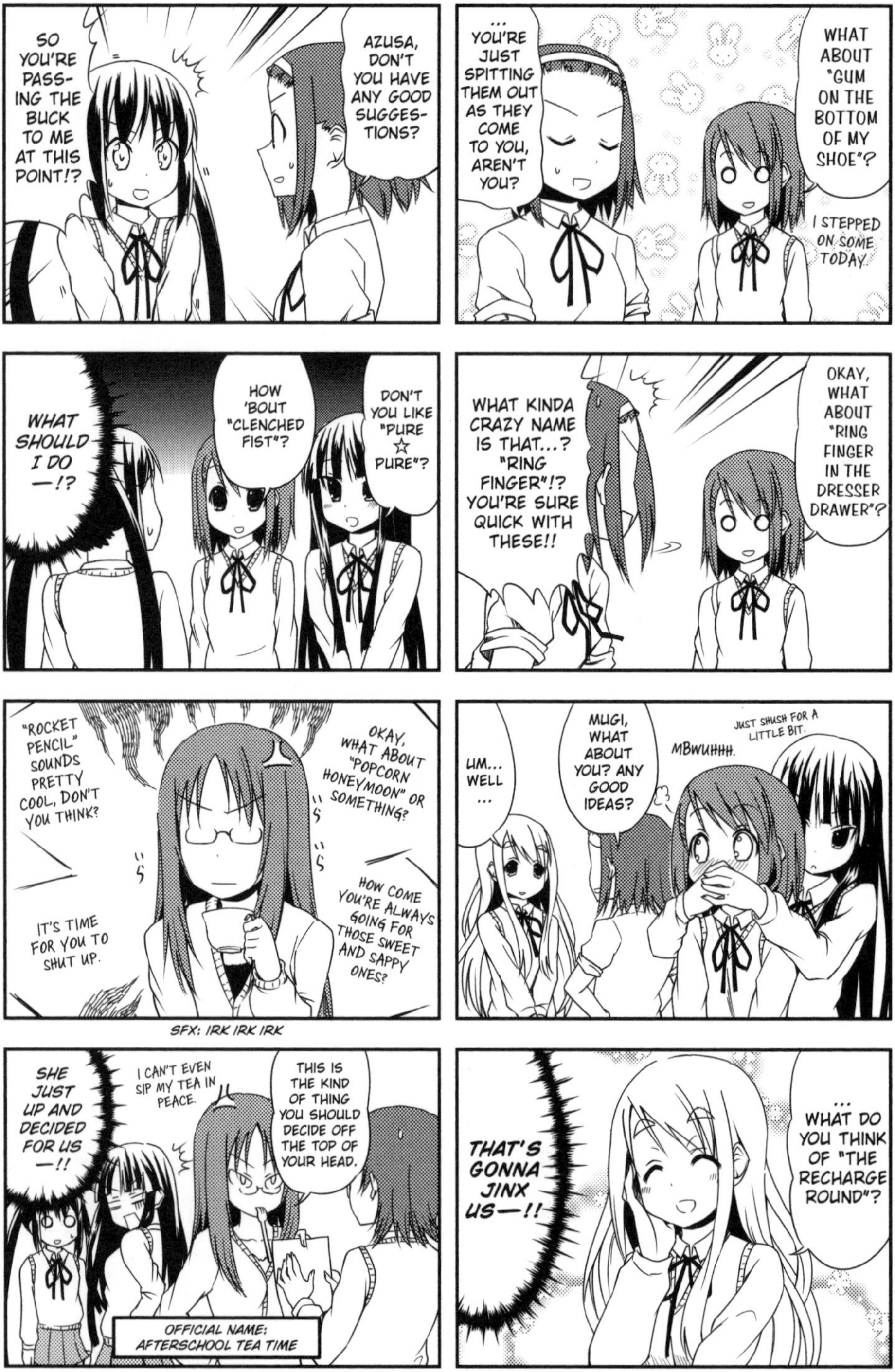
WHAT ABOUT "GUM ON THE BOTTOM OF MY SHOE"?
I STEPPED ON SOME TODAY.
... YOU'RE JUST SPITTING THEM OUT AS THEY COME TO YOU, AREN'T YOU?
OKAY, WHAT ABOUT "RING FINGER IN THE DRESSER DRAWER"?
WHAT KINDA CRAZY NAME IS THAT...? "RING FINGER"!? YOU'RE SURE QUICK WITH THESE!!
JUST SHUSH FOR A LITTLE BIT.
MBWUHHH.
MUGI, WHAT ABOUT YOU? ANY GOOD IDEAS?
UM... WELL ...
... WHAT DO YOU THINK OF "THE RECHARGE ROUND"?
THAT'S GONNA JINX US—!!
AZUSA, DON'T YOU HAVE ANY GOOD SUGGES-TIONS?
SO YOU'RE PASS-ING THE BUCK TO ME AT THIS POINT!?
DON'T YOU LIKE "PURE ☆ PURE"?
HOW 'BOUT "CLENCHED FIST"?
WHAT SHOULD I DO —!?
OKAY, WHAT ABOUT "POPCORN HONEYMOON" OR SOMETHING?
HOW COME YOU'RE ALWAYS GOING FOR THOSE SWEET AND SAPPY ONES?
"ROCKET PENCIL" SOUNDS PRETTY COOL, DON'T YOU THINK?
IT'S TIME FOR YOU TO SHUT UP.
SFX: IRK IRK IRK
THIS IS THE KIND OF THING YOU SHOULD DECIDE OFF THE TOP OF YOUR HEAD.
I CAN'T EVEN SIP MY TEA IN PEACE.
SHE JUST UP AND DECIDED FOR US —!!
OFFICIAL NAME: AFTERSCHOOL TEA TIME

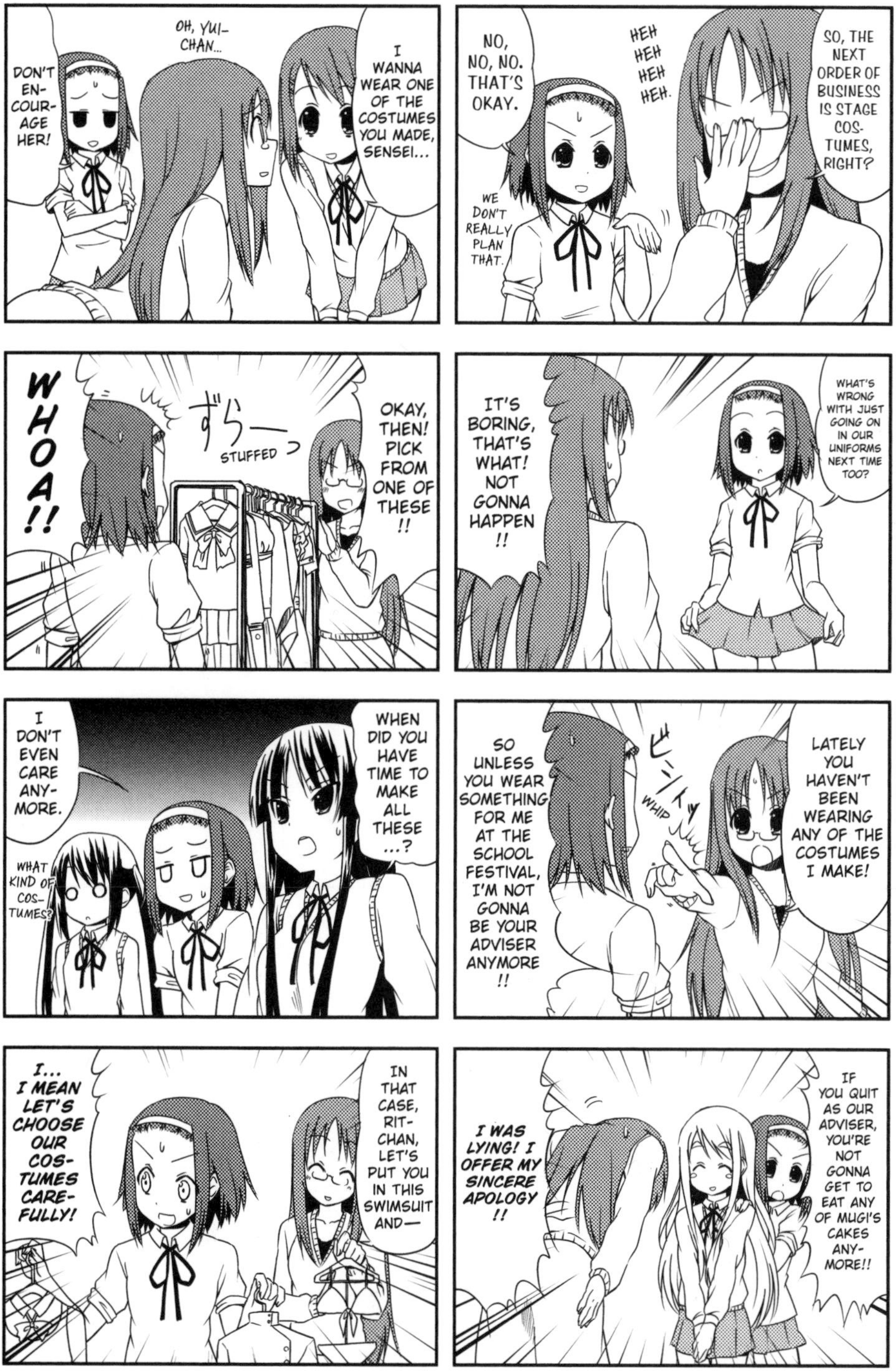
SO, THE NEXT ORDER OF BUSINESS IS STAGE COS-TUMES, RIGHT?
HEH HEH HEH HEH.
NO, NO, NO. THAT'S OKAY.
WE DON'T REALLY PLAN THAT.
I WANNA WEAR ONE OF THE COSTUMES YOU MADE, SENSEI...
OH, YUI-CHAN...
DON'T EN-COUR-AGE HER!
WHAT'S WRONG WITH JUST GOING ON IN OUR UNIFORMS NEXT TIME TOO?
IT'S BORING, THAT'S WHAT! NOT GONNA HAPPEN!!
OKAY, THEN! PICK FROM ONE OF THESE!!
ずらー
STUFFED
WHOA!!
LATELY YOU HAVEN'T BEEN WEARING ANY OF THE COSTUMES I MAKE!
ビシィッ
WHIP
SO UNLESS YOU WEAR SOMETHING FOR ME AT THE SCHOOL FESTIVAL, I'M NOT GONNA BE YOUR ADVISER ANYMORE!!
WHEN DID YOU HAVE TIME TO MAKE ALL THESE...?
I DON'T EVEN CARE ANY-MORE.
WHAT KIND OF COS-TUMES?
IF YOU QUIT AS OUR ADVISER, YOU'RE NOT GONNA GET TO EAT ANY OF MUGI'S CAKES ANY-MORE!!
I WAS LYING! I OFFER MY SINCERE APOLOGY!!
IN THAT CASE, RIT-CHAN, LET'S PUT YOU IN THIS SWIMSUIT AND—
I... I MEAN LET'S CHOOSE OUR COS-TUMES CARE-FULLY!

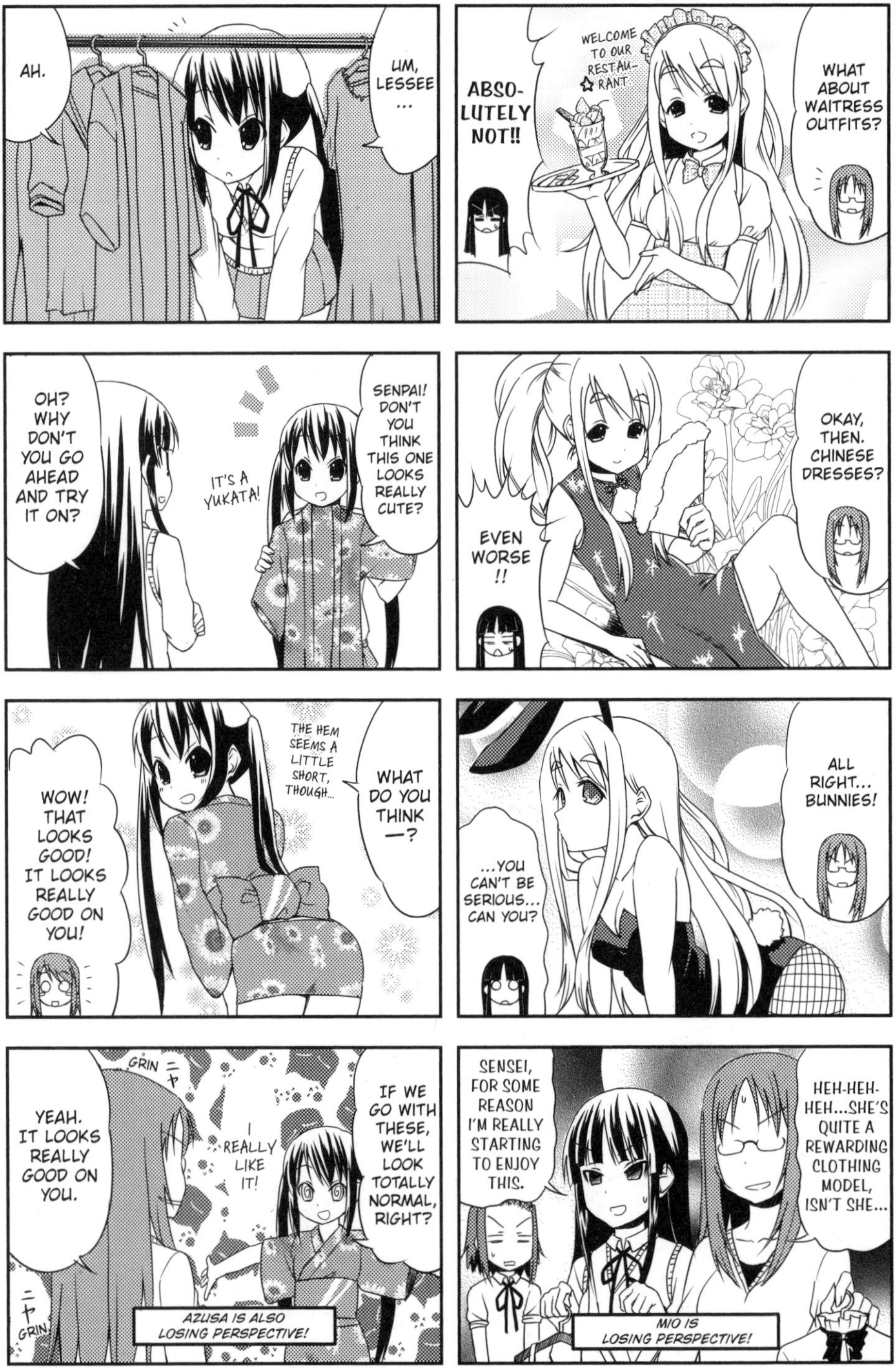
WHAT ABOUT WAITRESS OUTFITS?
WELCOME TO OUR RESTAURANT ☆
ABSOLUTELY NOT!!
OKAY, THEN. CHINESE DRESSES?
EVEN WORSE !!
ALL RIGHT... BUNNIES!
...YOU CAN'T BE SERIOUS... CAN YOU?
HEH-HEH-HEH...SHE'S QUITE A REWARDING CLOTHING MODEL, ISN'T SHE...
SENSEI, FOR SOME REASON I'M REALLY STARTING TO ENJOY THIS.
MIO IS LOSING PERSPECTIVE!
UM, LESSEE ...
AH.
SENPAI! DON'T YOU THINK THIS ONE LOOKS REALLY CUTE?
IT'S A YUKATA!
OH? WHY DON'T YOU GO AHEAD AND TRY IT ON?
WHAT DO YOU THINK—?
THE HEM SEEMS A LITTLE SHORT, THOUGH...
WOW! THAT LOOKS GOOD! IT LOOKS REALLY GOOD ON YOU!
IF WE GO WITH THESE, WE'LL LOOK TOTALLY NORMAL, RIGHT?
I REALLY LIKE IT!
GRIN ニヤ
YEAH. IT LOOKS REALLY GOOD ON YOU.
ニヤ GRIN
AZUSA IS ALSO LOSING PERSPECTIVE!

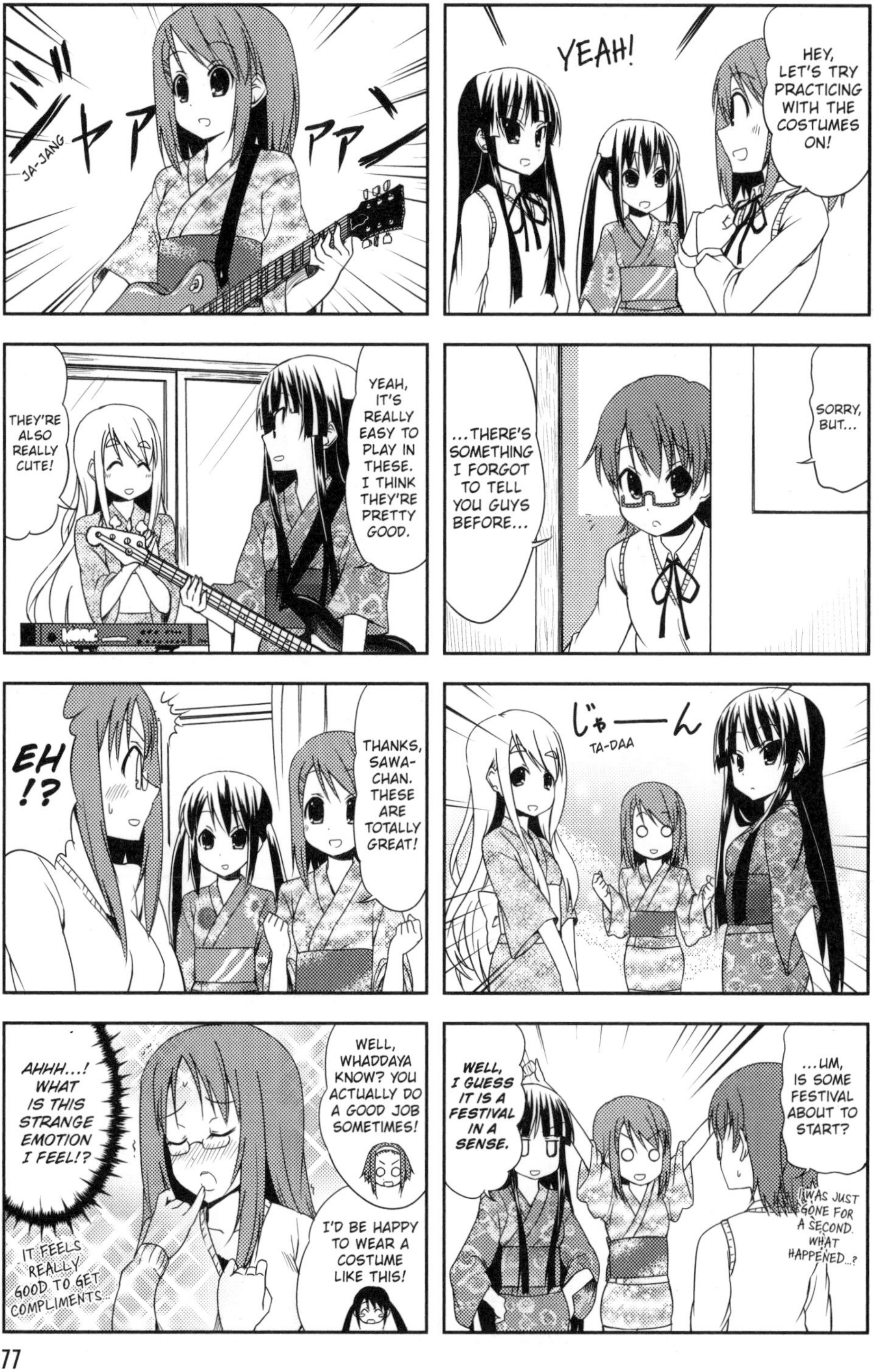
HEY, LET'S TRY PRACTICING WITH THE COSTUMES ON!
YEAH!
ジャアアア
JA-JANG
SORRY, BUT...
...THERE'S SOMETHING I FORGOT TO TELL YOU GUYS BEFORE...
YEAH, IT'S REALLY EASY TO PLAY IN THESE. I THINK THEY'RE PRETTY GOOD.
THEY'RE ALSO REALLY CUTE!
じゃーん
TA-DAA
THANKS, SAWA-CHAN. THESE ARE TOTALLY GREAT!
EH!?
...UM, IS SOME FESTIVAL ABOUT TO START?
I WAS JUST GONE FOR A SECOND. WHAT HAPPENED...?
WELL, I GUESS IT IS A FESTIVAL IN A SENSE.
WELL, WHADDAYA KNOW? YOU ACTUALLY DO A GOOD JOB SOMETIMES!
I'D BE HAPPY TO WEAR A COSTUME LIKE THIS!
AHHH...! WHAT IS THIS STRANGE EMOTION I FEEL!?
IT FEELS REALLY GOOD TO GET COMPLIMENTS.

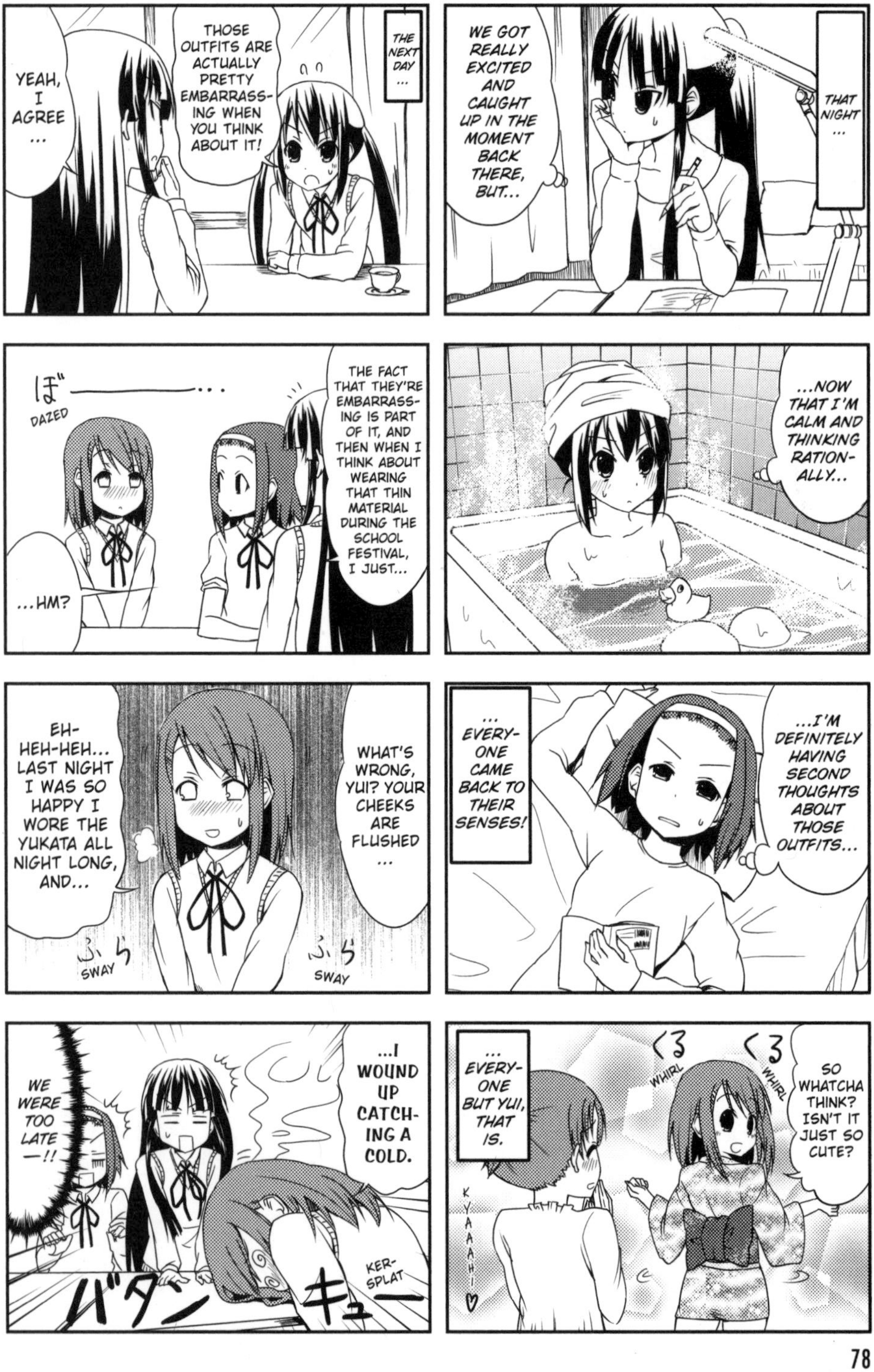
THAT NIGHT ...
WE GOT REALLY EXCITED AND CAUGHT UP IN THE MOMENT BACK THERE, BUT...
...NOW THAT I'M CALM AND THINKING RATION-ALLY...
... EVERY-ONE CAME BACK TO THEIR SENSES!
...I'M DEFINITELY HAVING SECOND THOUGHTS ABOUT THOSE OUTFITS...
... EVERY-ONE BUT YUI, THAT IS.
くる WHIRL
くる WHIRL
SO WHATCHA THINK? ISN'T IT JUST SO CUTE?
KYAAAH! ♥
THE NEXT DAY ...
THOSE OUTFITS ARE ACTUALLY PRETTY EMBARRASS-ING WHEN YOU THINK ABOUT IT!
YEAH, I AGREE ...
THE FACT THAT THEY'RE EMBARRASS-ING IS PART OF IT, AND THEN WHEN I THINK ABOUT WEARING THAT THIN MATERIAL DURING THE SCHOOL FESTIVAL, I JUST...
ぼ――――...
DAZED
...HM?
WHAT'S WRONG, YUI? YOUR CHEEKS ARE FLUSHED ...
EH-HEH-HEH... LAST NIGHT I WAS SO HAPPY I WORE THE YUKATA ALL NIGHT LONG, AND...
ふら SWAY
ふら SWAY
...I WOUND UP CATCHING A COLD.
WE WERE TOO LATE —!!
バタン KER-SPLAT
キュー

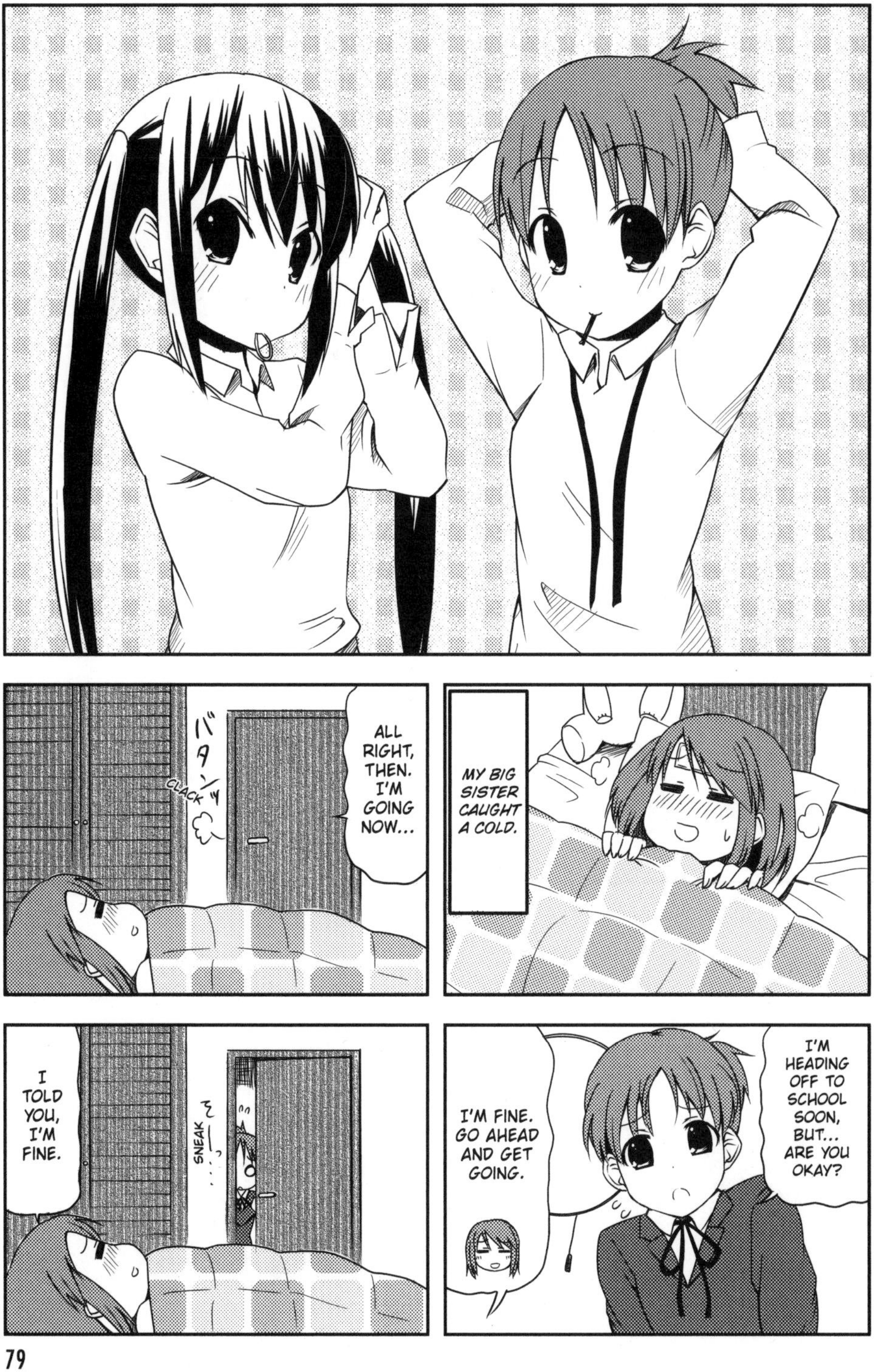
MY BIG SISTER CAUGHT A COLD.
ALL RIGHT, THEN. I'M GOING NOW...
バタン
CLACK
I'M HEADING OFF TO SCHOOL SOON, BUT... ARE YOU OKAY?
I'M FINE. GO AHEAD AND GET GOING.
SNEAK
I TOLD YOU, I'M FINE.

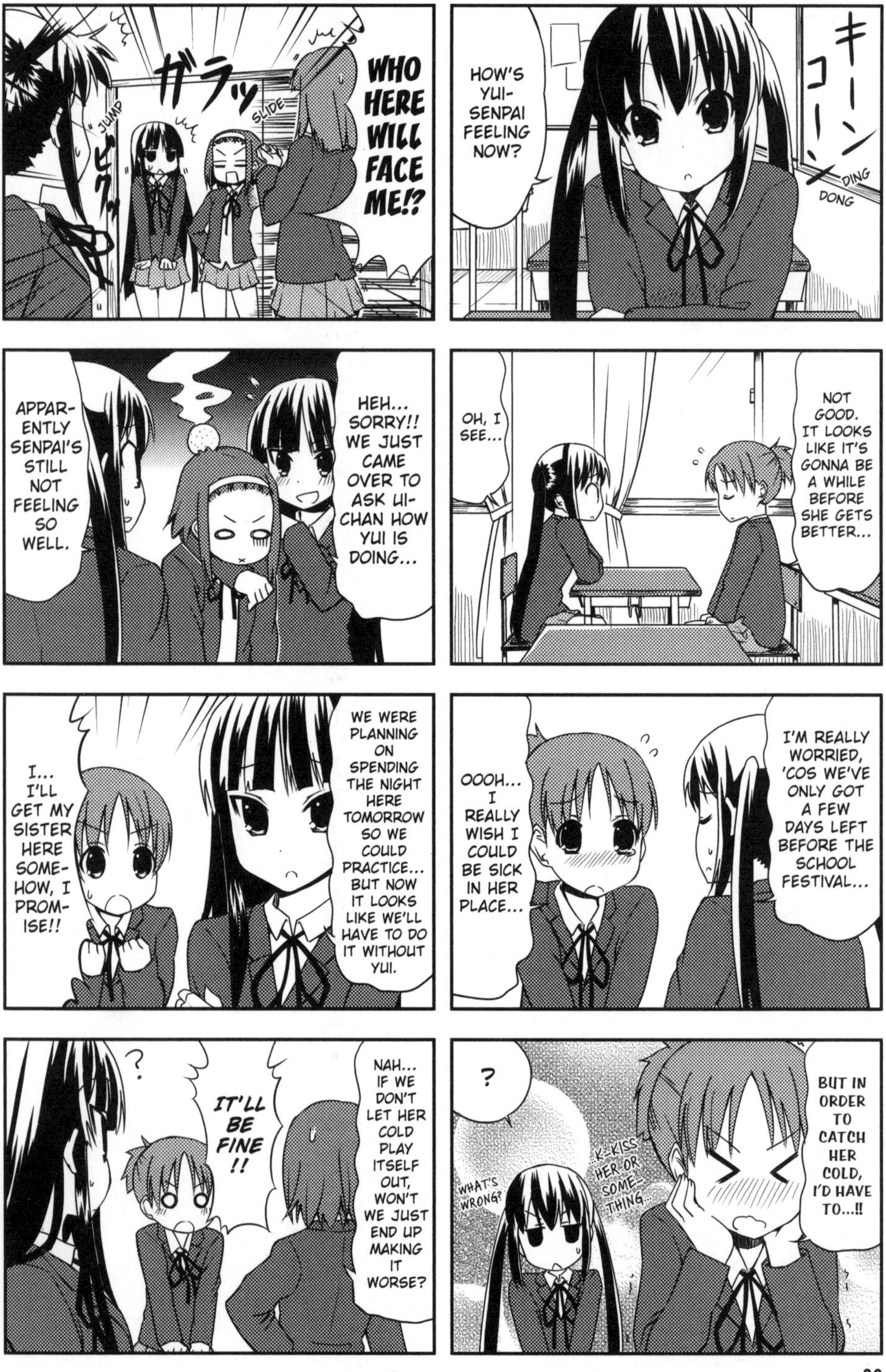
キーンコーン
DING DONG
HOW'S YUI-SENPAI FEELING NOW?
NOT GOOD. IT LOOKS LIKE IT'S GONNA BE A WHILE BEFORE SHE GETS BETTER...
OH, I SEE...
I'M REALLY WORRIED, 'COS WE'VE ONLY GOT A FEW DAYS LEFT BEFORE THE SCHOOL FESTIVAL...
OOOH... I REALLY WISH I COULD BE SICK IN HER PLACE...
BUT IN ORDER TO CATCH HER COLD, I'D HAVE TO...!!
K-KISS HER OR SOME-THING...
?
WHAT'S WRONG?
ガラッ
SLIDE
WHO HERE WILL FACE ME!?
ビクッ
JUMP
HEH... SORRY!! WE JUST CAME OVER TO ASK UI-CHAN HOW YUI IS DOING...
APPAR-ENTLY SENPAI'S STILL NOT FEELING SO WELL.
WE WERE PLANNING ON SPENDING THE NIGHT HERE TOMORROW SO WE COULD PRACTICE... BUT NOW IT LOOKS LIKE WE'LL HAVE TO DO IT WITHOUT YUI.
I... I'LL GET MY SISTER HERE SOME-HOW, I PROM-ISE!!
NAH... IF WE DON'T LET HER COLD PLAY ITSELF OUT, WON'T WE JUST END UP MAKING IT WORSE?
IT'LL BE FINE!!
?

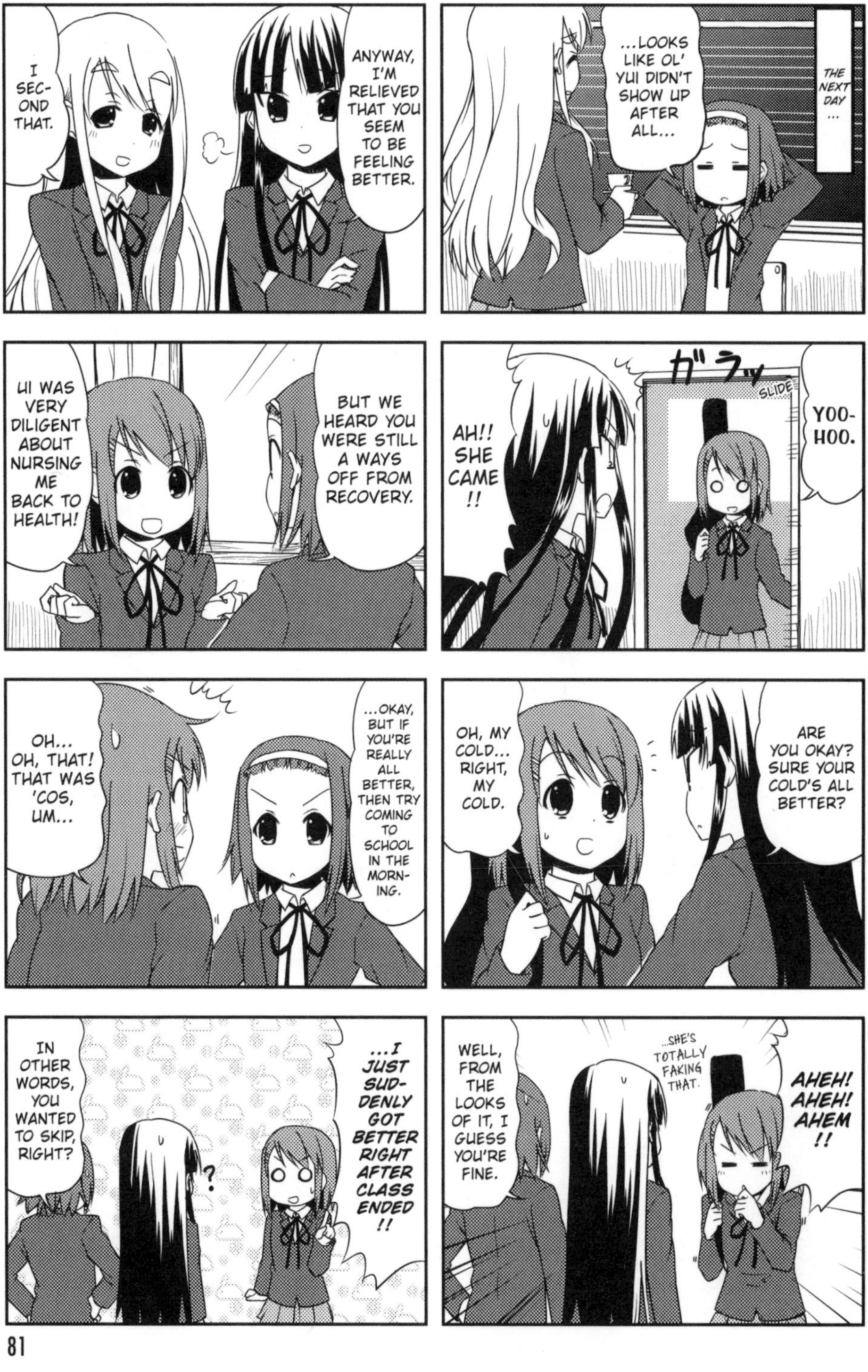
THE NEXT DAY...
...LOOKS LIKE OL' YUI DIDN'T SHOW UP AFTER ALL...
ANYWAY, I'M RELIEVED THAT YOU SEEM TO BE FEELING BETTER.
I SECOND THAT.
ガラッ
SLIDE
YOO-HOO.
AH!! SHE CAME!!
BUT WE HEARD YOU WERE STILL A WAYS OFF FROM RECOVERY.
UI WAS VERY DILIGENT ABOUT NURSING ME BACK TO HEALTH!
ARE YOU OKAY? SURE YOUR COLD'S ALL BETTER?
OH, MY COLD... RIGHT, MY COLD.
...OKAY, BUT IF YOU'RE REALLY ALL BETTER, THEN TRY COMING TO SCHOOL IN THE MORNING.
OH... OH, THAT! THAT WAS 'COS, UM...
AHEH! AHEH! AHEM!!
...SHE'S TOTALLY FAKING THAT.
WELL, FROM THE LOOKS OF IT, I GUESS YOU'RE FINE.
...I JUST SUDDENLY GOT BETTER RIGHT AFTER CLASS ENDED!!
IN OTHER WORDS, YOU WANTED TO SKIP, RIGHT?

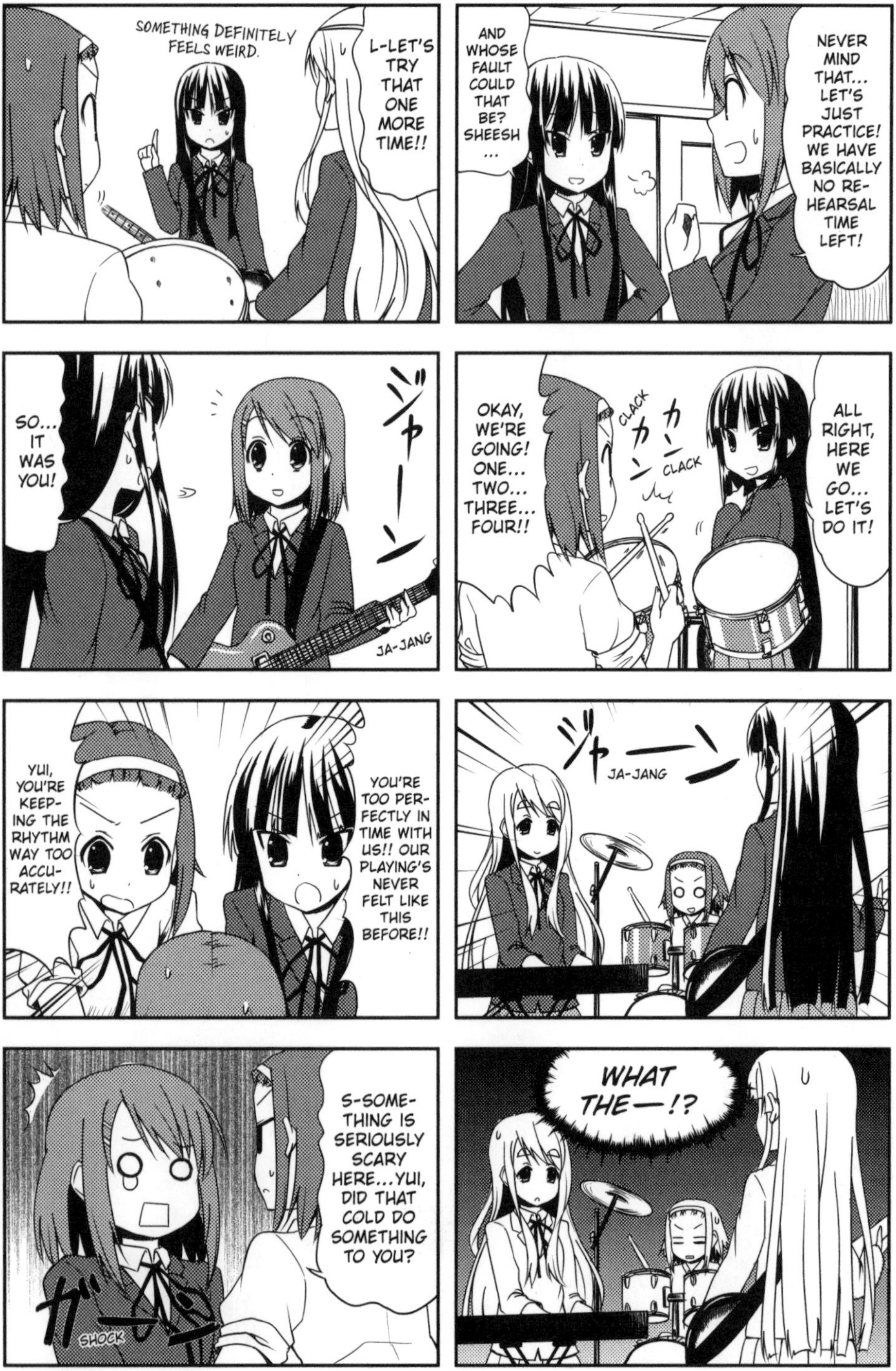
NEVER MIND THAT... LET'S JUST PRACTICE! WE HAVE BASICALLY NO RE-HEARSAL TIME LEFT!
AND WHOSE FAULT COULD THAT BE? SHEESH...
ALL RIGHT, HERE WE GO... LET'S DO IT!
CLACK
CLACK
OKAY, WE'RE GOING! ONE... TWO... THREE... FOUR!!
JA-JANG
WHAT THE—!?
SOMETHING DEFINITELY FEELS WEIRD.
L-LET'S TRY THAT ONE MORE TIME!!
JA-JANG
SO... IT WAS YOU!
YOU'RE TOO PER-FECTLY IN TIME WITH US!! OUR PLAYING'S NEVER FELT LIKE THIS BEFORE!!
YUI, YOU'RE KEEP-ING THE RHYTHM WAY TOO ACCU-RATELY!!
S-SOME-THING IS SERIOUSLY SCARY HERE...YUI, DID THAT COLD DO SOMETHING TO YOU?
SHOCK

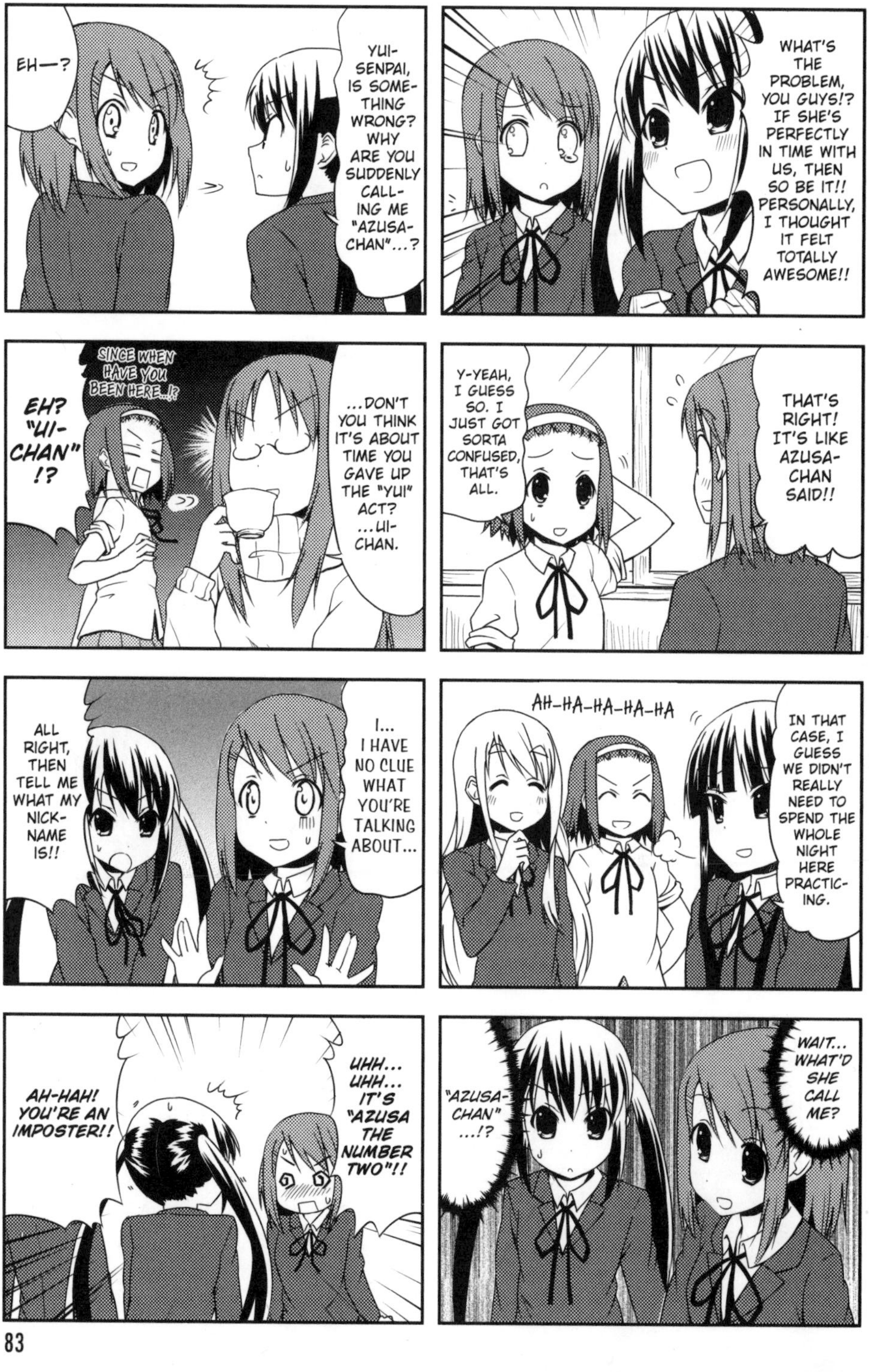
WHAT'S THE PROBLEM, YOU GUYS!? IF SHE'S PERFECTLY IN TIME WITH US, THEN SO BE IT!! PERSONALLY, I THOUGHT IT FELT TOTALLY AWESOME!!
YUI-SENPAI, IS SOMETHING WRONG? WHY ARE YOU SUDDENLY CALLING ME "AZUSA-CHAN"...?
EH—?
THAT'S RIGHT! IT'S LIKE AZUSA-CHAN SAID!!
Y-YEAH, I GUESS SO. I JUST GOT SORTA CONFUSED, THAT'S ALL.
...DON'T YOU THINK IT'S ABOUT TIME YOU GAVE UP THE "YUI" ACT? ...UI-CHAN.
SINCE WHEN HAVE YOU BEEN HERE...!?
EH? "UI-CHAN" !?
IN THAT CASE, I GUESS WE DIDN'T REALLY NEED TO SPEND THE WHOLE NIGHT HERE PRACTICING.
AH-HA-HA-HA-HA
I... I HAVE NO CLUE WHAT YOU'RE TALKING ABOUT...
ALL RIGHT, THEN TELL ME WHAT MY NICKNAME IS!!
WAIT... WHAT'D SHE CALL ME?
"AZUSA-CHAN" ...!?
UHH... UHH... IT'S "AZUSA THE NUMBER TWO"!!
AH-HAH! YOU'RE AN IMPOSTER!!

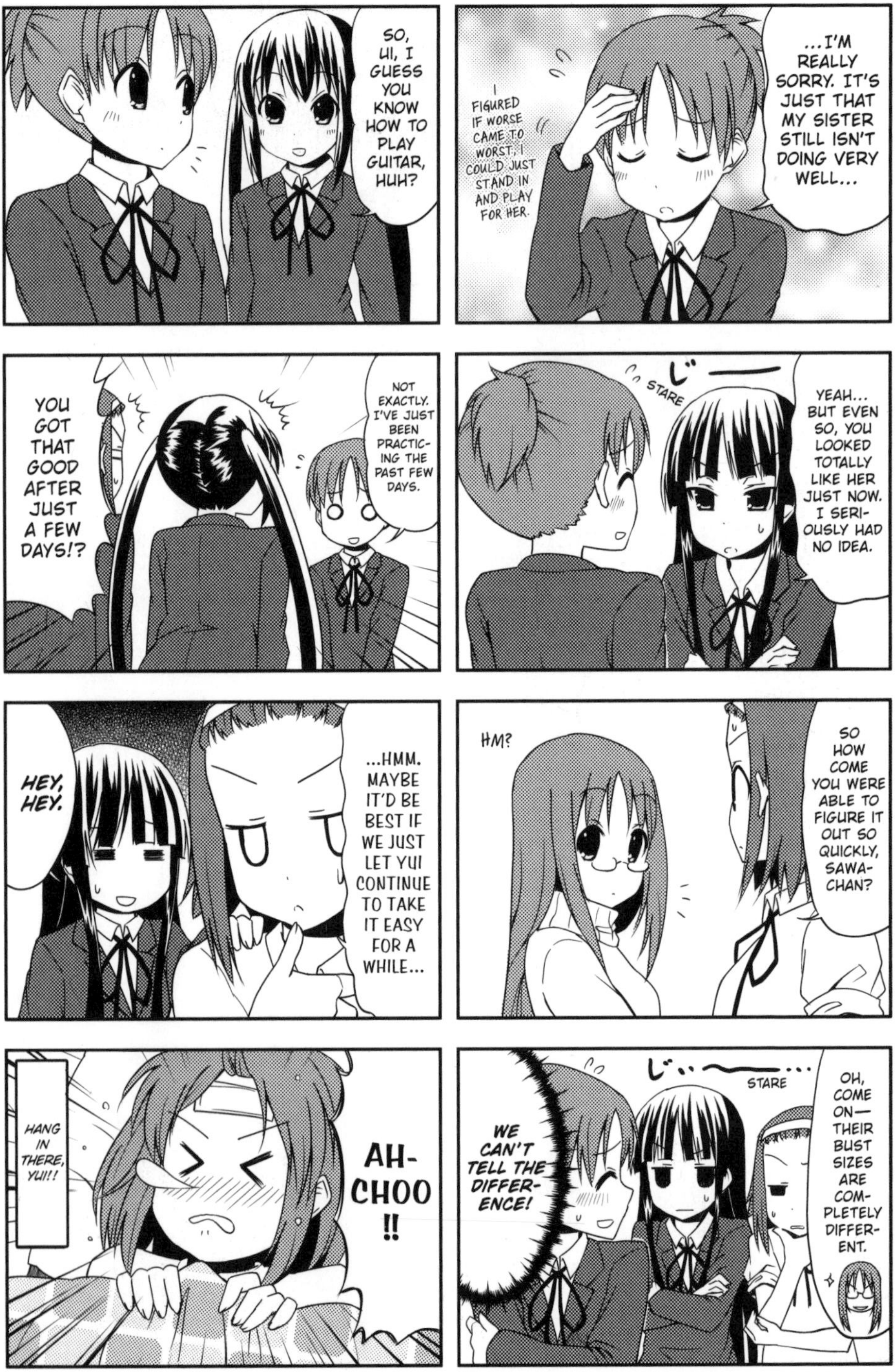
...I'M REALLY SORRY. IT'S JUST THAT MY SISTER STILL ISN'T DOING VERY WELL...
I FIGURED IF WORSE CAME TO WORST, I COULD JUST STAND IN AND PLAY FOR HER.
SO, UI, I GUESS YOU KNOW HOW TO PLAY GUITAR, HUH?
YEAH... BUT EVEN SO, YOU LOOKED TOTALLY LIKE HER JUST NOW. I SERIOUSLY HAD NO IDEA.
じーー
STARE
NOT EXACTLY. I'VE JUST BEEN PRACTICING THE PAST FEW DAYS.
YOU GOT THAT GOOD AFTER JUST A FEW DAYS!?
SO HOW COME YOU WERE ABLE TO FIGURE IT OUT SO QUICKLY, SAWA-CHAN?
HM?
...HMM. MAYBE IT'D BE BEST IF WE JUST LET YUI CONTINUE TO TAKE IT EASY FOR A WHILE...
HEY, HEY.
OH, COME ON—THEIR BUST SIZES ARE COMPLETELY DIFFERENT.
じぃ〜ー…
STARE
WE CAN'T TELL THE DIFFERENCE!
AH-CHOO!!
HANG IN THERE, YUI!!

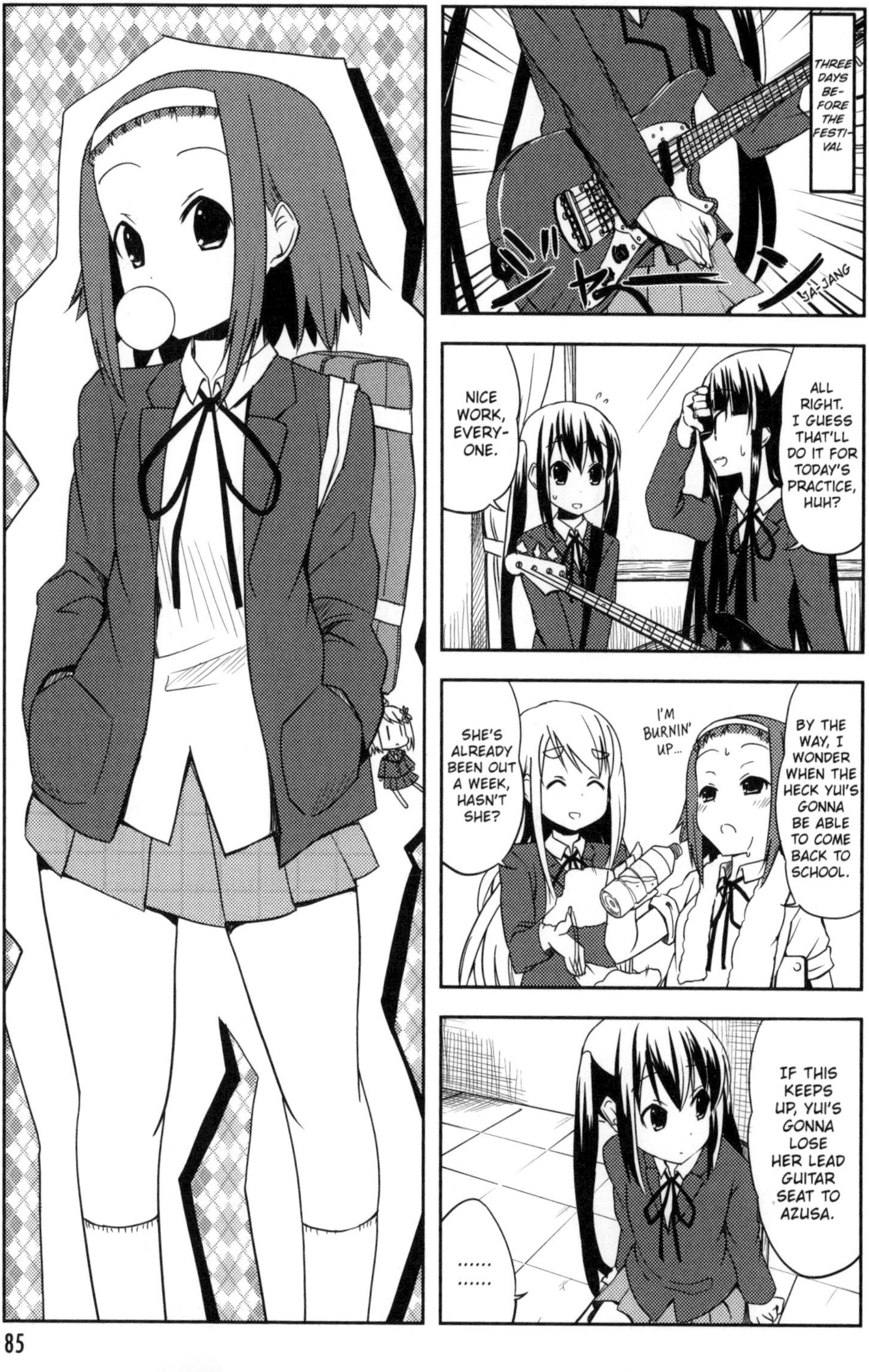
THREE DAYS BEFORE THE FESTIVAL
JA-JANG
ALL RIGHT. I GUESS THAT'LL DO IT FOR TODAY'S PRACTICE, HUH?
NICE WORK, EVERYONE.
BY THE WAY, I WONDER WHEN THE HECK YUI'S GONNA BE ABLE TO COME BACK TO SCHOOL.
I'M BURNIN' UP...
SHE'S ALREADY BEEN OUT A WEEK, HASN'T SHE?
IF THIS KEEPS UP, YUI'S GONNA LOSE HER LEAD GUITAR SEAT TO AZUSA.
......
......

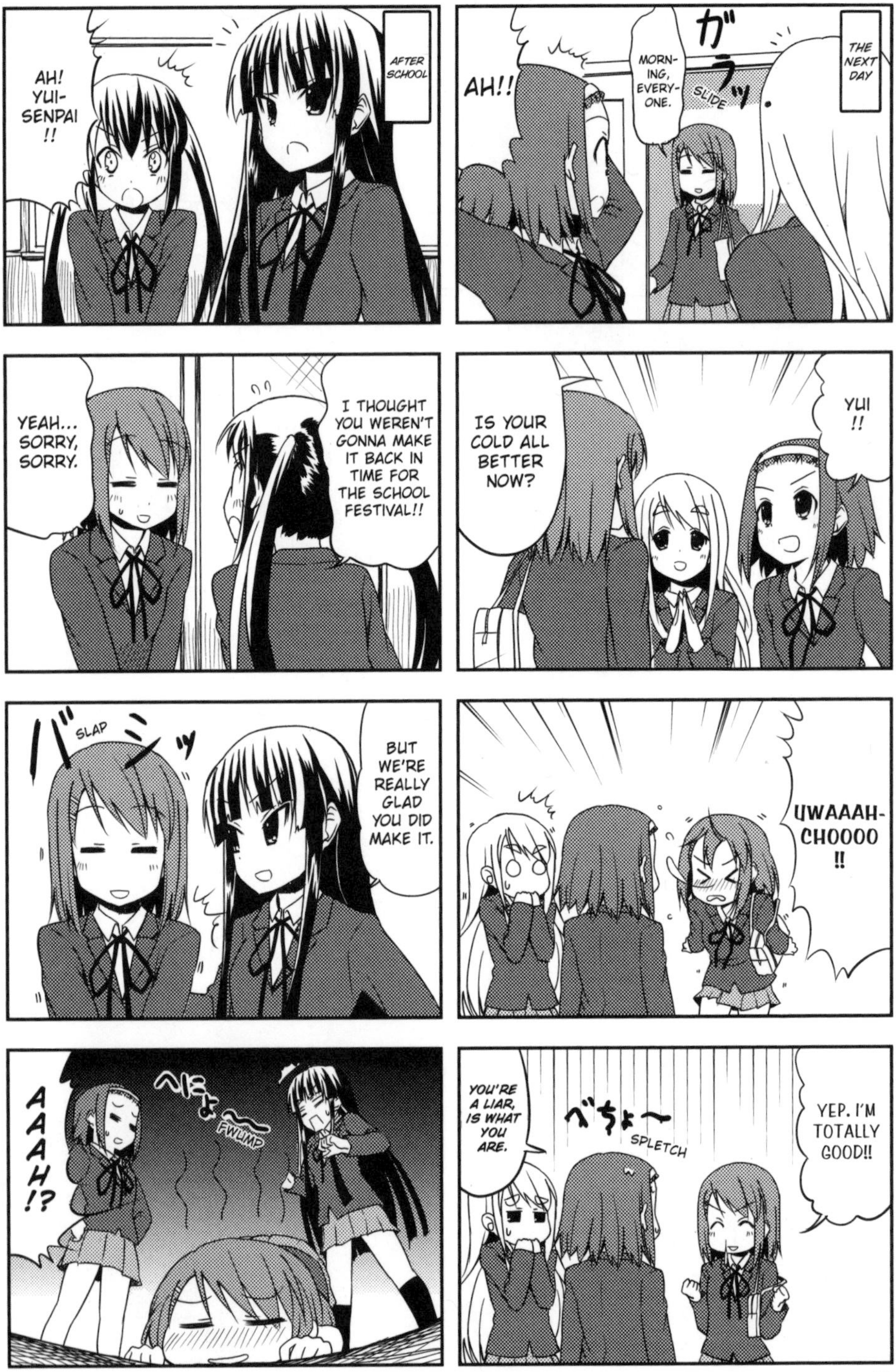
THE NEXT DAY
ガラッ
MORNING, EVERYONE.
SLIDE
AH!!
YUI!!
IS YOUR COLD ALL BETTER NOW?
UWAAAH-CHOOOO!!
YEP. I'M TOTALLY GOOD!!
べちょ~
SPLETCH
YOU'RE A LIAR, IS WHAT YOU ARE.
AFTER SCHOOL
AH! YUI-SENPAI!!
I THOUGHT YOU WEREN'T GONNA MAKE IT BACK IN TIME FOR THE SCHOOL FESTIVAL!!
YEAH... SORRY, SORRY.
BUT WE'RE REALLY GLAD YOU DID MAKE IT.
バミッ
SLAP
へにょ~
FWUMP
AAAAH!?

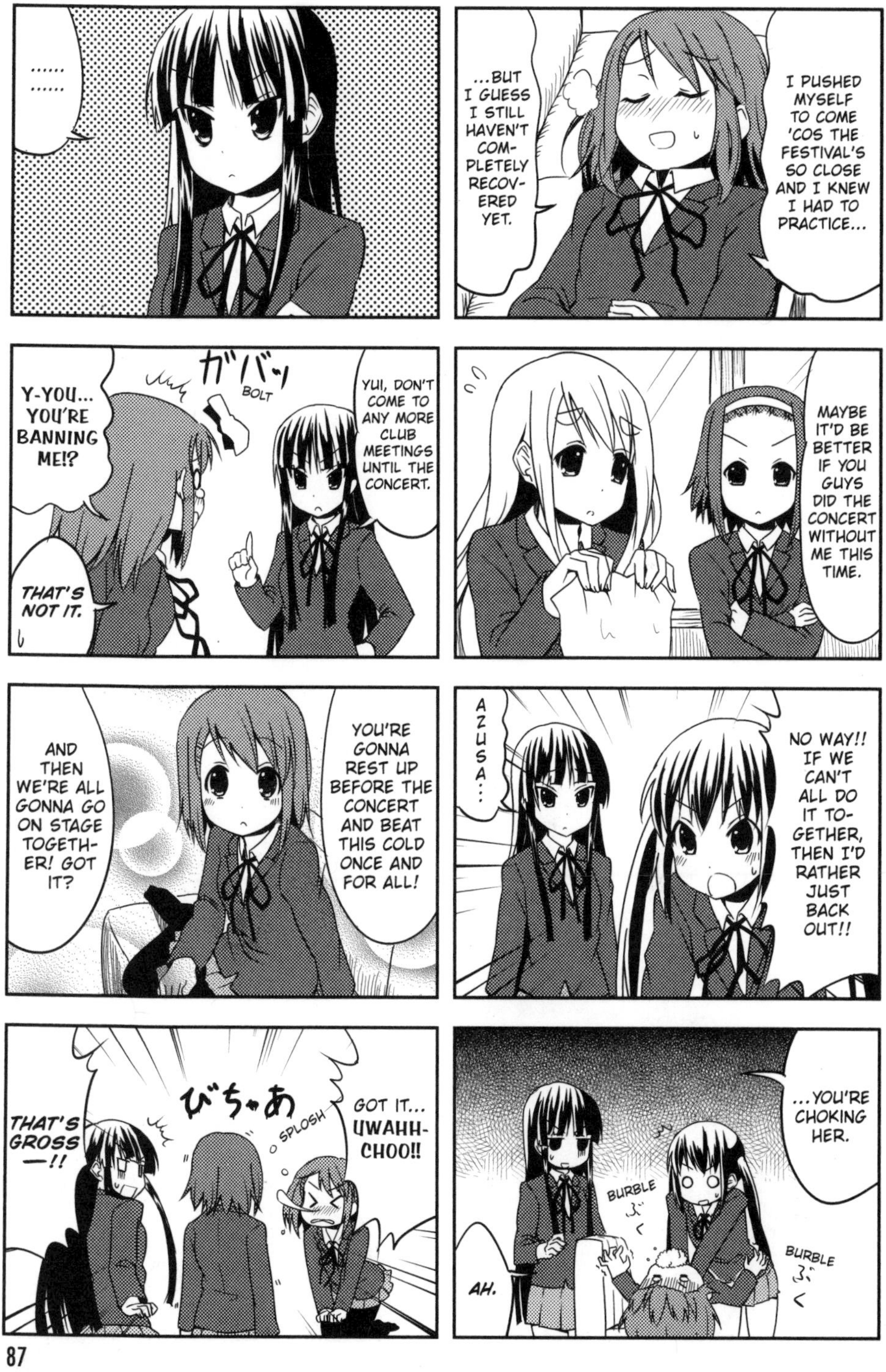

I PUSHED MYSELF TO COME 'COS THE FESTIVAL'S SO CLOSE AND I KNEW I HAD TO PRACTICE...
...BUT I GUESS I STILL HAVEN'T COMPLETELY RECOVERED YET.
....
MAYBE IT'D BE BETTER IF YOU GUYS DID THE CONCERT WITHOUT ME THIS TIME.
YUI, DON'T COME TO ANY MORE CLUB MEETINGS UNTIL THE CONCERT.
ガバッ
BOLT
Y-YOU... YOU'RE BANNING ME!?
THAT'S NOT IT.
NO WAY!! IF WE CAN'T ALL DO IT TOGETHER, THEN I'D RATHER JUST BACK OUT!!
AZUSA...
YOU'RE GONNA REST UP BEFORE THE CONCERT AND BEAT THIS COLD ONCE AND FOR ALL!
AND THEN WE'RE ALL GONNA GO ON STAGE TOGETHER! GOT IT?
...YOU'RE CHOKING HER.
BURBLE ぶく
BURBLE ぶく
AH.
GOT IT... UWAHH-CHOO!!
びちゃあ
SPLOSH
THAT'S GROSS—!!

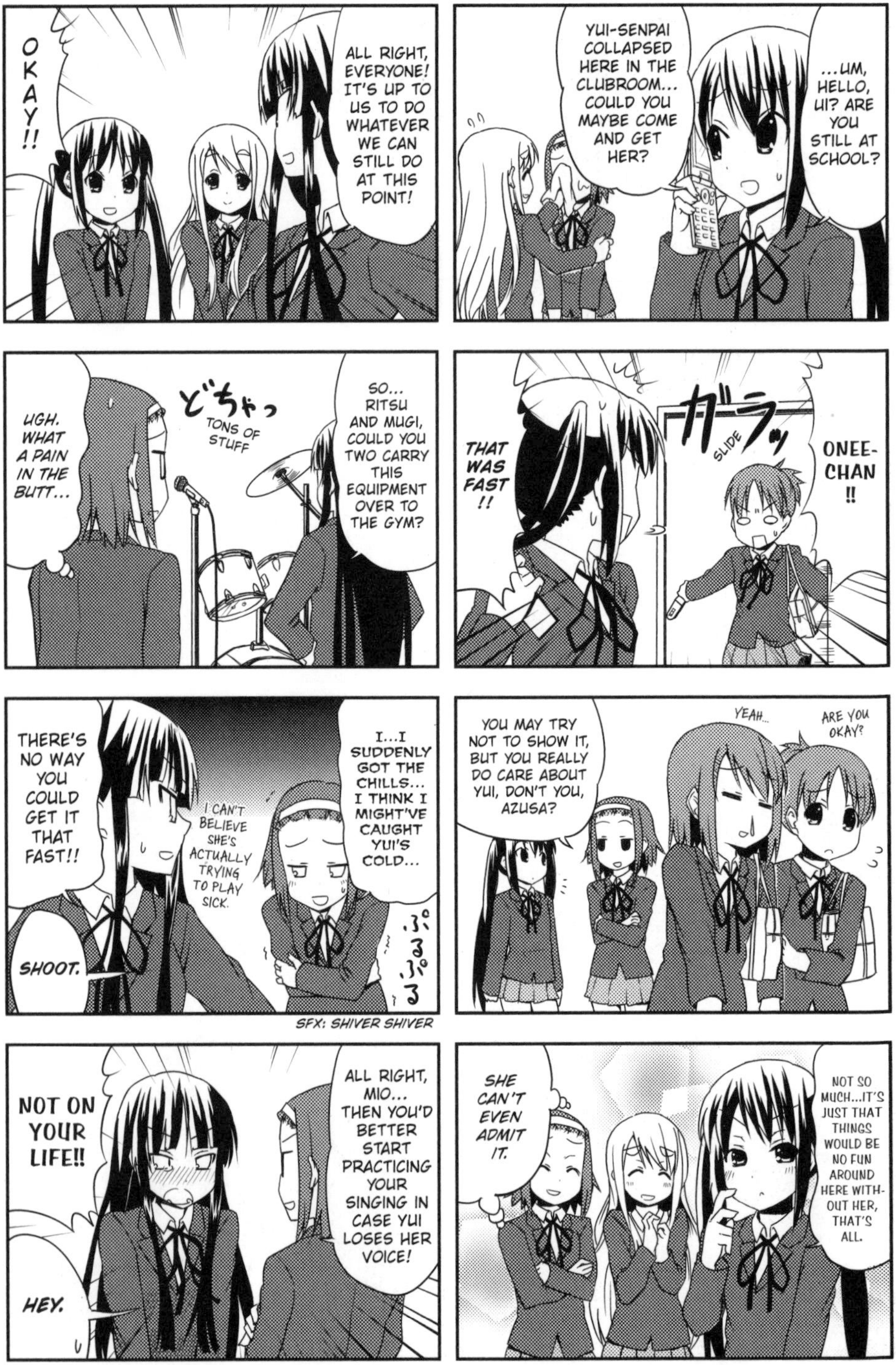
...UM, HELLO, UI? ARE YOU STILL AT SCHOOL?
YUI-SENPAI COLLAPSED HERE IN THE CLUBROOM... COULD YOU MAYBE COME AND GET HER?
ONEE-CHAN!!
ガラッ
SLIDE
THAT WAS FAST!!
ARE YOU OKAY?
YEAH...
YOU MAY TRY NOT TO SHOW IT, BUT YOU REALLY DO CARE ABOUT YUI, DON'T YOU, AZUSA?
NOT SO MUCH...IT'S JUST THAT THINGS WOULD BE NO FUN AROUND HERE WITH-OUT HER, THAT'S ALL.
SHE CAN'T EVEN ADMIT IT.
ALL RIGHT, EVERYONE! IT'S UP TO US TO DO WHATEVER WE CAN STILL DO AT THIS POINT!
OKAY!!
SO... RITSU AND MUGI, COULD YOU TWO CARRY THIS EQUIPMENT OVER TO THE GYM?
どちゃっ
TONS OF STUFF
UGH. WHAT A PAIN IN THE BUTT...
I...I SUDDENLY GOT THE CHILLS... I THINK I MIGHT'VE CAUGHT YUI'S COLD...
ぷるぷる
I CAN'T BELIEVE SHE'S ACTUALLY TRYING TO PLAY SICK.
THERE'S NO WAY YOU COULD GET IT THAT FAST!!
SHOOT.
SFX: SHIVER SHIVER
ALL RIGHT, MIO... THEN YOU'D BETTER START PRACTICING YOUR SINGING IN CASE YUI LOSES HER VOICE!
NOT ON YOUR LIFE!!
HEY.

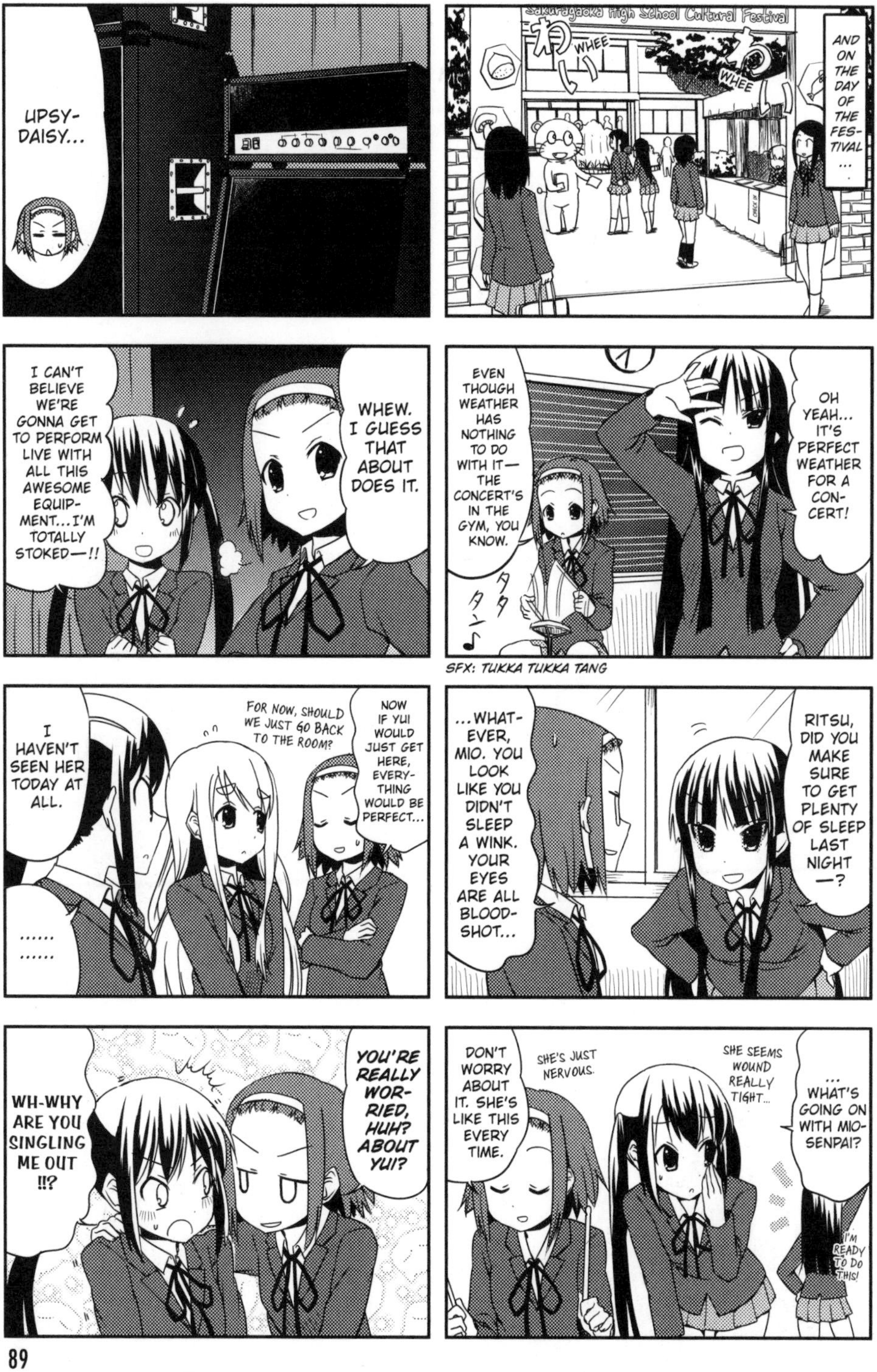
Sakuragaoka High School Cultural Festival
WHEE
WHEE
AND ON THE DAY OF THE FES-TIVAL......
UPSY-DAISY...
OH YEAH... IT'S PERFECT WEATHER FOR A CON-CERT!
EVEN THOUGH WEATHER HAS NOTHING TO DO WITH IT—THE CONCERT'S IN THE GYM, YOU KNOW.
SFX: TUKKA TUKKA TANG
WHEW. I GUESS THAT ABOUT DOES IT.
I CAN'T BELIEVE WE'RE GONNA GET TO PERFORM LIVE WITH ALL THIS AWESOME EQUIP-MENT...I'M TOTALLY STOKED—!!
RITSU, DID YOU MAKE SURE TO GET PLENTY OF SLEEP LAST NIGHT—?
...WHAT-EVER, MIO. YOU LOOK LIKE YOU DIDN'T SLEEP A WINK. YOUR EYES ARE ALL BLOOD-SHOT...
NOW IF YUI WOULD JUST GET HERE, EVERY-THING WOULD BE PERFECT...
FOR NOW, SHOULD WE JUST GO BACK TO THE ROOM?
I HAVEN'T SEEN HER TODAY AT ALL.
....
... WHAT'S GOING ON WITH MIO-SENPAI?
I'M READY TO DO THIS!
SHE SEEMS WOUND REALLY TIGHT...
SHE'S JUST NERVOUS.
DON'T WORRY ABOUT IT. SHE'S LIKE THIS EVERY TIME.
YOU'RE REALLY WOR-RIED, HUH? ABOUT YUI?
WH-WHY ARE YOU SINGLING ME OUT!!?

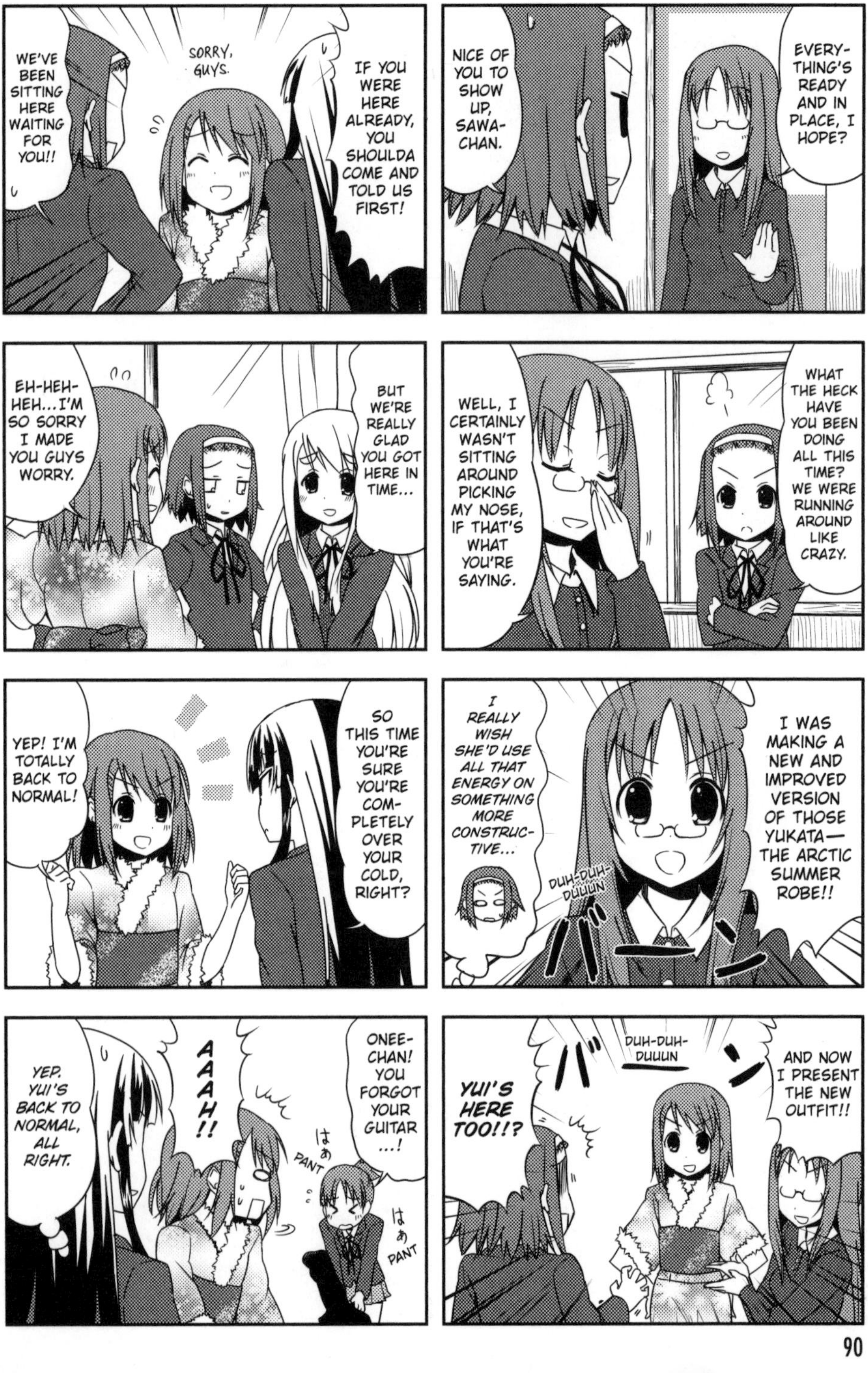
EVERYTHING'S READY AND IN PLACE, I HOPE?
NICE OF YOU TO SHOW UP, SAWA-CHAN.
WHAT THE HECK HAVE YOU BEEN DOING ALL THIS TIME? WE WERE RUNNING AROUND LIKE CRAZY.
WELL, I CERTAINLY WASN'T SITTING AROUND PICKING MY NOSE, IF THAT'S WHAT YOU'RE SAYING.
I WAS MAKING A NEW AND IMPROVED VERSION OF THOSE YUKATA—THE ARCTIC SUMMER ROBE!!
DUH-DUH-DUUUN
I REALLY WISH SHE'D USE ALL THAT ENERGY ON SOMETHING MORE CONSTRUCTIVE...
AND NOW I PRESENT THE NEW OUTFIT!!
DUH-DUH-DUUUN
YUI'S HERE TOO!!?
IF YOU WERE HERE ALREADY, YOU SHOULDA COME AND TOLD US FIRST!
SORRY, GUYS.
WE'VE BEEN SITTING HERE WAITING FOR YOU!!
BUT WE'RE REALLY GLAD YOU GOT HERE IN TIME...
EH-HEH-HEH...I'M SO SORRY I MADE YOU GUYS WORRY.
SO THIS TIME YOU'RE SURE YOU'RE COMPLETELY OVER YOUR COLD, RIGHT?
YEP! I'M TOTALLY BACK TO NORMAL!
ONEE-CHAN! YOU FORGOT YOUR GUITAR...!
はあ PANT
はあ PANT
AAAAH!!
YEP. YUI'S BACK TO NORMAL, ALL RIGHT.

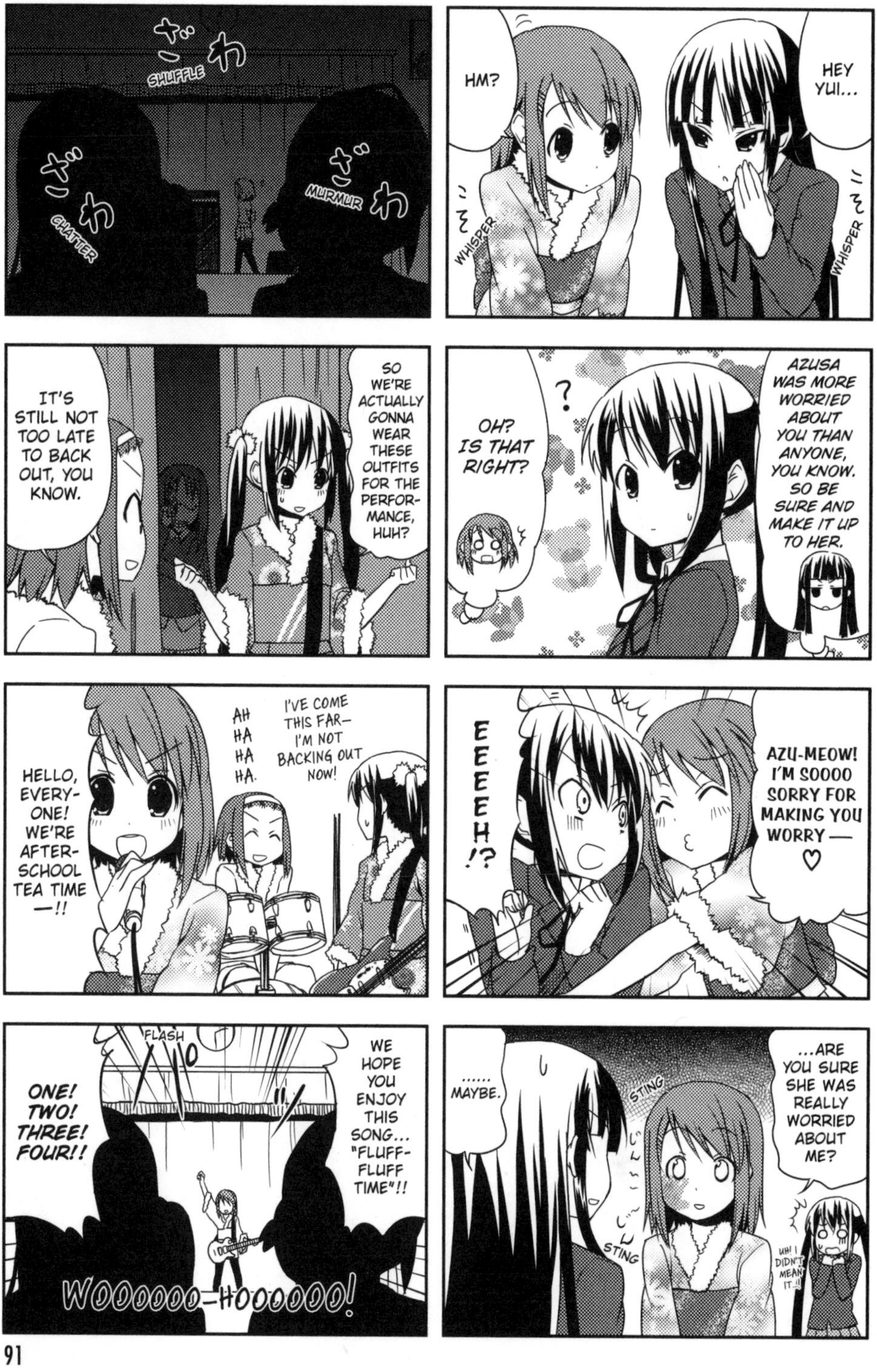
HEY YUI...
HM?
ひそ
WHISPER
ひそ
WHISPER
ざわ
SHUFFLE
ざわ
MURMUR
ざわ
CHATTER
AZUSA WAS MORE WORRIED ABOUT YOU THAN ANYONE, YOU KNOW. SO BE SURE AND MAKE IT UP TO HER.
?
OH? IS THAT RIGHT?
SO WE'RE ACTUALLY GONNA WEAR THESE OUTFITS FOR THE PERFORMANCE, HUH?
IT'S STILL NOT TOO LATE TO BACK OUT, YOU KNOW.
AZU-MEOW! I'M SOOOO SORRY FOR MAKING YOU WORRY—♡
EEEEEH!?
I'VE COME THIS FAR—I'M NOT BACKING OUT NOW!
AH HA HA HA.
HELLO, EVERYONE! WE'RE AFTER-SCHOOL TEA TIME—!!
...ARE YOU SURE SHE WAS REALLY WORRIED ABOUT ME?
STING
......MAYBE.
UH! I DIDN'T MEAN IT..!!
STING
WE HOPE YOU ENJOY THIS SONG... "FLUFF-FLUFF TIME"!!
FLASH
ONE! TWO! THREE! FOUR!!
WOOOOOO-HOOOOOO!

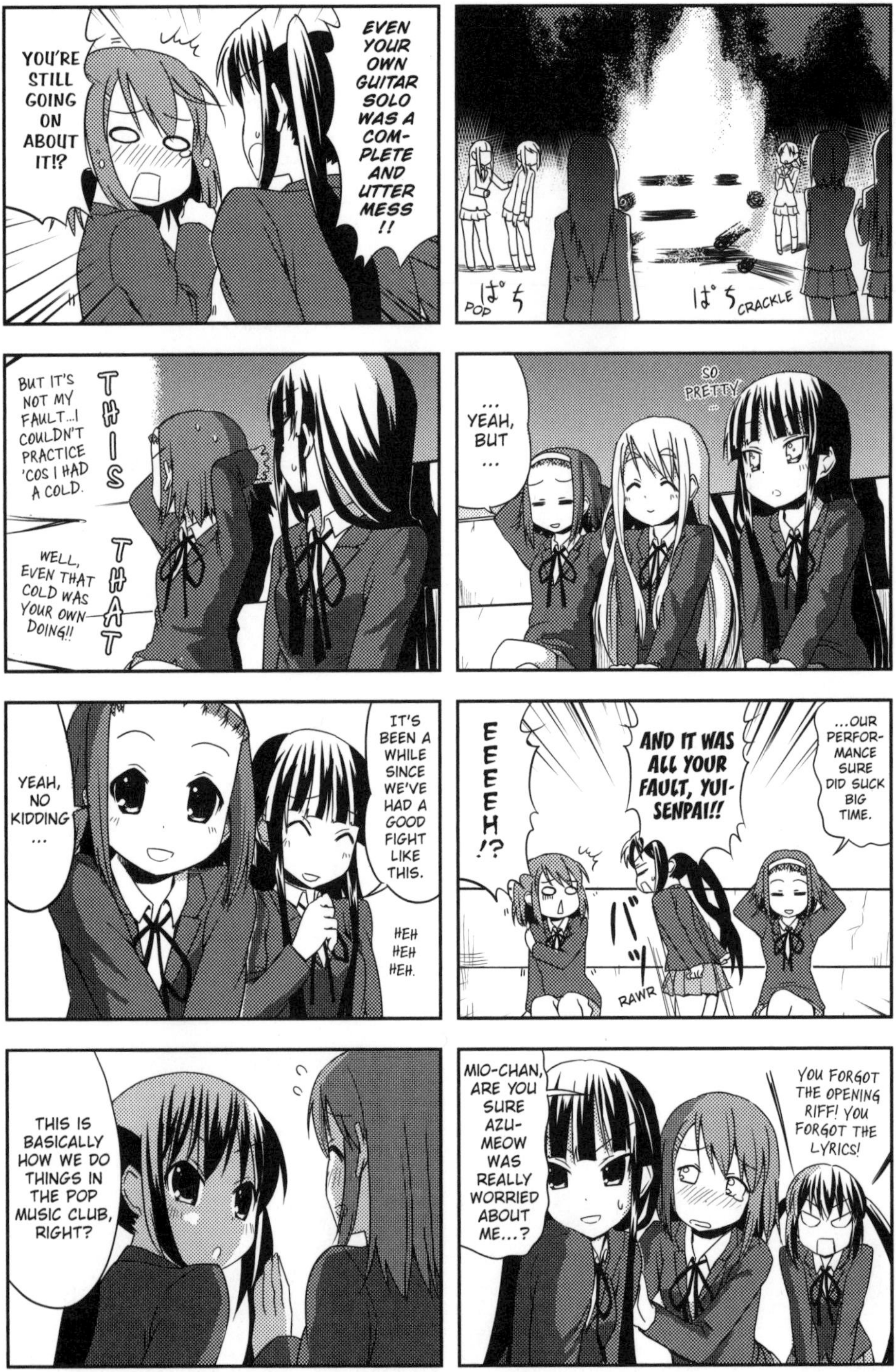

ぱち POP
ぱち CRACKLE
EVEN YOUR OWN GUITAR SOLO WAS A COMPLETE AND UTTER MESS!!
YOU'RE STILL GOING ON ABOUT IT!?
SO PRETTY...
...YEAH, BUT...
THIS THAT
BUT IT'S NOT MY FAULT...I COULDN'T PRACTICE 'COS I HAD A COLD.
WELL, EVEN THAT COLD WAS YOUR OWN DOING!!
...OUR PERFORMANCE SURE DID SUCK BIG TIME.
AND IT WAS ALL YOUR FAULT, YUI-SENPAI!!
EEEEEH!?
バッ
RAWR
IT'S BEEN A WHILE SINCE WE'VE HAD A GOOD FIGHT LIKE THIS.
HEH HEH HEH.
YEAH, NO KIDDING...
YOU FORGOT THE OPENING RIFF! YOU FORGOT THE LYRICS!
MIO-CHAN, ARE YOU SURE AZU-MEOW WAS REALLY WORRIED ABOUT ME...?
THIS IS BASICALLY HOW WE DO THINGS IN THE POP MUSIC CLUB, RIGHT?

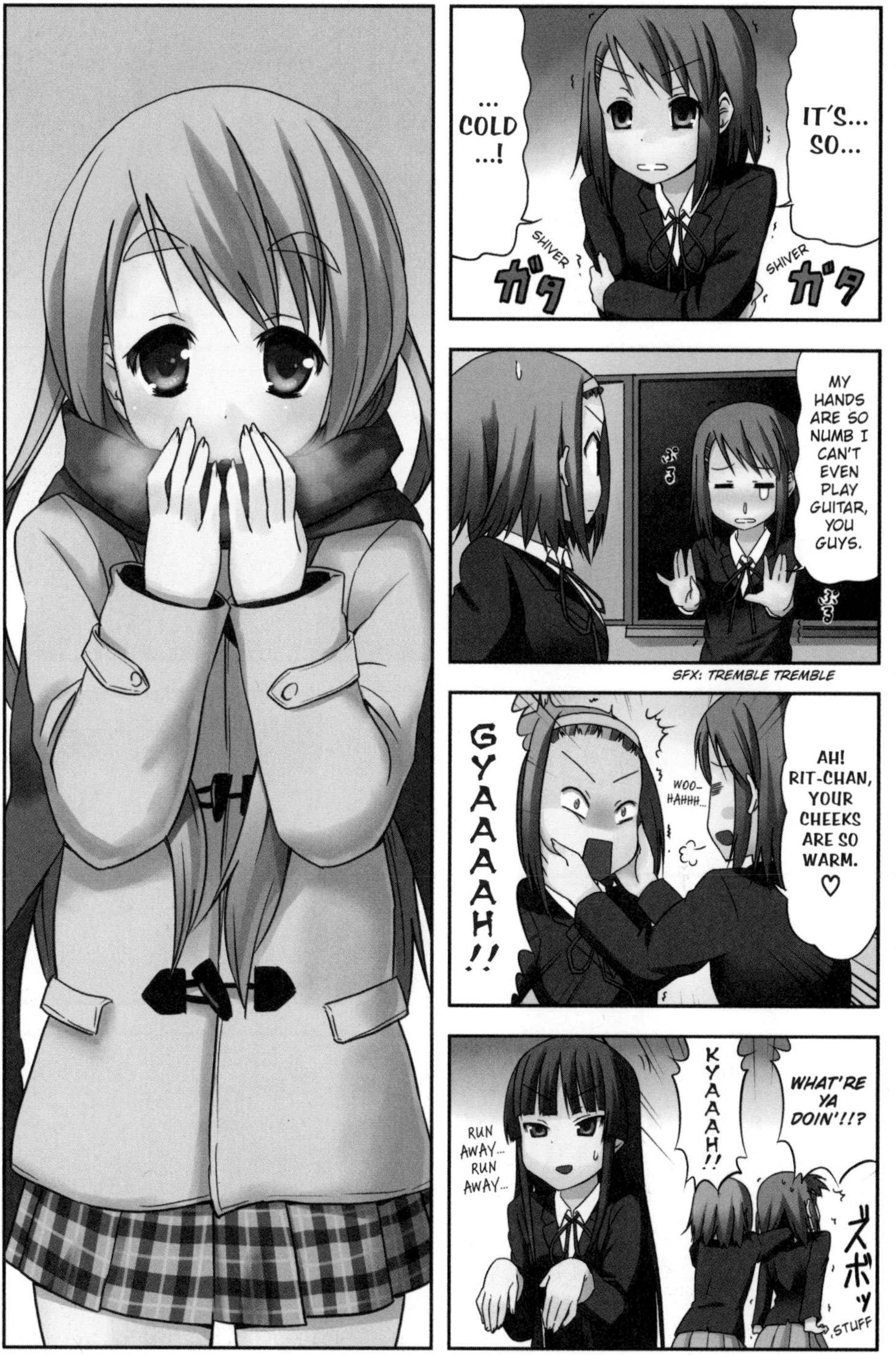
IT'S... SO...
... COLD ...!
SHIVER ガタ
SHIVER ガタ
MY HANDS ARE SO NUMB I CAN'T EVEN PLAY GUITAR, YOU GUYS.
ぷる
ぷる
SFX: TREMBLE TREMBLE
AH! RIT-CHAN, YOUR CHEEKS ARE SO WARM. ♡
WOO-HAHHH...
GYAAAAAH!!
WHAT'RE YA DOIN'!!?
KYAAAAH!!
RUN AWAY... RUN AWAY...
ズボッ
STUFF

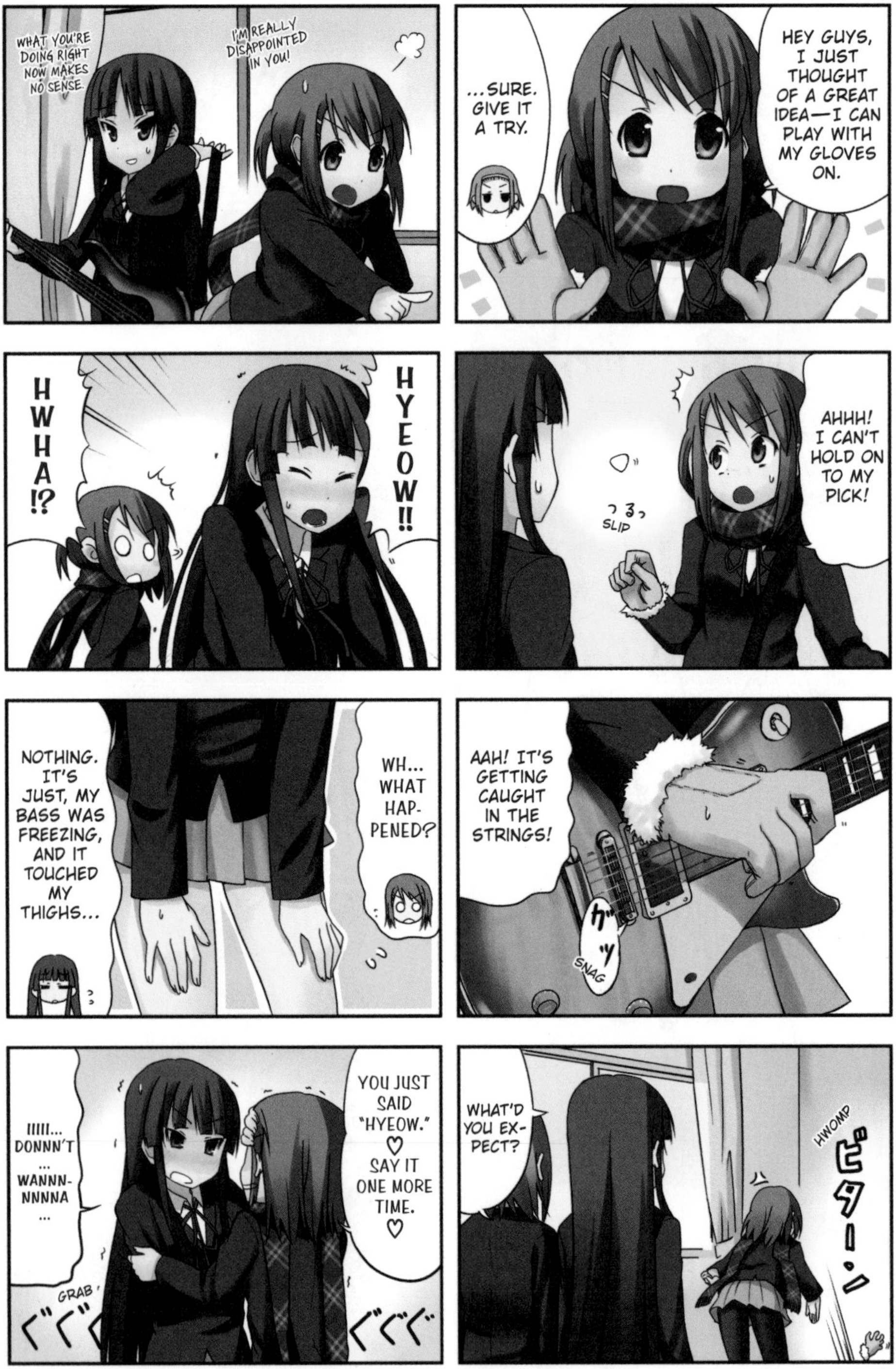
HEY GUYS, I JUST THOUGHT OF A GREAT IDEA—I CAN PLAY WITH MY GLOVES ON.
...SURE. GIVE IT A TRY.
I'M REALLY DISAPPOINTED IN YOU!
WHAT YOU'RE DOING RIGHT NOW MAKES NO SENSE.
AHHH! I CAN'T HOLD ON TO MY PICK!
つるっ SLIP
HYEOW!!
HWHA!?
AAH! IT'S GETTING CAUGHT IN THE STRINGS!
ガッ SNAG
WH... WHAT HAP-PENED?
NOTHING. IT'S JUST, MY BASS WAS FREEZING, AND IT TOUCHED MY THIGHS...
HWOMP
WHAT'D YOU EXPECT?
YOU JUST SAID "HYEOW." ♡ SAY IT ONE MORE TIME. ♡
ぐぐぐ
IIIII... DONNN'T ... WANNN-NNNNA ...
GRAB ぐぐぐ

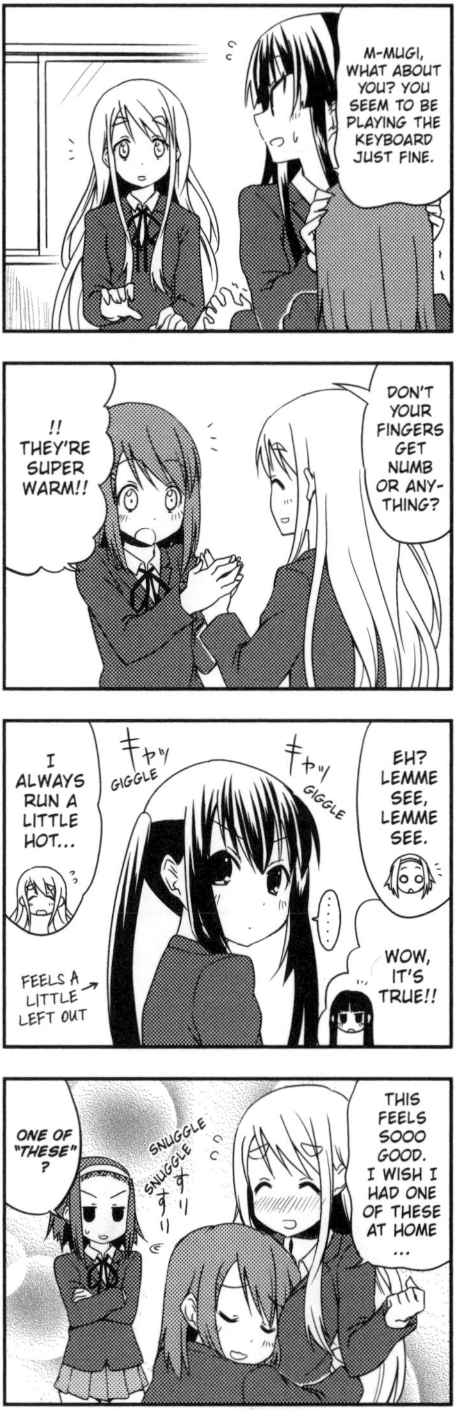
M-MUGI, WHAT ABOUT YOU? YOU SEEM TO BE PLAYING THE KEYBOARD JUST FINE.
DON'T YOUR FINGERS GET NUMB OR ANYTHING?
!! THEY'RE SUPER WARM!!
EH? LEMME SEE, LEMME SEE.
キャッ GIGGLE
キャッ GIGGLE
I ALWAYS RUN A LITTLE HOT...
WOW, IT'S TRUE!!
FEELS A LITTLE LEFT OUT
THIS FEELS SOOO GOOD. I WISH I HAD ONE OF THESE AT HOME ...
すり SNUGGLE
すり SNUGGLE
ONE OF "THESE"?

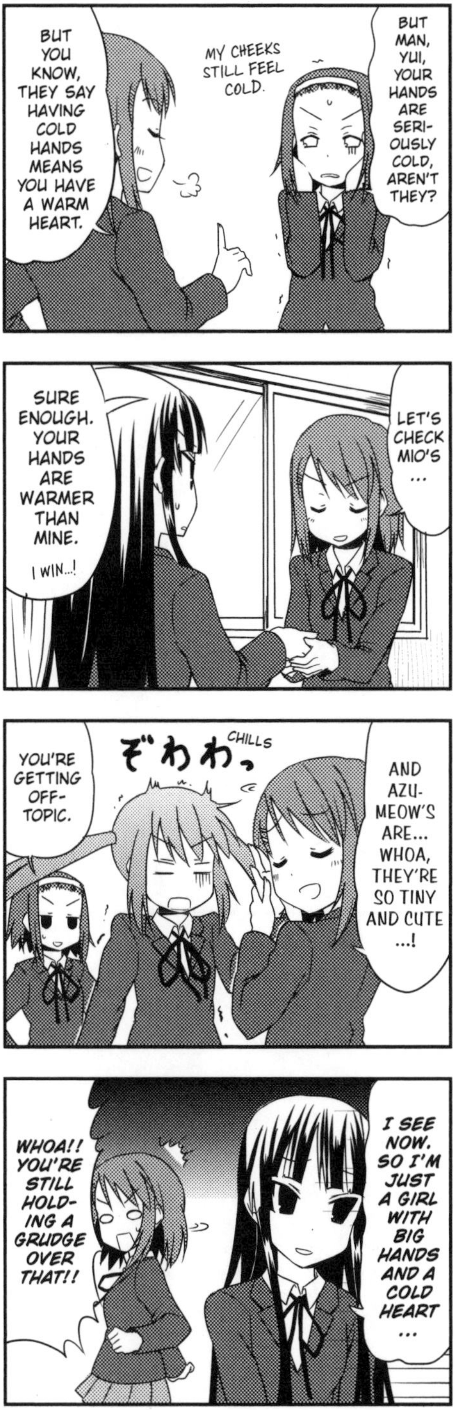
BUT MAN, YUI, YOUR HANDS ARE SERIOUSLY COLD, AREN'T THEY?
MY CHEEKS STILL FEEL COLD.
BUT YOU KNOW, THEY SAY HAVING COLD HANDS MEANS YOU HAVE A WARM HEART.
LET'S CHECK MIO'S ...
SURE ENOUGH. YOUR HANDS ARE WARMER THAN MINE.
I WIN...!
AND AZU-MEOW'S ARE... WHOA, THEY'RE SO TINY AND CUTE ...!
ぞわわっ CHILLS
YOU'RE GETTING OFF-TOPIC.
I SEE NOW. SO I'M JUST A GIRL WITH BIG HANDS AND A COLD HEART ...
WHOA!! YOU'RE STILL HOLDING A GRUDGE OVER THAT!!

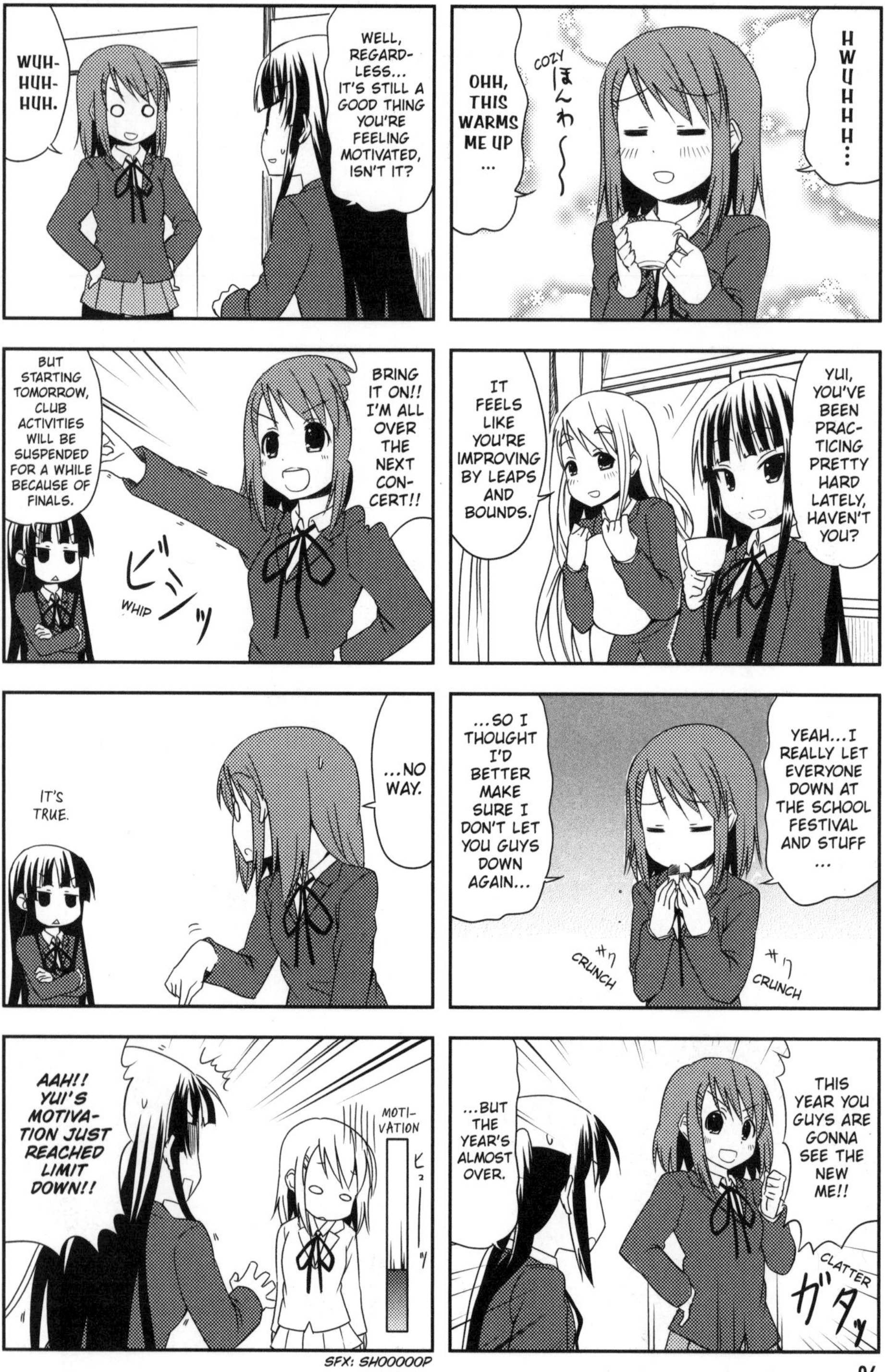
HWUHHHH…
COZY ほんわ～～
OHH, THIS WARMS ME UP…
YUI, YOU'VE BEEN PRAC-TICING PRETTY HARD LATELY, HAVEN'T YOU?
IT FEELS LIKE YOU'RE IMPROVING BY LEAPS AND BOUNDS.
YEAH…I REALLY LET EVERYONE DOWN AT THE SCHOOL FESTIVAL AND STUFF…
…SO I THOUGHT I'D BETTER MAKE SURE I DON'T LET YOU GUYS DOWN AGAIN…
サク CRUNCH
サク CRUNCH
THIS YEAR YOU GUYS ARE GONNA SEE THE NEW ME!!
CLATTER ガタッ
…BUT THE YEAR'S ALMOST OVER.
WELL, REGARD-LESS… IT'S STILL A GOOD THING YOU'RE FEELING MOTIVATED, ISN'T IT?
WUH-HUH-HUH.
BRING IT ON!! I'M ALL OVER THE NEXT CON-CERT!!
BUT STARTING TOMORROW, CLUB ACTIVITIES WILL BE SUSPENDED FOR A WHILE BECAUSE OF FINALS.
ビシッ WHIP
…NO WAY.
IT'S TRUE.
MOTI-VATION
ヒュ～ッ
AAH!! YUI'S MOTIVA-TION JUST REACHED LIMIT DOWN!!

SFX: SHOOOOOP

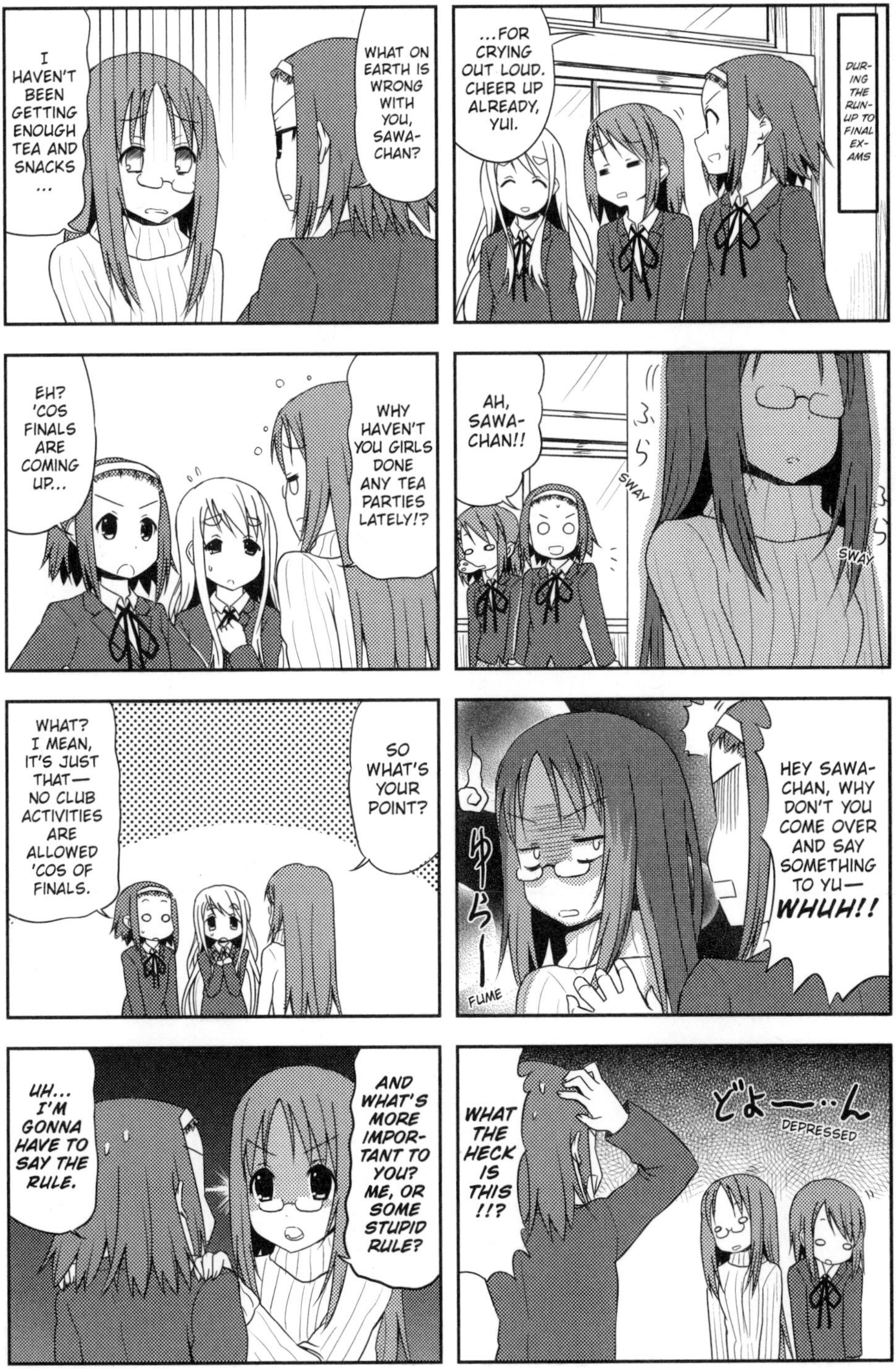
DURING THE RUN-UP TO FINAL EXAMS
...FOR CRYING OUT LOUD. CHEER UP ALREADY, YUI.
WHAT ON EARTH IS WRONG WITH YOU, SAWA-CHAN?
I HAVEN'T BEEN GETTING ENOUGH TEA AND SNACKS...
ふら
SWAY
AH, SAWA-CHAN!!
ふら
SWAY
WHY HAVEN'T YOU GIRLS DONE ANY TEA PARTIES LATELY!?
EH? 'COS FINALS ARE COMING UP...
HEY SAWA-CHAN, WHY DON'T YOU COME OVER AND SAY SOMETHING TO YU— WHUH!!
ゆら〜
FUME
SO WHAT'S YOUR POINT?
WHAT? I MEAN, IT'S JUST THAT— NO CLUB ACTIVITIES ARE ALLOWED 'COS OF FINALS.
どよ〜…ん
DEPRESSED
WHAT THE HECK IS THIS !!?
AND WHAT'S MORE IMPORTANT TO YOU? ME, OR SOME STUPID RULE?
UH... I'M GONNA HAVE TO SAY THE RULE.

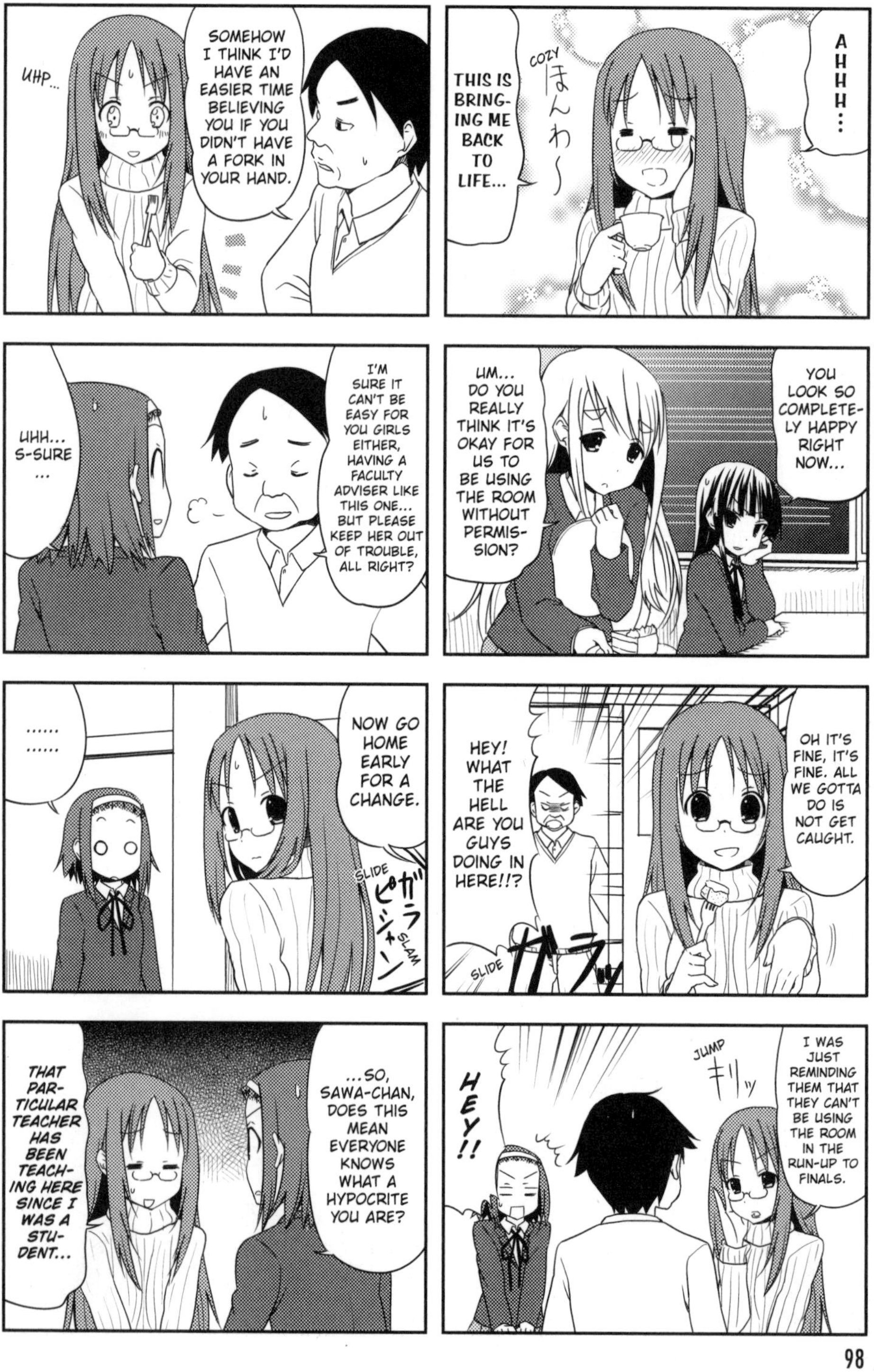
AHHH...
COZY
ほんわ～
THIS IS BRINGING ME BACK TO LIFE...
YOU LOOK SO COMPLETELY HAPPY RIGHT NOW...
UM... DO YOU REALLY THINK IT'S OKAY FOR US TO BE USING THE ROOM WITHOUT PERMISSION?
OH IT'S FINE, IT'S FINE. ALL WE GOTTA DO IS NOT GET CAUGHT.
HEY! WHAT THE HELL ARE YOU GUYS DOING IN HERE!!?
SLIDE
ガラッ
I WAS JUST REMINDING THEM THAT THEY CAN'T BE USING THE ROOM IN THE RUN-UP TO FINALS.
JUMP
キリッ
HEY!!
SOMEHOW I THINK I'D HAVE AN EASIER TIME BELIEVING YOU IF YOU DIDN'T HAVE A FORK IN YOUR HAND.
UHP...
I'M SURE IT CAN'T BE EASY FOR YOU GIRLS EITHER, HAVING A FACULTY ADVISER LIKE THIS ONE... BUT PLEASE KEEP HER OUT OF TROUBLE, ALL RIGHT?
UHH... S-SURE ...
NOW GO HOME EARLY FOR A CHANGE.
SLIDE
ガラ
ピシャン
SLAM
......
......
...SO, SAWA-CHAN, DOES THIS MEAN EVERYONE KNOWS WHAT A HYPOCRITE YOU ARE?
THAT PARTICULAR TEACHER HAS BEEN TEACHING HERE SINCE I WAS A STUDENT...

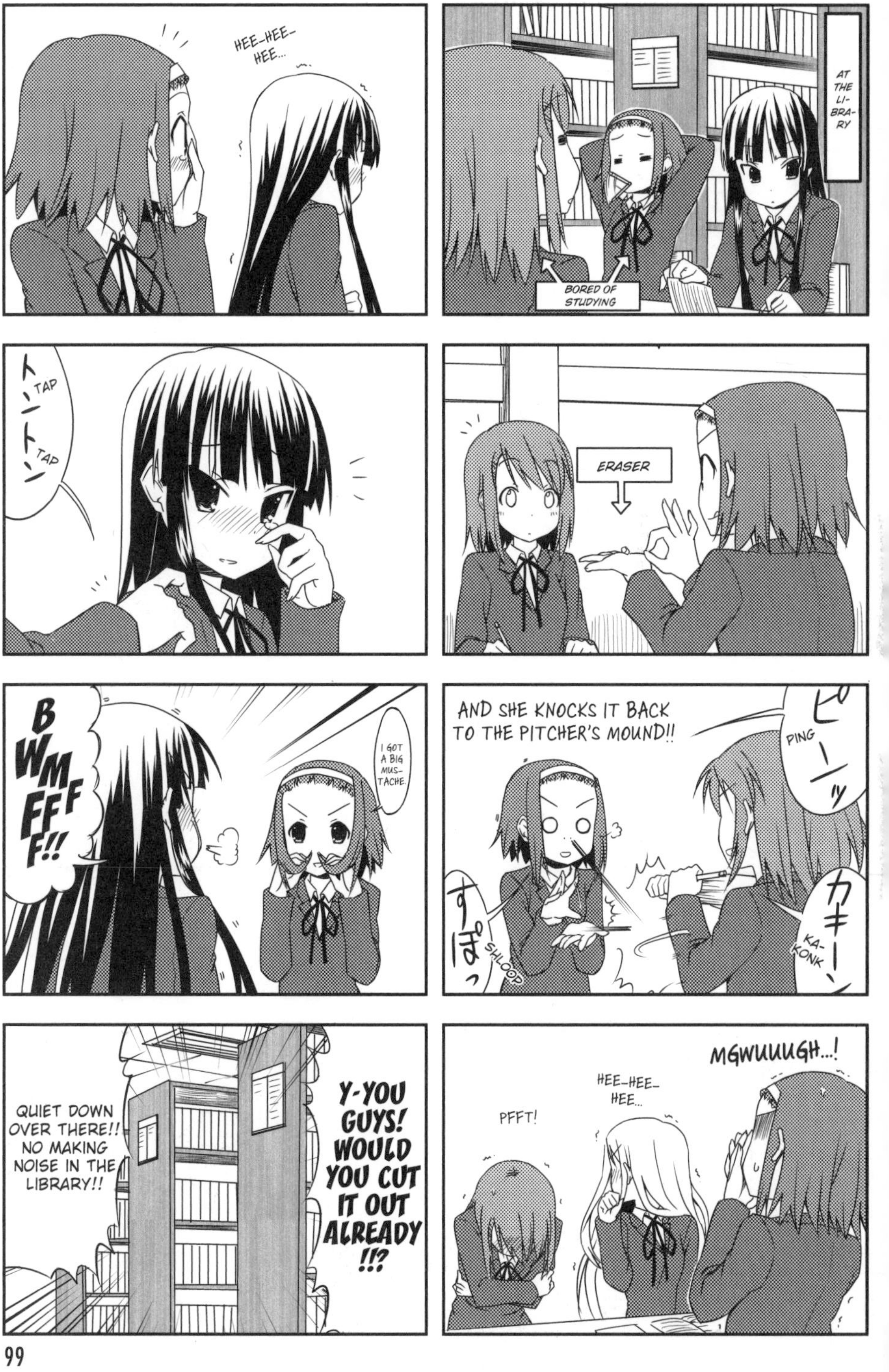
AT THE LI-BRA-RY
BORED OF STUDYING
HEE-HEE-HEE...
ERASER
トントン
TAP TAP
ピーンッ
PING
AND SHE KNOCKS IT BACK TO THE PITCHER'S MOUND!!
カキーン
KA-KONK
すぽっ
SHLOOP
I GOT A BIG MUS-TACHE.
BWMFFFF!!
MGWUUUGH...!
HEE-HEE-HEE...
PFFT!
Y-YOU GUYS! WOULD YOU CUT IT OUT ALREADY!!?
QUIET DOWN OVER THERE!! NO MAKING NOISE IN THE LIBRARY!!

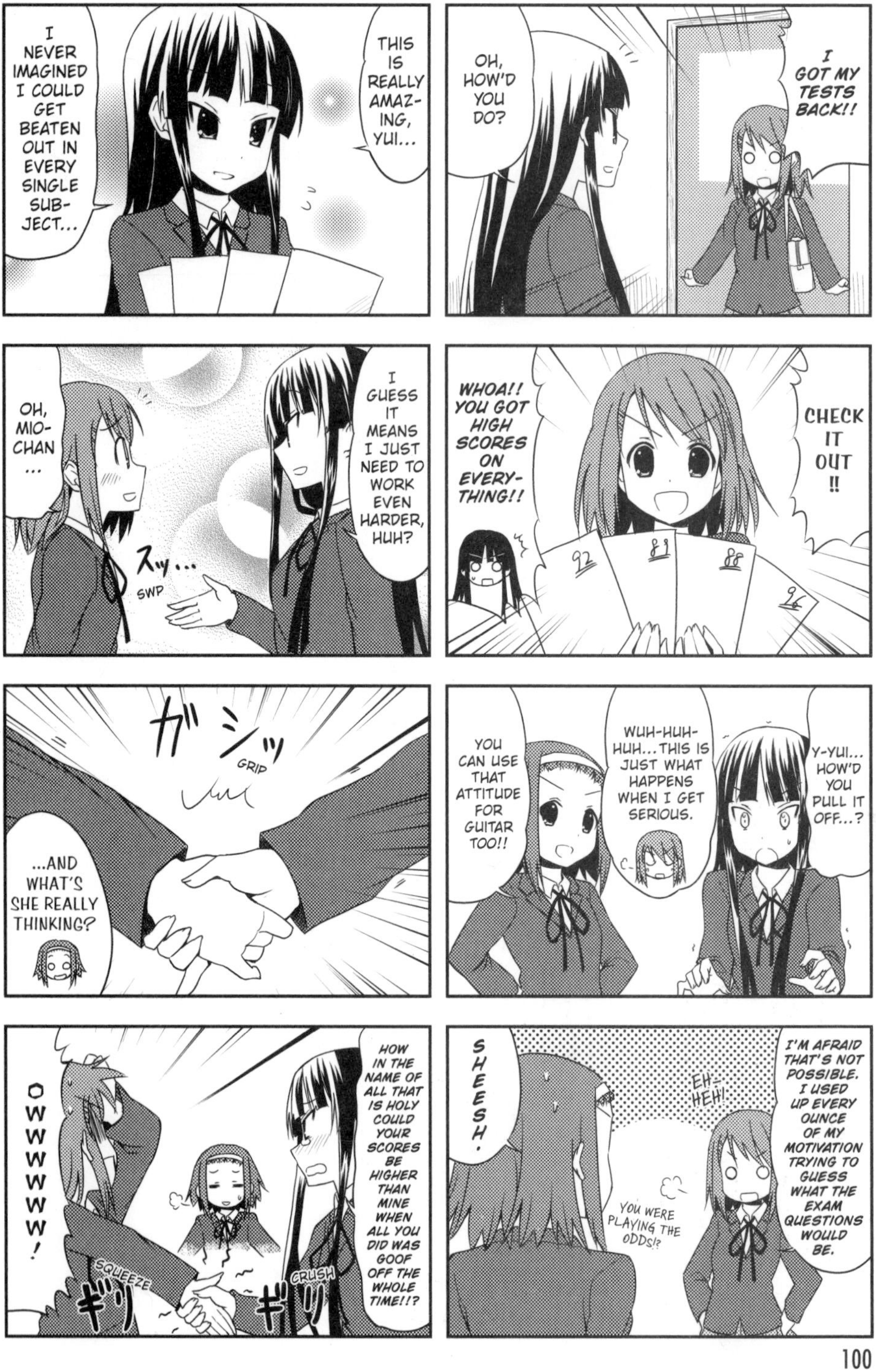
I GOT MY TESTS BACK!!
OH, HOW'D YOU DO?
CHECK IT OUT!!
WHOA!! YOU GOT HIGH SCORES ON EVERYTHING!!
Y-YUI... HOW'D YOU PULL IT OFF...?
WUH-HUH-HUH... THIS IS JUST WHAT HAPPENS WHEN I GET SERIOUS.
YOU CAN USE THAT ATTITUDE FOR GUITAR TOO!!
I'M AFRAID THAT'S NOT POSSIBLE. I USED UP EVERY OUNCE OF MY MOTIVATION TRYING TO GUESS WHAT THE EXAM QUESTIONS WOULD BE.
EH-HEH!
YOU WERE PLAYING THE ODDS!?
SHEESH.
THIS IS REALLY AMAZING, YUI...
I NEVER IMAGINED I COULD GET BEATEN OUT IN EVERY SINGLE SUBJECT...
I GUESS IT MEANS I JUST NEED TO WORK EVEN HARDER, HUH?
OH, MIO-CHAN...
スッ...
SWP
ガシッ
GRIP
...AND WHAT'S SHE REALLY THINKING?
HOW IN THE NAME OF ALL THAT IS HOLY COULD YOUR SCORES BE HIGHER THAN MINE WHEN ALL YOU DID WAS GOOF OFF THE WHOLE TIME!!?
ギリ
CRUSH
ギリ
SQUEEZE
OWWWWWWWW!

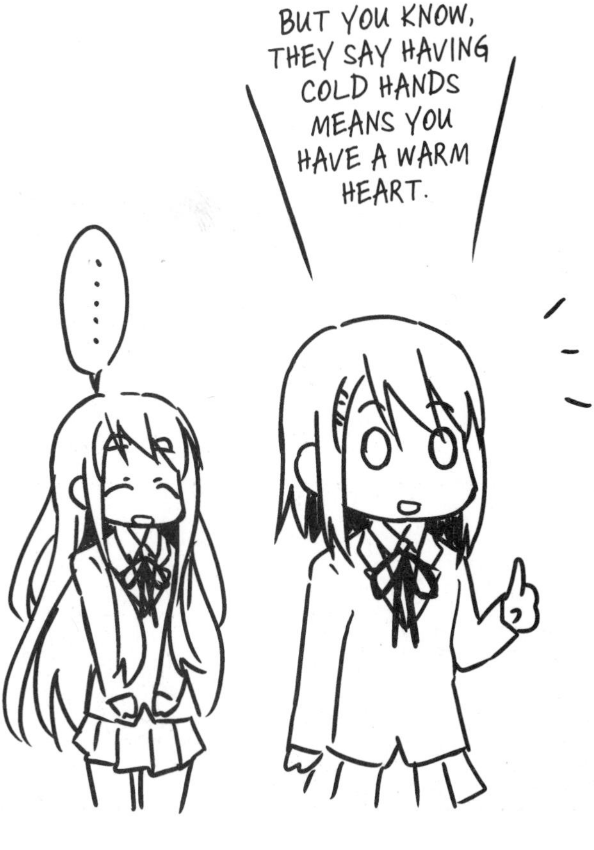
BUT YOU KNOW, THEY SAY HAVING COLD HANDS MEANS YOU HAVE A WARM HEART.
......

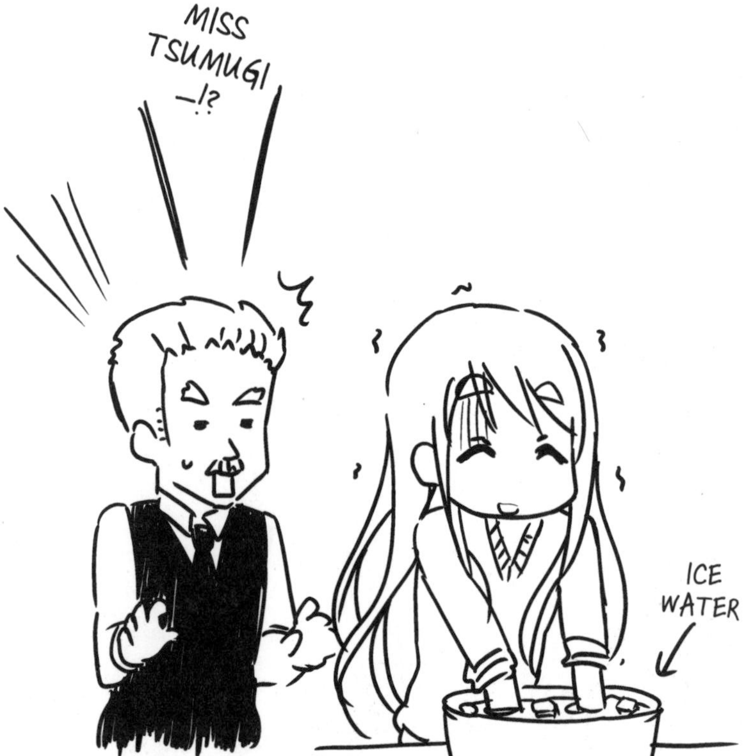
MISS TSUMUGI—!?
ICE WATER

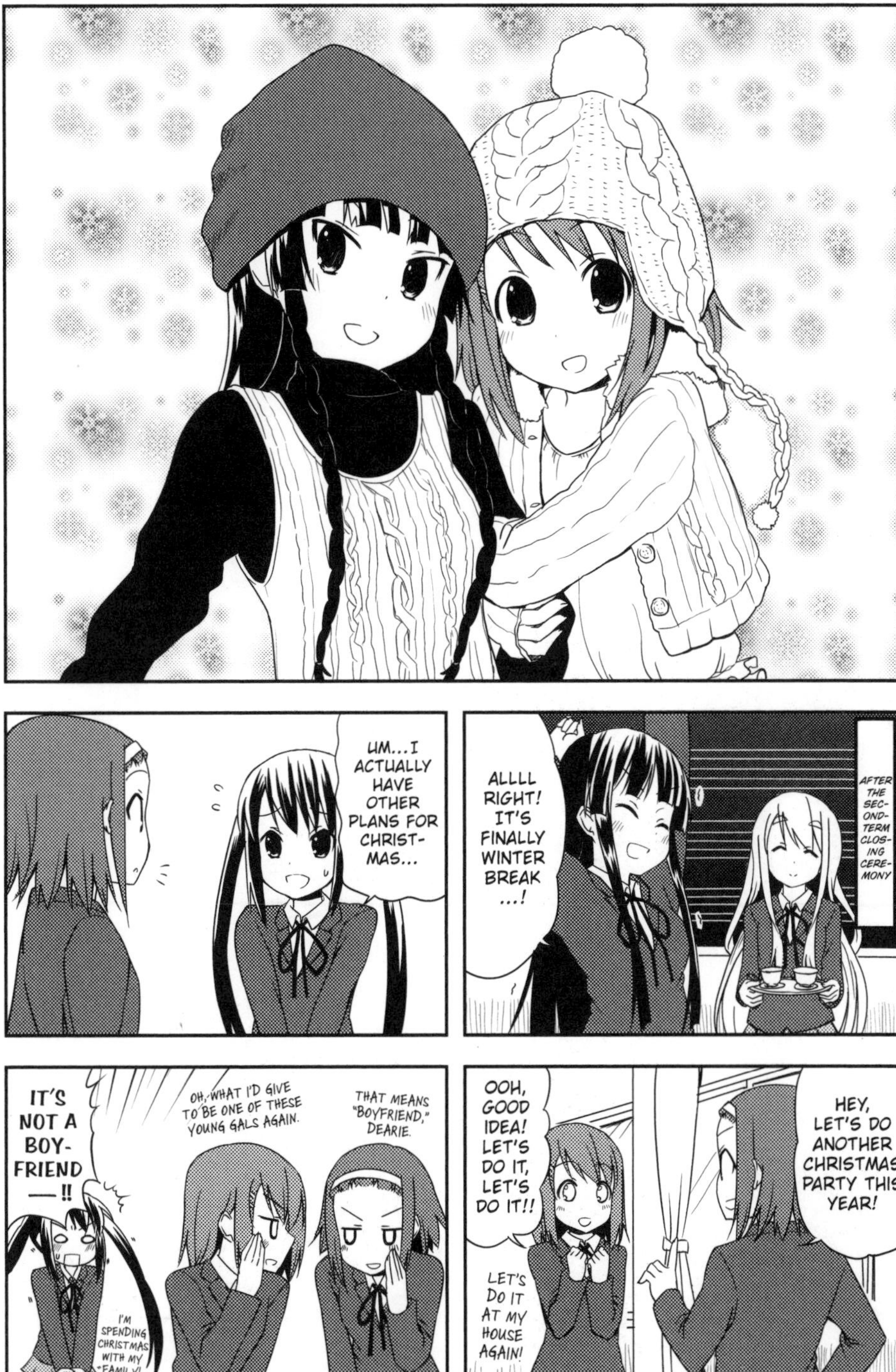
AFTER THE SECOND-TERM CLOSING CEREMONY
ALLLL RIGHT! IT'S FINALLY WINTER BREAK ...!
HEY, LET'S DO ANOTHER CHRISTMAS PARTY THIS YEAR!
OOH, GOOD IDEA! LET'S DO IT, LET'S DO IT!!
LET'S DO IT AT MY HOUSE AGAIN!
UM...I ACTUALLY HAVE OTHER PLANS FOR CHRIST-MAS...
THAT MEANS "BOYFRIEND," DEARIE.
OH, WHAT I'D GIVE TO BE ONE OF THESE YOUNG GALS AGAIN.
IT'S NOT A BOY-FRIEND —!!
I'M SPENDING CHRISTMAS WITH MY *FAMILY!

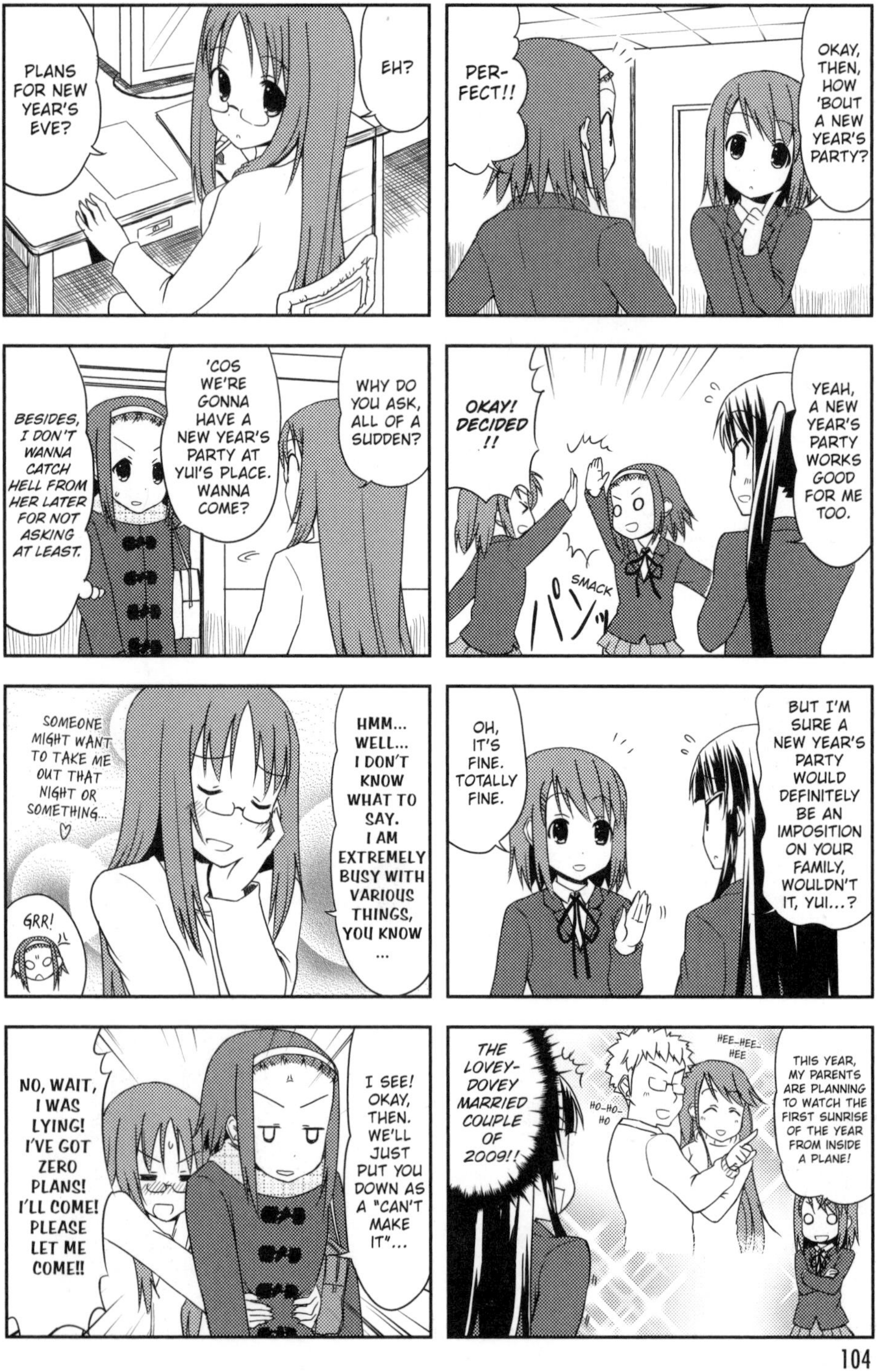
OKAY, THEN, HOW 'BOUT A NEW YEAR'S PARTY?
PER-FECT!!
EH?
PLANS FOR NEW YEAR'S EVE?
YEAH, A NEW YEAR'S PARTY WORKS GOOD FOR ME TOO.
OKAY! DECIDED!!
SMACK
WHY DO YOU ASK, ALL OF A SUDDEN?
'COS WE'RE GONNA HAVE A NEW YEAR'S PARTY AT YUI'S PLACE. WANNA COME?
BESIDES, I DON'T WANNA CATCH HELL FROM HER LATER FOR NOT ASKING AT LEAST.
BUT I'M SURE A NEW YEAR'S PARTY WOULD DEFINITELY BE AN IMPOSITION ON YOUR FAMILY, WOULDN'T IT, YUI...?
OH, IT'S FINE. TOTALLY FINE.
HMM... WELL... I DON'T KNOW WHAT TO SAY. I AM EXTREMELY BUSY WITH VARIOUS THINGS, YOU KNOW ...
SOMEONE MIGHT WANT TO TAKE ME OUT THAT NIGHT OR SOMETHING... ♡
GRR!
THIS YEAR, MY PARENTS ARE PLANNING TO WATCH THE FIRST SUNRISE OF THE YEAR FROM INSIDE A PLANE!
HEE-HEE-HEE
HO-HO-HO
THE LOVEY-DOVEY MARRIED COUPLE OF 2009!!
I SEE! OKAY, THEN. WE'LL JUST PUT YOU DOWN AS A "CAN'T MAKE IT"...
NO, WAIT, I WAS LYING! I'VE GOT ZERO PLANS! I'LL COME! PLEASE LET ME COME!!

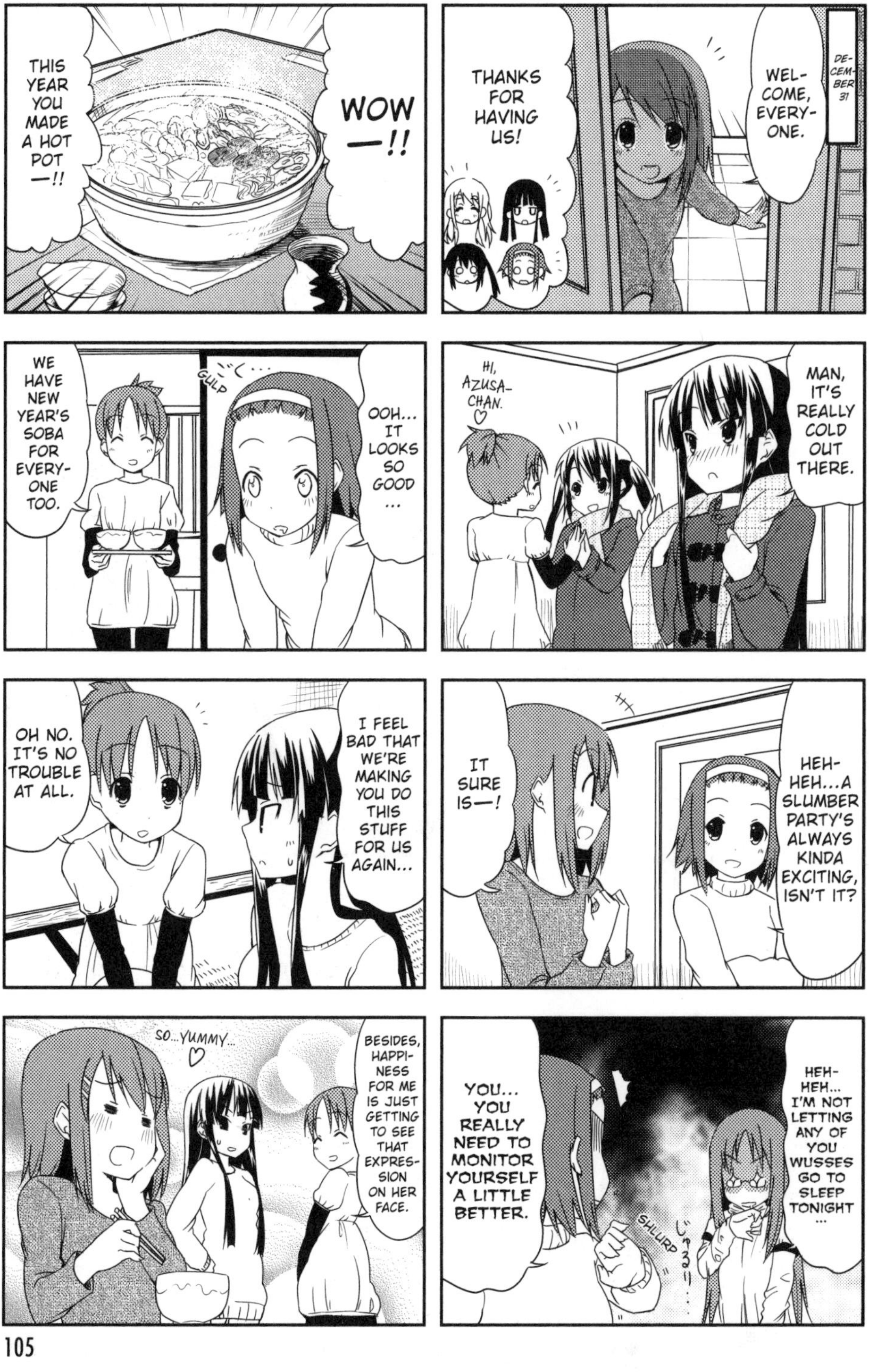
DECEMBER 31
WELCOME, EVERYONE.
THANKS FOR HAVING US!
WOW—!!
THIS YEAR YOU MADE A HOT POT—!!
MAN, IT'S REALLY COLD OUT THERE.
HI, AZUSA-CHAN. ♡
OOH... IT LOOKS SO GOOD...
GULP
WE HAVE NEW YEAR'S SOBA FOR EVERYONE TOO.
HEH-HEH...A SLUMBER PARTY'S ALWAYS KINDA EXCITING, ISN'T IT?
IT SURE IS—!
I FEEL BAD THAT WE'RE MAKING YOU DO THIS STUFF FOR US AGAIN...
OH NO. IT'S NO TROUBLE AT ALL.
HEH-HEH... I'M NOT LETTING ANY OF YOU WUSSES GO TO SLEEP TONIGHT...
SHLURP
YOU... YOU REALLY NEED TO MONITOR YOURSELF A LITTLE BETTER.
BESIDES, HAPPINESS FOR ME IS JUST GETTING TO SEE THAT EXPRESSION ON HER FACE.
SO...YUMMY... ♡

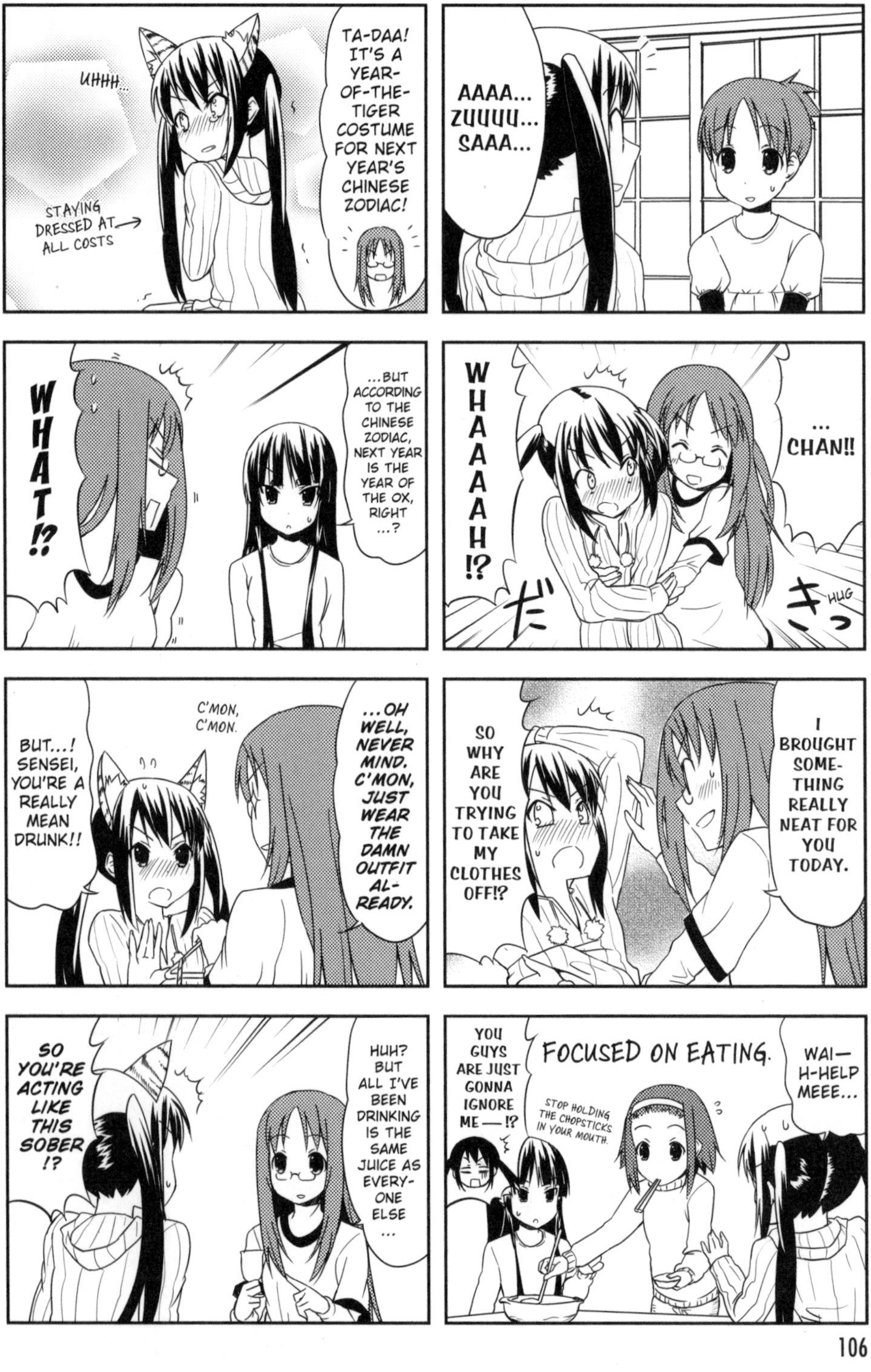
AAAA... ZUUUU... SAAA...
TA-DAA! IT'S A YEAR-OF-THE-TIGER COSTUME FOR NEXT YEAR'S CHINESE ZODIAC!
UHHH...
STAYING DRESSED AT ALL COSTS
... CHAN!!
WHAAAAAH!?
HUG
...BUT ACCORDING TO THE CHINESE ZODIAC, NEXT YEAR IS THE YEAR OF THE OX, RIGHT ...?
WHAT!?
I BROUGHT SOME-THING REALLY NEAT FOR YOU TODAY.
SO WHY ARE YOU TRYING TO TAKE MY CLOTHES OFF!?
...OH WELL, NEVER MIND. C'MON, JUST WEAR THE DAMN OUTFIT AL-READY.
C'MON, C'MON.
BUT...! SENSEI, YOU'RE A REALLY MEAN DRUNK!!
WAI—H-HELP MEEE...
FOCUSED ON EATING.
YOU GUYS ARE JUST GONNA IGNORE ME—!?
STOP HOLDING THE CHOPSTICKS IN YOUR MOUTH.
HUH? BUT ALL I'VE BEEN DRINKING IS THE SAME JUICE AS EVERY-ONE ELSE ...
SO YOU'RE ACTING LIKE THIS SOBER !?

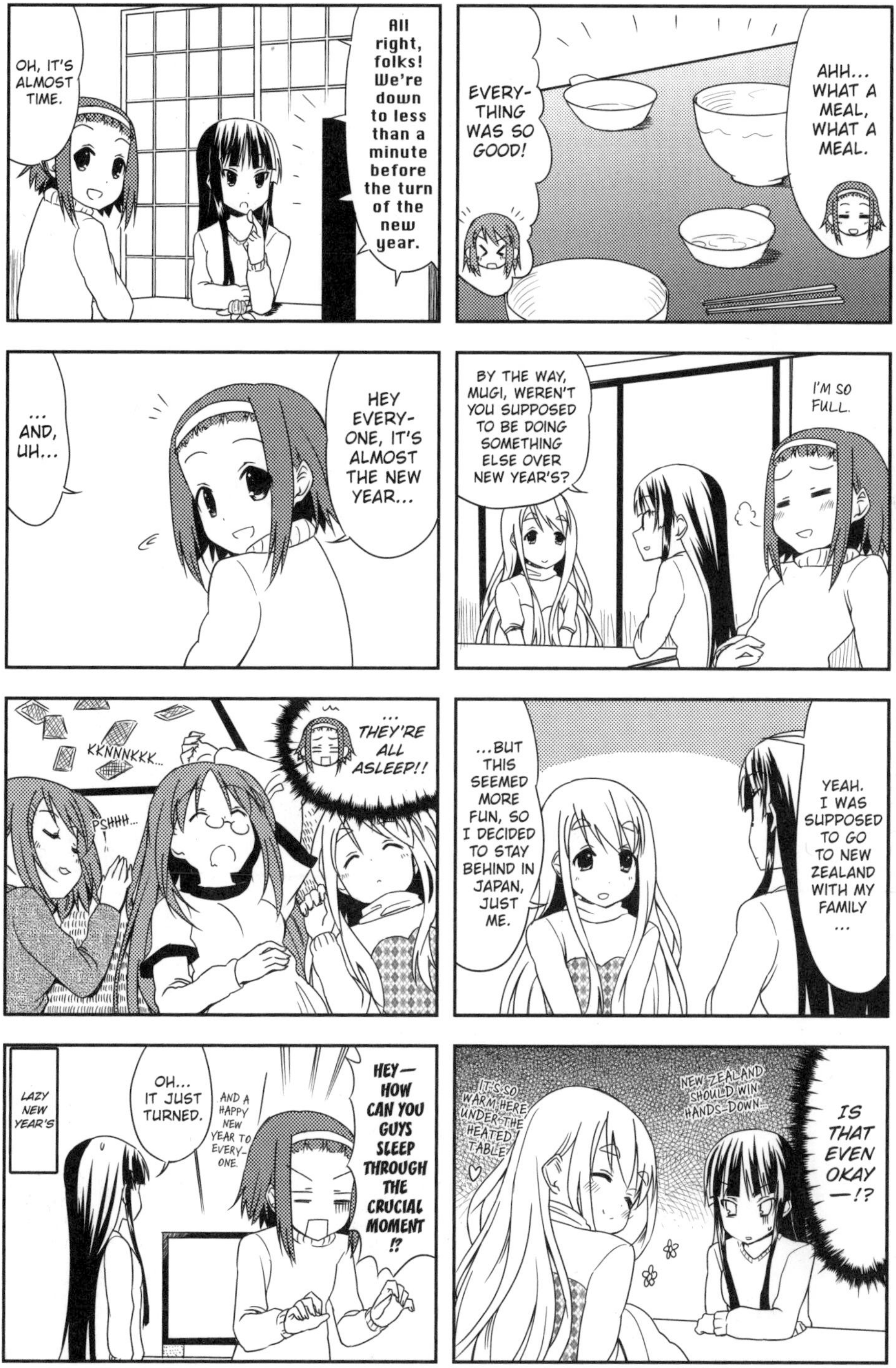

AHH... WHAT A MEAL, WHAT A MEAL.
EVERYTHING WAS SO GOOD!
All right, folks! We're down to less than a minute before the turn of the new year.
OH, IT'S ALMOST TIME.
I'M SO FULL.
BY THE WAY, MUGI, WEREN'T YOU SUPPOSED TO BE DOING SOMETHING ELSE OVER NEW YEAR'S?
HEY EVERYONE, IT'S ALMOST THE NEW YEAR...
...AND, UH...
YEAH. I WAS SUPPOSED TO GO TO NEW ZEALAND WITH MY FAMILY...
...BUT THIS SEEMED MORE FUN, SO I DECIDED TO STAY BEHIND IN JAPAN, JUST ME.
...THEY'RE ALL ASLEEP!!
KKNNNKKK...
PSHHH...
IS THAT EVEN OKAY—!?
NEW ZEALAND SHOULD WIN HANDS-DOWN...
IT'S SO WARM HERE UNDER THE HEATED TABLE.
HEY—HOW CAN YOU GUYS SLEEP THROUGH THE CRUCIAL MOMENT!?
AND A HAPPY NEW YEAR TO EVERYONE.
OH... IT JUST TURNED.
LAZY NEW YEAR'S

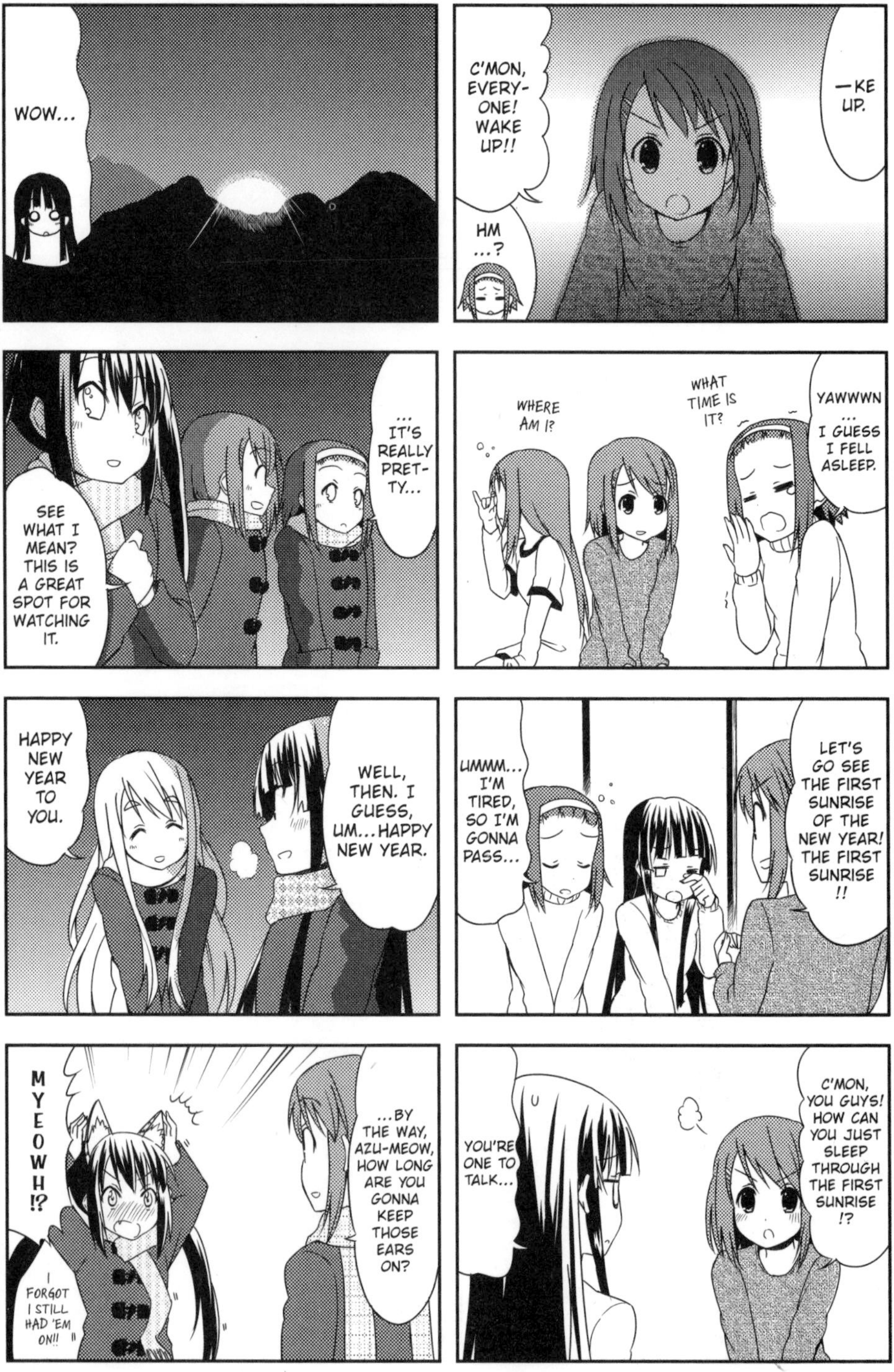
—KE UP.
C'MON, EVERY-ONE! WAKE UP!!
HM ...?
YAWWWN ... I GUESS I FELL ASLEEP.
WHAT TIME IS IT?
WHERE AM I?
LET'S GO SEE THE FIRST SUNRISE OF THE NEW YEAR! THE FIRST SUNRISE !!
UMMM... I'M TIRED, SO I'M GONNA PASS...
C'MON, YOU GUYS! HOW CAN YOU JUST SLEEP THROUGH THE FIRST SUNRISE !?
YOU'RE ONE TO TALK...
WOW...
... IT'S REALLY PRET-TY...
SEE WHAT I MEAN? THIS IS A GREAT SPOT FOR WATCHING IT.
WELL, THEN. I GUESS, UM...HAPPY NEW YEAR.
HAPPY NEW YEAR TO YOU.
...BY THE WAY, AZU-MEOW, HOW LONG ARE YOU GONNA KEEP THOSE EARS ON?
MYEOWH!?
I FORGOT I STILL HAD 'EM ON!!

SCALE

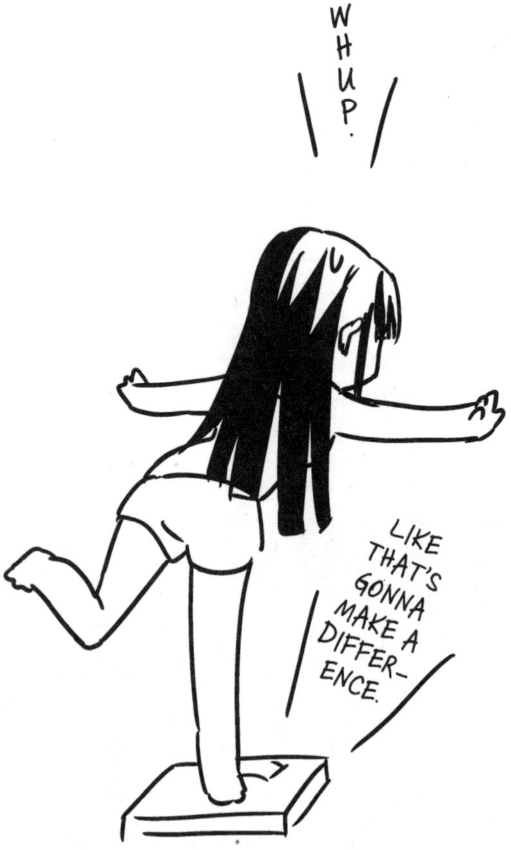
WHUP.
LIKE THAT'S GONNA MAKE A DIFFER-ENCE.

BONUS CHAPTER COMMEMORATING THE UPCOMING ANIME ADAPTATION

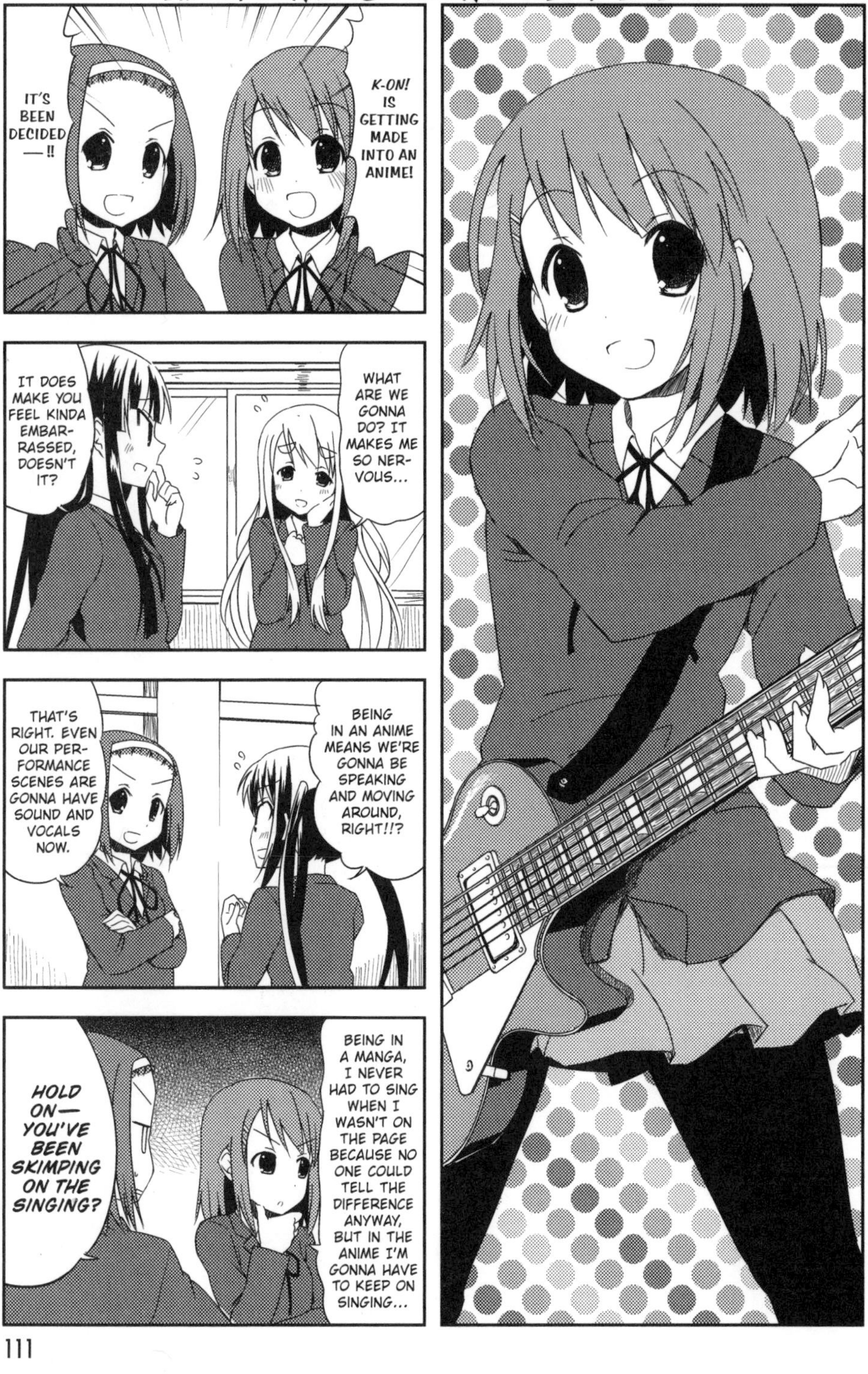
K-ON! IS GETTING MADE INTO AN ANIME!
IT'S BEEN DECIDED—!!
WHAT ARE WE GONNA DO? IT MAKES ME SO NERVOUS...
IT DOES MAKE YOU FEEL KINDA EMBARRASSED, DOESN'T IT?
BEING IN AN ANIME MEANS WE'RE GONNA BE SPEAKING AND MOVING AROUND, RIGHT!!?
THAT'S RIGHT. EVEN OUR PERFORMANCE SCENES ARE GONNA HAVE SOUND AND VOCALS NOW.
BEING IN A MANGA, I NEVER HAD TO SING WHEN I WASN'T ON THE PAGE BECAUSE NO ONE COULD TELL THE DIFFERENCE ANYWAY, BUT IN THE ANIME I'M GONNA HAVE TO KEEP ON SINGING...
HOLD ON— YOU'VE BEEN SKIMPING ON THE SINGING?

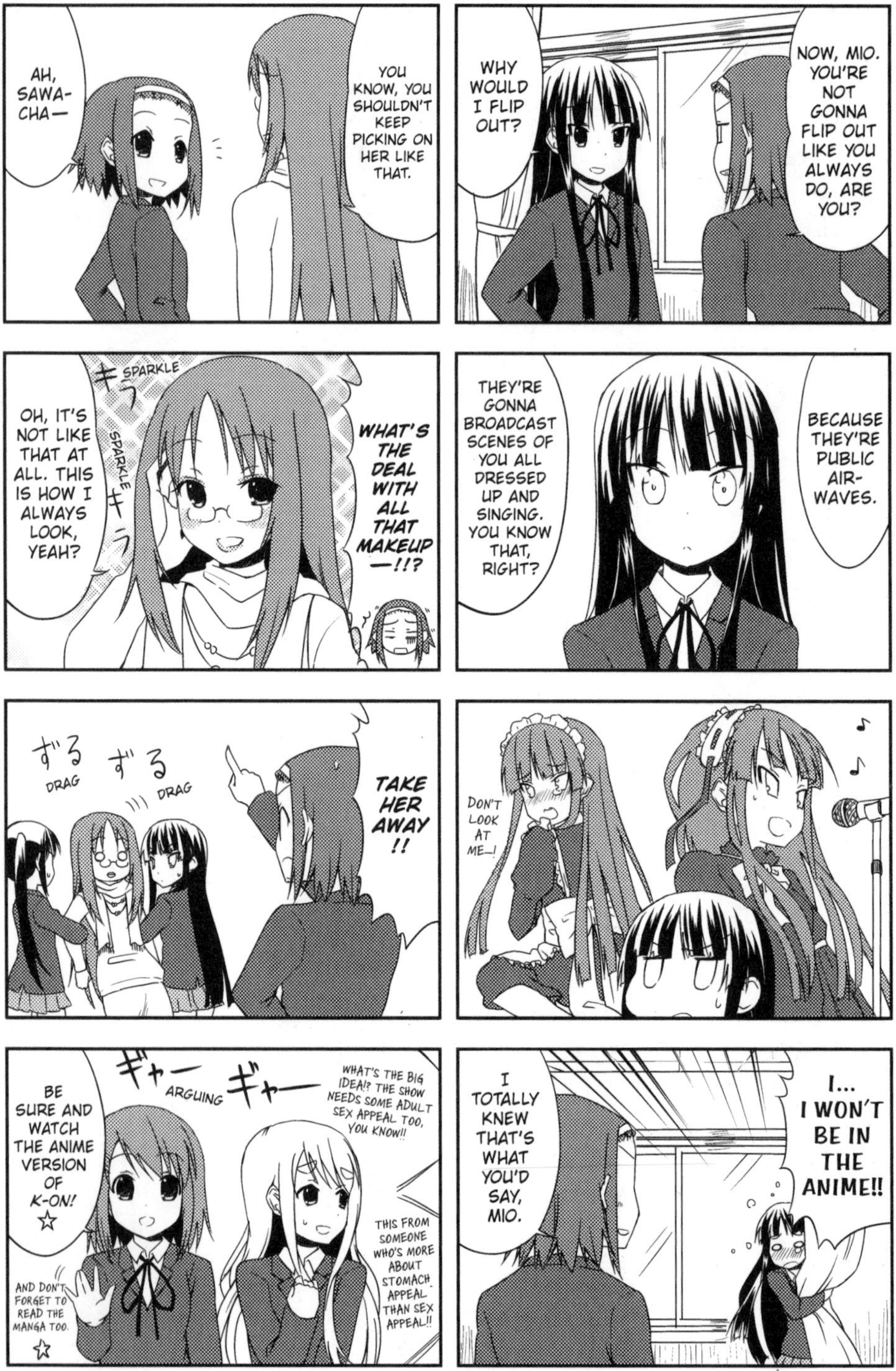
NOW, MIO. YOU'RE NOT GONNA FLIP OUT LIKE YOU ALWAYS DO, ARE YOU?
WHY WOULD I FLIP OUT?
YOU KNOW, YOU SHOULDN'T KEEP PICKING ON HER LIKE THAT.
AH, SAWA-CHA—
BECAUSE THEY'RE PUBLIC AIR-WAVES.
THEY'RE GONNA BROADCAST SCENES OF YOU ALL DRESSED UP AND SINGING. YOU KNOW THAT, RIGHT?
WHAT'S THE DEAL WITH ALL THAT MAKEUP—!!?
キラ SPARKLE
キラ SPARKLE
OH, IT'S NOT LIKE THAT AT ALL. THIS IS HOW I ALWAYS LOOK, YEAH?
DON'T LOOK AT ME—!
TAKE HER AWAY!!
ずる DRAG
ずる DRAG
I... I WON'T BE IN THE ANIME!!
I TOTALLY KNEW THAT'S WHAT YOU'D SAY, MIO.
WHAT'S THE BIG IDEA!? THE SHOW NEEDS SOME ADULT SEX APPEAL TOO, YOU KNOW!!
THIS FROM SOMEONE WHO'S MORE ABOUT STOMACH APPEAL THAN SEX APPEAL!!
ギャー ARGUING ギャー
BE SURE AND WATCH THE ANIME VERSION OF *K-ON!* ☆
AND DON'T FORGET TO READ THE MANGA TOO. ☆

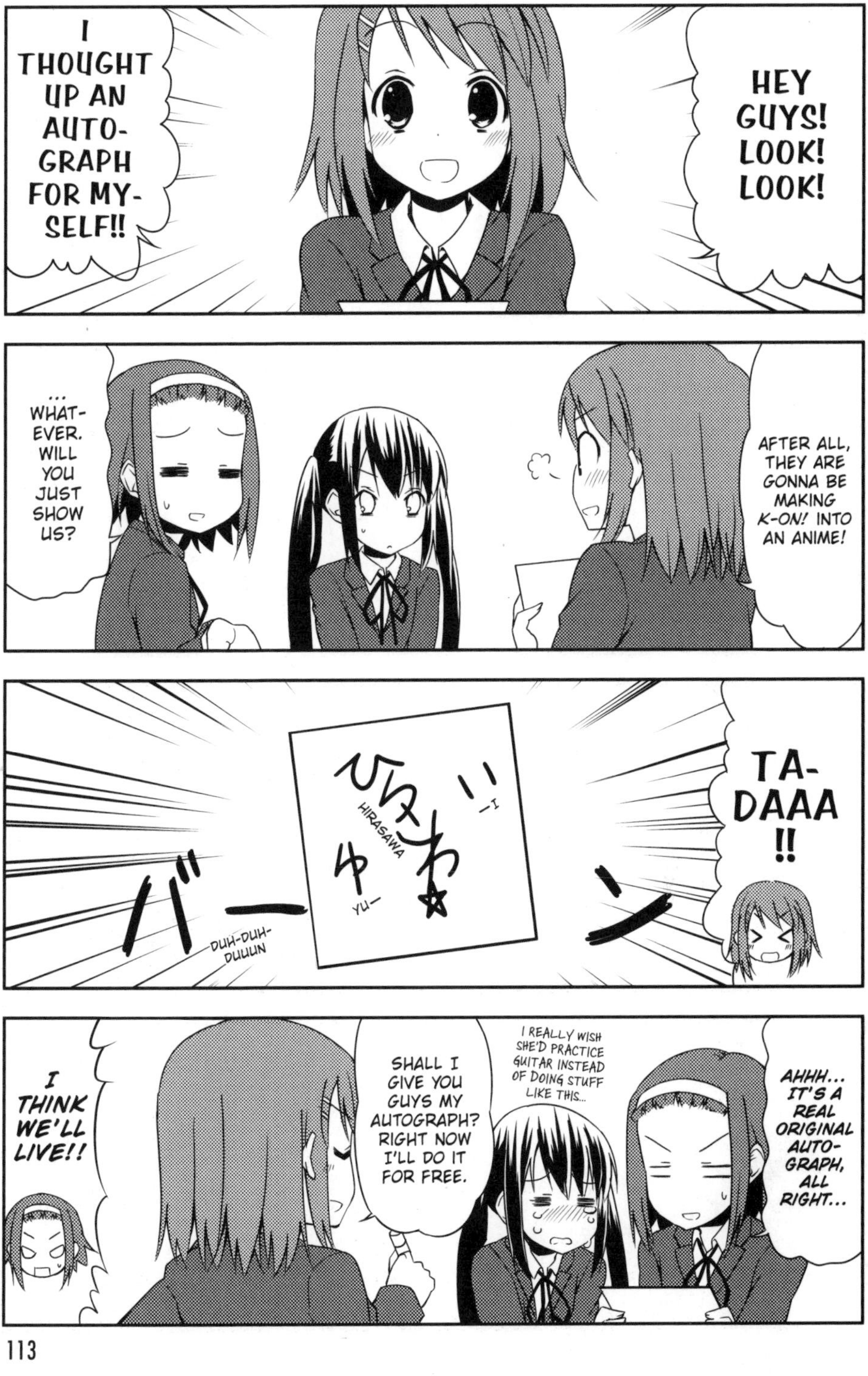
HEY GUYS! LOOK! LOOK!
I THOUGHT UP AN AUTO- GRAPH FOR MY- SELF!!
AFTER ALL, THEY ARE GONNA BE MAKING K-ON! INTO AN ANIME!
... WHAT- EVER. WILL YOU JUST SHOW US?
TA- DAAA !!
ひらさわ
HIRASAWA
ゆい☆
YU—
—I
バーン
DUH-DUH-DUUUN
AHHH... IT'S A REAL ORIGINAL AUTO- GRAPH, ALL RIGHT...
I REALLY WISH SHE'D PRACTICE GUITAR INSTEAD OF DOING STUFF LIKE THIS...
SHALL I GIVE YOU GUYS MY AUTOGRAPH? RIGHT NOW I'LL DO IT FOR FREE.
I THINK WE'LL LIVE!!

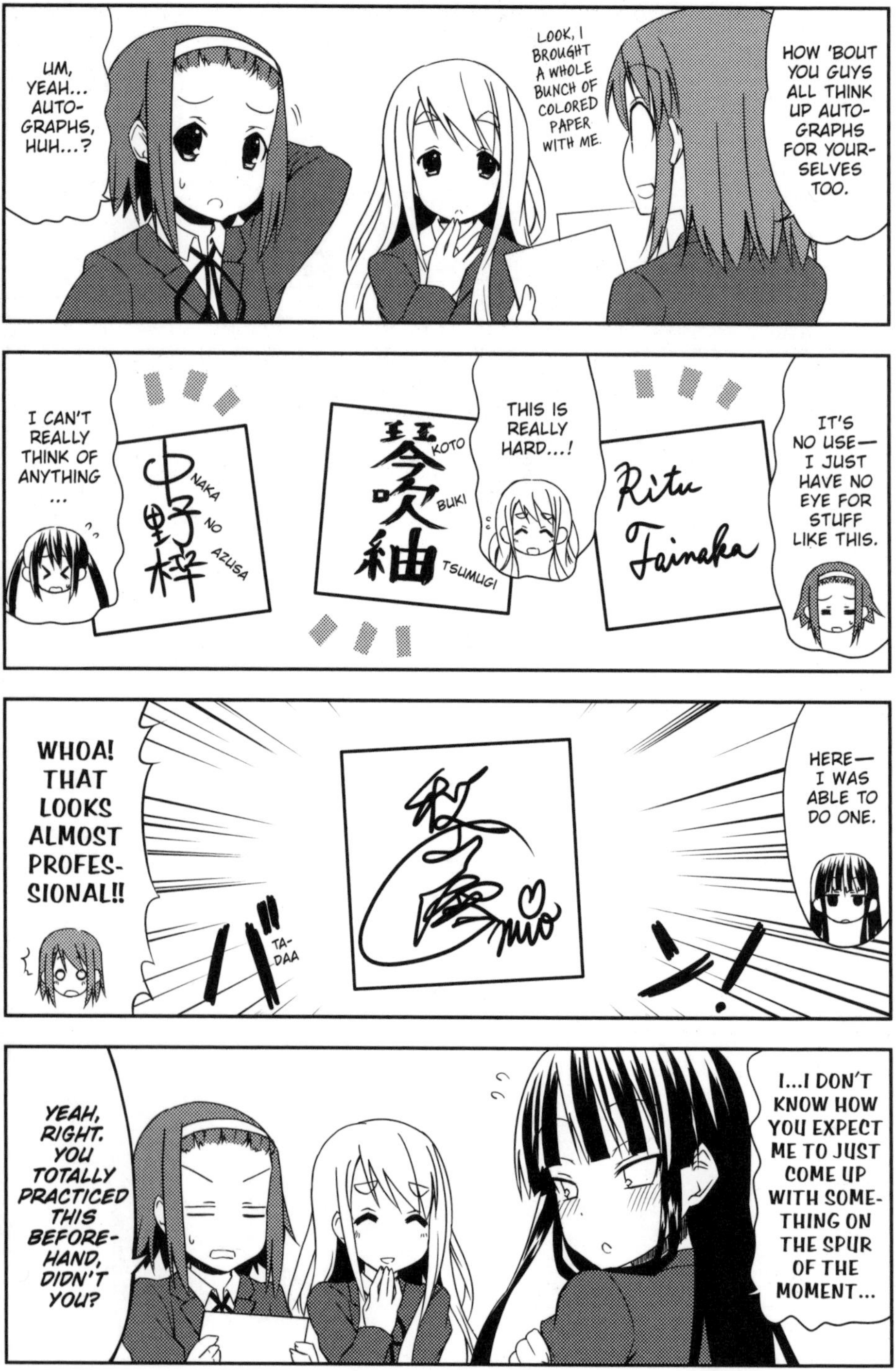
HOW 'BOUT YOU GUYS ALL THINK UP AUTOGRAPHS FOR YOURSELVES TOO.
LOOK, I BROUGHT A WHOLE BUNCH OF COLORED PAPER WITH ME.
UM, YEAH... AUTOGRAPHS, HUH...?
IT'S NO USE— I JUST HAVE NO EYE FOR STUFF LIKE THIS.
Ritu Tainaka
THIS IS REALLY HARD...!
琴吹紬
KOTO BUKI TSUMUGI
I CAN'T REALLY THINK OF ANYTHING...
中野梓
NAKA NO AZUSA
HERE— I WAS ABLE TO DO ONE.
mio
TA-DAA
WHOA! THAT LOOKS ALMOST PROFESSIONAL!!
I...I DON'T KNOW HOW YOU EXPECT ME TO JUST COME UP WITH SOMETHING ON THE SPUR OF THE MOMENT...
YEAH, RIGHT. YOU TOTALLY PRACTICED THIS BEFOREHAND, DIDN'T YOU?

K-ON!

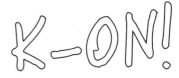

CONGRATULATIONS ON *K-ON!* GETTING MADE INTO AN ANIME! I'M REALLY LOOKING FORWARD TO SEEING YUI AND HER FRIENDS MOVING AROUND ON SCREEN.

-DAIOKI

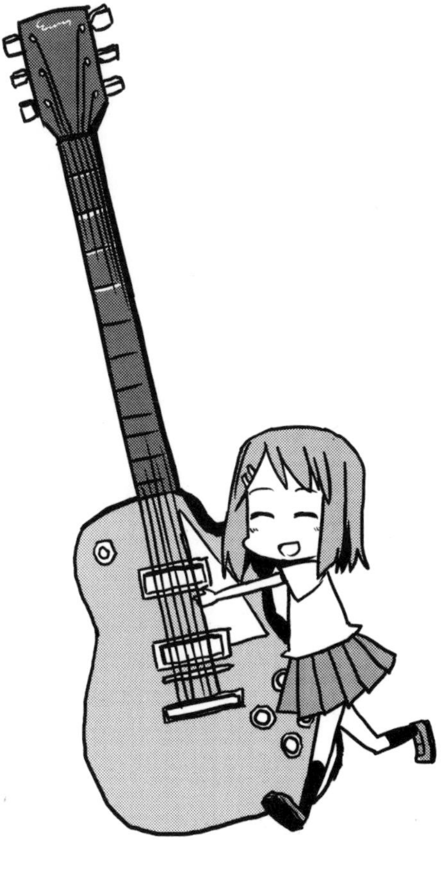

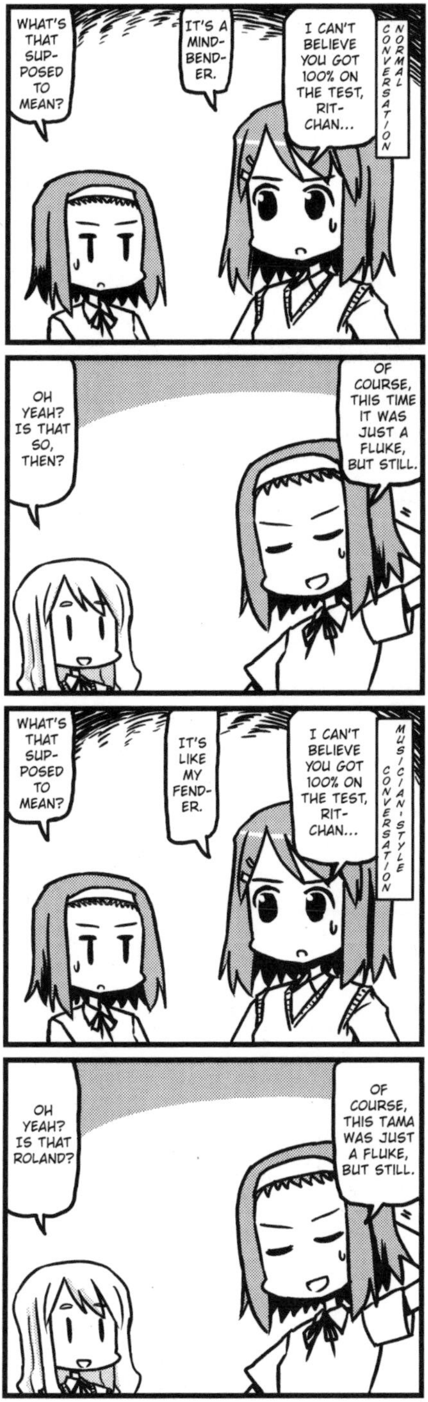
NORMAL CONVERSATION
I CAN'T BELIEVE YOU GOT 100% ON THE TEST, RIT-CHAN...
IT'S A MIND-BENDER.
WHAT'S THAT SUP-POSED TO MEAN?
OF COURSE, THIS TIME IT WAS JUST A FLUKE, BUT STILL.
OH YEAH? IS THAT SO, THEN?
MUSICIAN-STYLE CONVERSATION
I CAN'T BELIEVE YOU GOT 100% ON THE TEST, RIT-CHAN...
IT'S LIKE MY FEND-ER.
WHAT'S THAT SUP-POSED TO MEAN?
OF COURSE, THIS TAMA WAS JUST A FLUKE, BUT STILL.
OH YEAH? IS THAT ROLAND?

CONGRATULATIONS ON THE SECOND VOLUME GOING ON SALE AND ON THE ANIME ADAPTATION!!

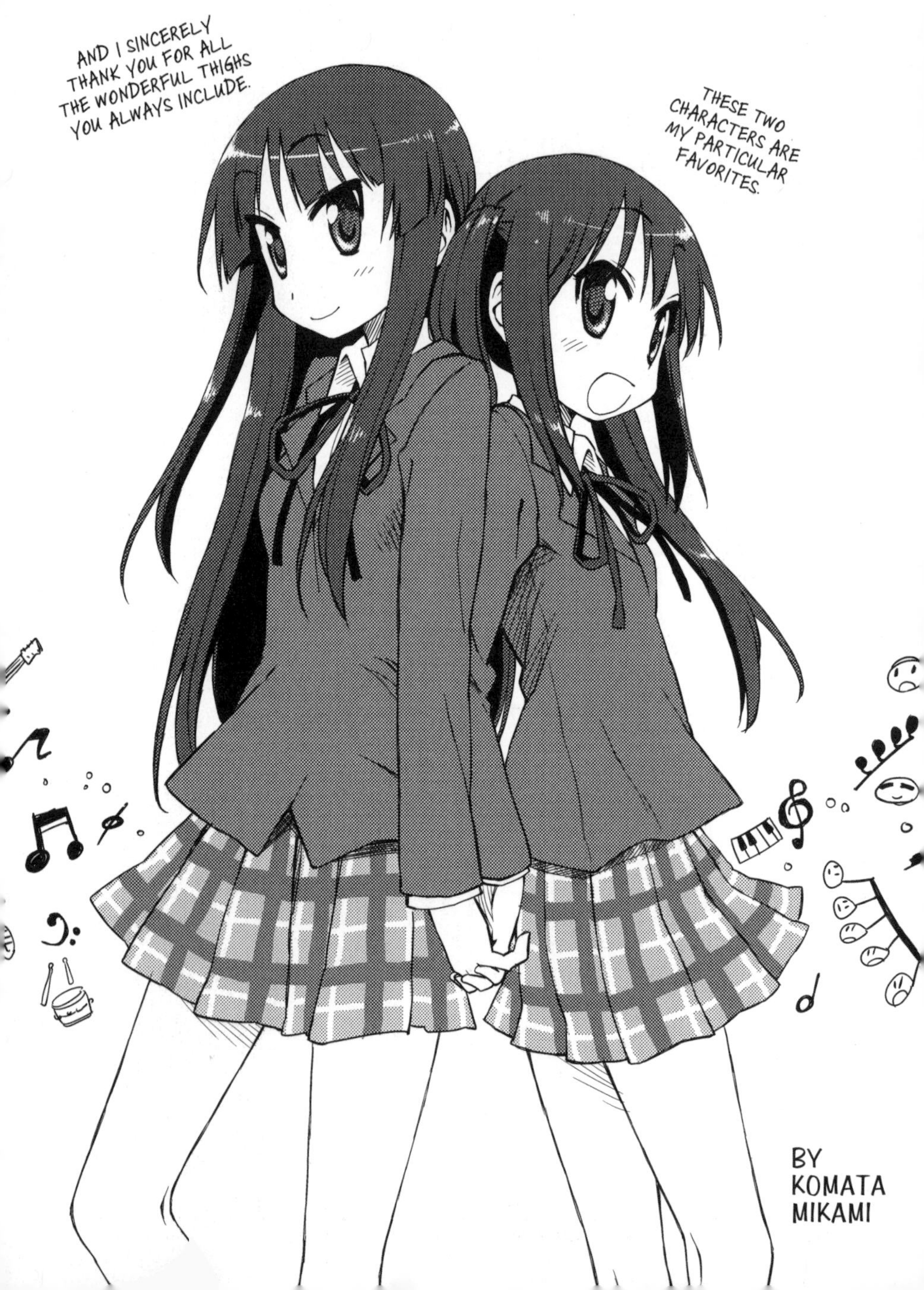
THESE TWO CHARACTERS ARE MY PARTICULAR FAVORITES.
AND I SINCERELY THANK YOU FOR ALL THE WONDERFUL THIGHS YOU ALWAYS INCLUDE.
BY KOMATA MIKAMI

BONUS PAGE

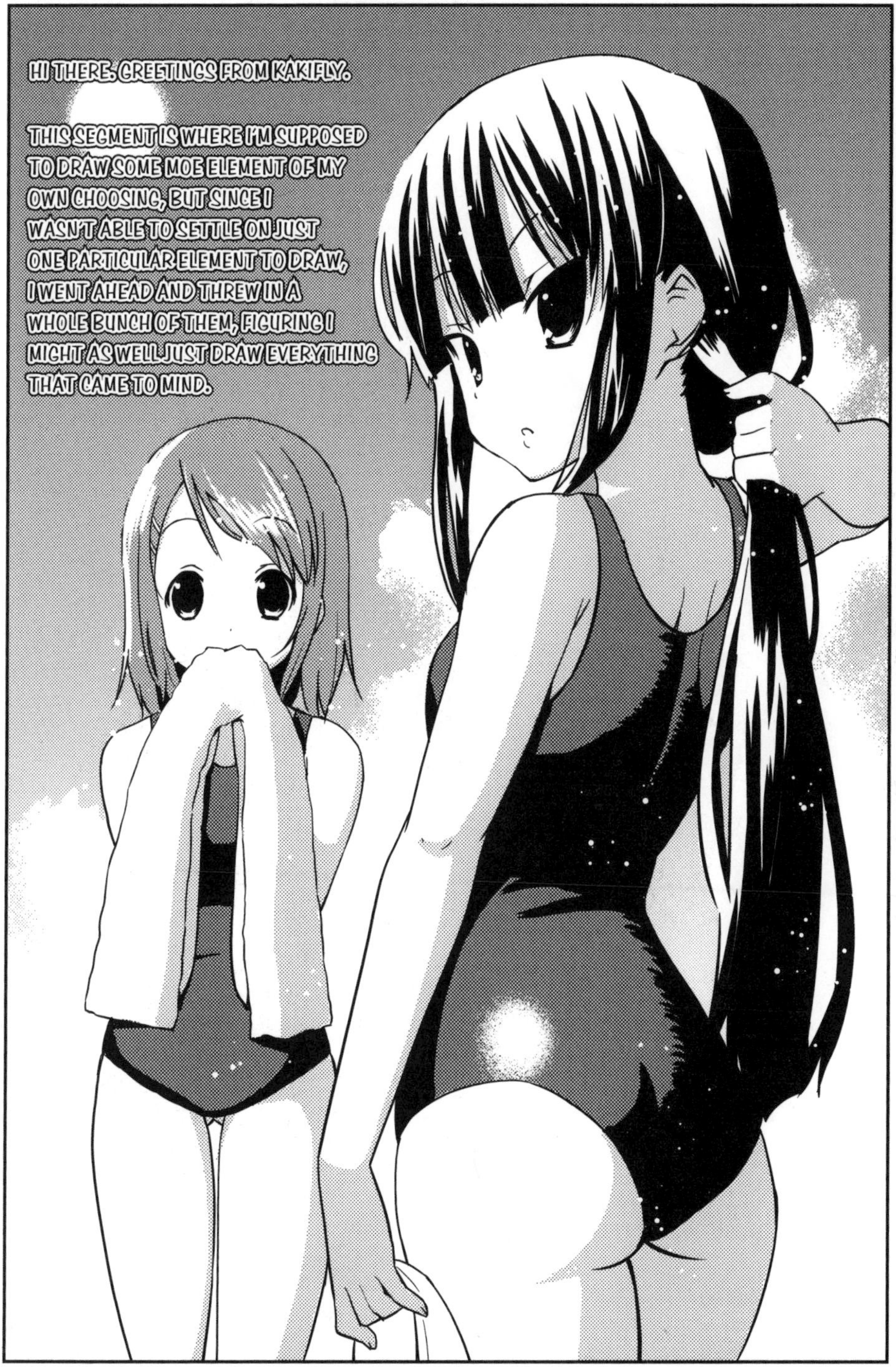
HI THERE. GREETINGS FROM KAKIFLY.
THIS SEGMENT IS WHERE I'M SUPPOSED TO DRAW SOME MOE ELEMENT OF MY OWN CHOOSING, BUT SINCE I WASN'T ABLE TO SETTLE ON JUST ONE PARTICULAR ELEMENT TO DRAW, I WENT AHEAD AND THREW IN A WHOLE BUNCH OF THEM, FIGURING I MIGHT AS WELL JUST DRAW EVERYTHING THAT CAME TO MIND.

(ORIGINALLY APPEARED IN THE RELAY ESSAY "MY PRIVATE D☆V" IN THE JUNE 2008 ISSUE OF MANGA TIME KIRARA.)

HELLO, MY NAME IS KAKIFLY. WE'RE ON THE SECOND VOLUME. THAT'S CRAZY. AND ON TOP OF THAT, THERE'S THE FACT THAT THE SERIES HAS BEEN LICENSED FOR AN ANIME ADAPTATION. WITH ALL THIS GOING ON, IT FEELS LIKE I DON'T EVEN KNOW WHAT'S WHAT ANYMORE. BUT ALL OF IT'S THANKS TO YOU, THE ONES WHO'VE BEEN SUPPORTING ME BY READING *K-ON!* I HONESTLY CAN'T THANK YOU ENOUGH. TRULY, THANK YOU FROM THE BOTTOM OF MY HEART! AND IF YOU COULD ALL PLEASE CONTINUE TO WAIT PATIENTLY FOR THE RELEASE OF THE THIRD VOLUME OF THE SERIES, NOTHING WOULD MAKE ME HAPPIER.

ALSO, I'D LIKE TO THANK MY GUEST ARTISTS DAIOKI, WHO KINDLY AGREED TO DRAW A BONUS MANGA PAGE FOR THIS VOLUME TOO, AND MIKAMI AS WELL. TO BOTH OF YOU, THANK YOU SO, SO MUCH!!!

KAKIFLY

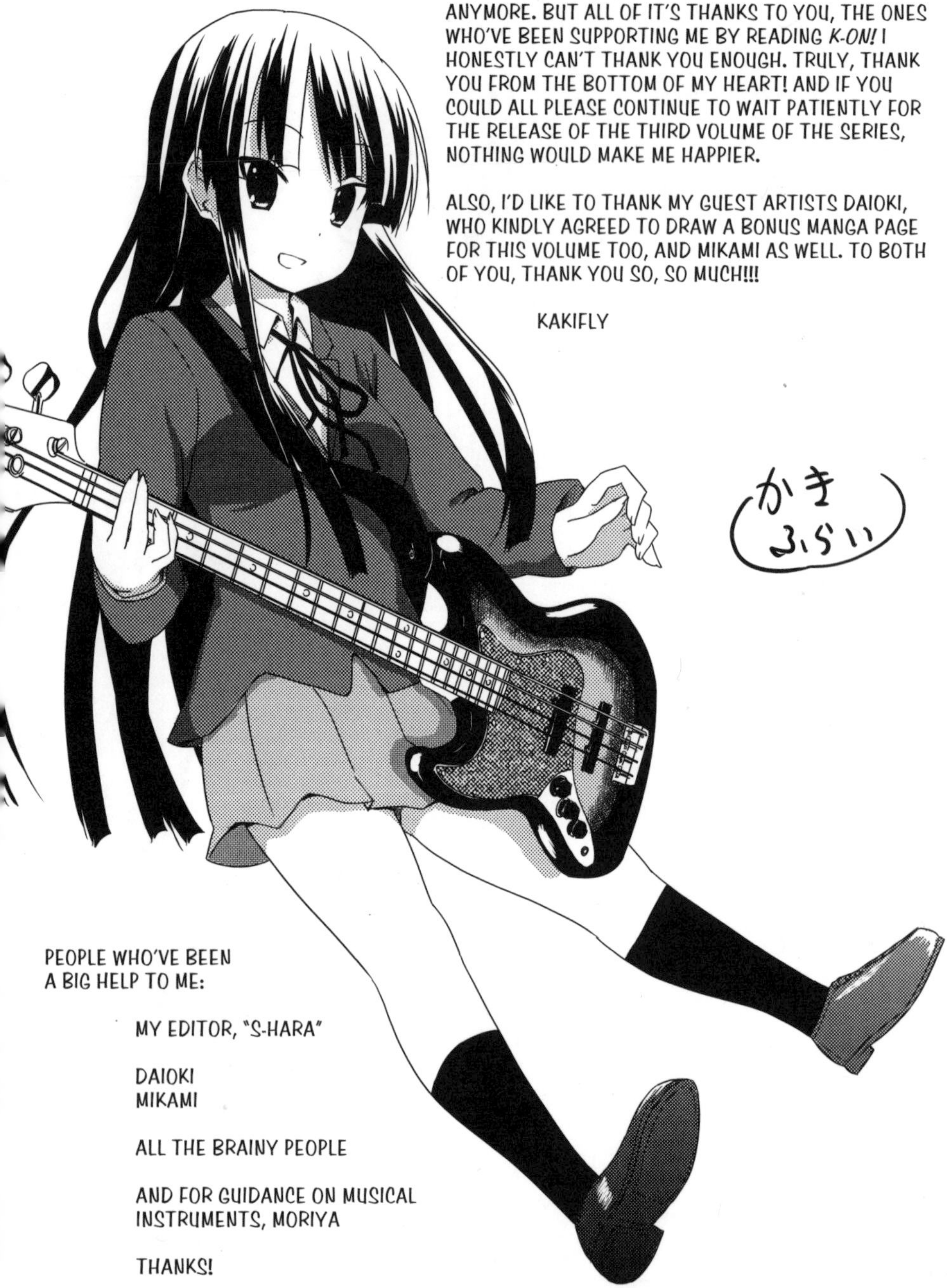
かき
ふらい

PEOPLE WHO'VE BEEN A BIG HELP TO ME:

MY EDITOR, "S-HARA"

DAIOKI
MIKAMI

ALL THE BRAINY PEOPLE

AND FOR GUIDANCE ON MUSICAL INSTRUMENTS, MORIYA

THANKS!

kakifly

C O M M E N T S

Hi, my name is kakifly.
I am now able to eat
oysters. Thank you so much
for buying my manga.

THANKS FOR
READING!

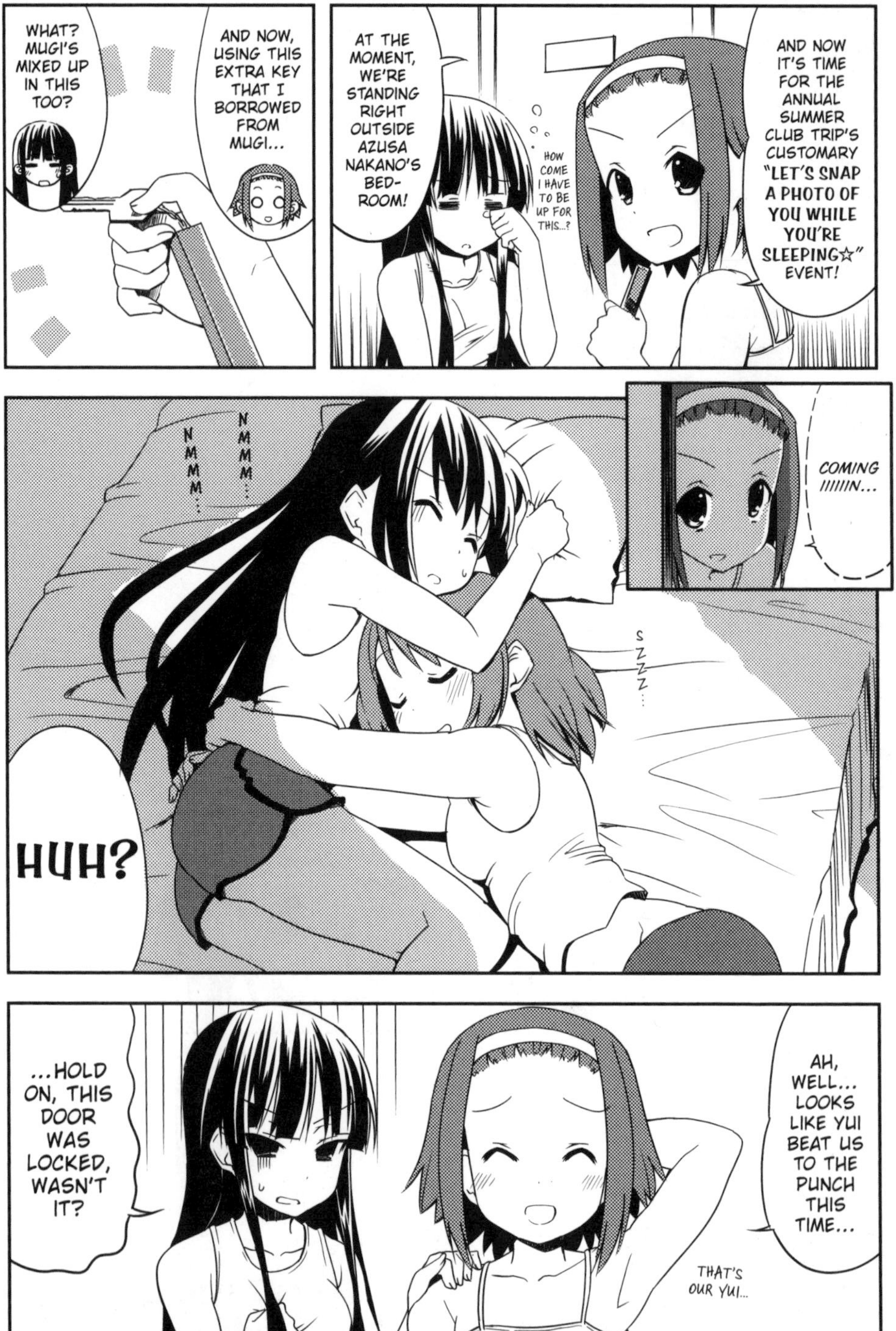
AND NOW IT'S TIME FOR THE ANNUAL SUMMER CLUB TRIP'S CUSTOMARY "LET'S SNAP A PHOTO OF YOU WHILE YOU'RE SLEEPING☆" EVENT!
AT THE MOMENT, WE'RE STANDING RIGHT OUTSIDE AZUSA NAKANO'S BED-ROOM!
HOW COME I HAVE TO BE UP FOR THIS...?
AND NOW, USING THIS EXTRA KEY THAT I BORROWED FROM MUGI...
WHAT? MUGI'S MIXED UP IN THIS TOO?
COMING IIIIIIN...
NMMM...
NMMM...
SZZZ...
HUH?
AH, WELL... LOOKS LIKE YUI BEAT US TO THE PUNCH THIS TIME...
THAT'S OUR YUI...
...HOLD ON, THIS DOOR WAS LOCKED, WASN'T IT?

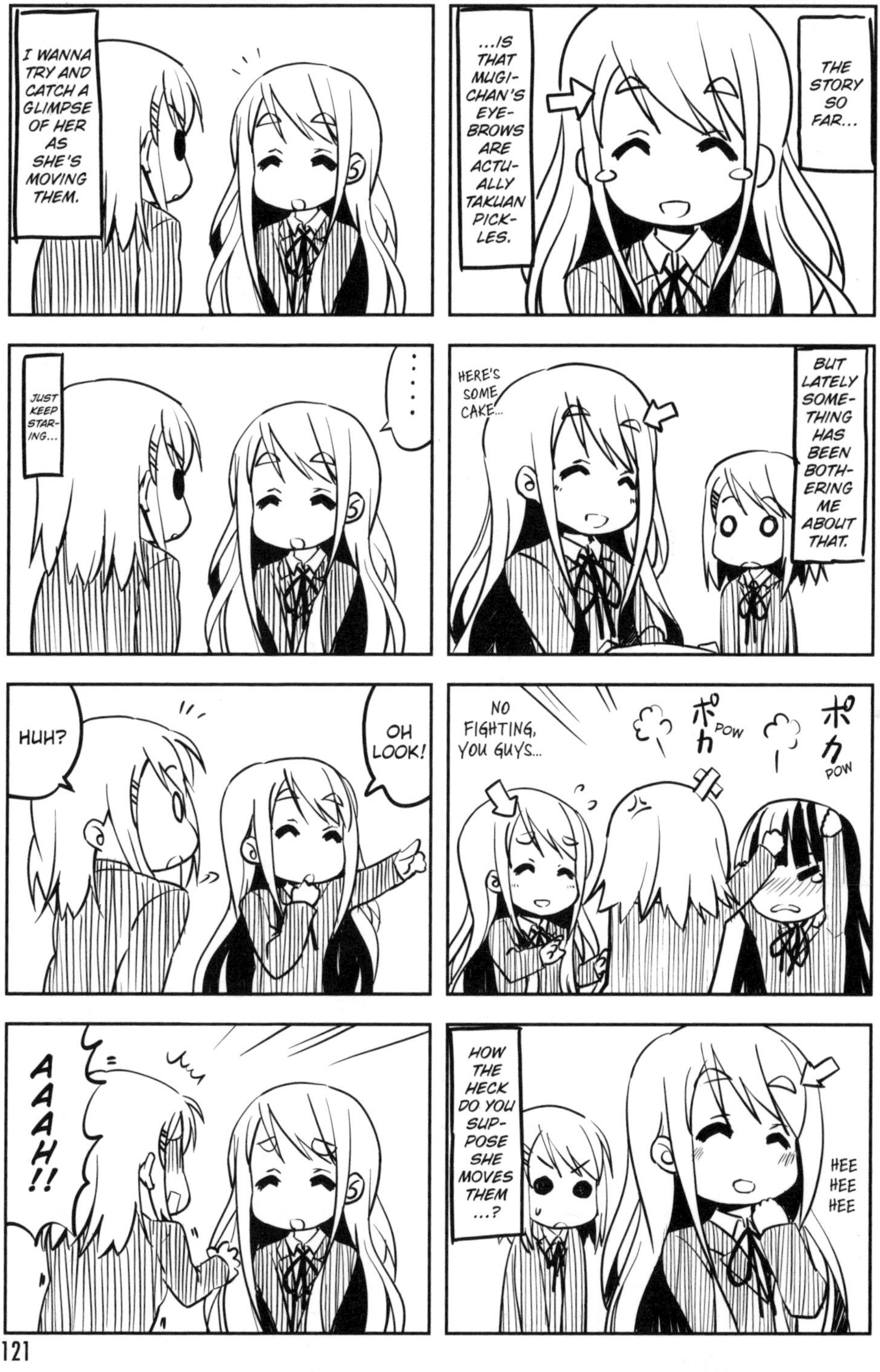

THE STORY SO FAR...
...IS THAT MUGI-CHAN'S EYEBROWS ARE ACTUALLY TAKUAN PICKLES.
BUT LATELY SOMETHING HAS BEEN BOTHERING ME ABOUT THAT.
HERE'S SOME CAKE...
ポカ POW
ポカ POW
NO FIGHTING, YOU GUYS...
HEE HEE HEE
HOW THE HECK DO YOU SUPPOSE SHE MOVES THEM ...?
I WANNA TRY AND CATCH A GLIMPSE OF HER AS SHE'S MOVING THEM.
.....
JUST KEEP STARING...
OH LOOK!
HUH?
AAAAH!!

around from room to room and participate in different class groupings like U.S. students do. Instead, they belong to a fixed "cohort" (*kumi*) that stays grouped in the same room all year, and teachers for each subject visit the room during the appropriate times.

PAGE 12
Mio's Song Titles
All of these songs were actually created and performed for the anime version of *K-ON!*, released on a soundtrack album titled *Hokago Tea Time* (Afterschool Tea Time). Musically speaking, the arrangements are punk-pop in flavor, with all instruments prominent in the mix.

PAGE 13
Yen Conversion
A general rule of thumb to use for converting Japanese yen to American dollars is ¥100 to 1 USD.

PAGE 14
Simple, Easy Music
The name of the club literally means "light music" (see *K-ON!* note above), which Yui initially interpreted as "easy music" because of the dual meaning of the prefix *kei–* (used in this context to contrast more traditional/classical music, not ease of playing).

PAGE 17
Blood Type
Asking someone's blood type in Japan is akin to asking about astrological signs in the U.S. The notion that personality is in some way determined by blood type has no scientific basis and is generally dismissed outside of Japan, but within Japan it's a popular belief that knowing someone's blood type gives one some insight into their attitude and behavior. The main personality types are:

Type O = outgoing social butterfly with a flexible outlook on life
Type A = high-strung perfectionist with strong artistic tendencies
Type B = easygoing individualist with a pragmatic, goal-oriented attitude
Type AB = unpredictable loose cannon with both artistic and pragmatic aspects

PAGE 27
"Nice try!!"
The joke here is based on a word pun: the Japanese word *oishii* (tasty) sounds similar to *oshii* (close, but no cigar).

PAGE 38
The Role of the Senpai
Traditionally in Japan, seniority takes precedence over ability in the assignment of leadership roles. It would've been impertinent for Azusa to suggest herself for the role of lead guitarist, even if she is the better player, and that's why she defers to Yui. However, leaders are also expected to show wisdom in judgment, so it seems a little arrogant of Yui to assert herself as lead guitarist when Azusa is the logical choice. In a "proper" interaction of this type, Azusa should immediately defer to Yui (which she does), and then Yui should display magnanimity by insisting that Azusa is the better choice (after which Azusa would offer a few token protests and then "reluctantly" accept the role).

PAGE 42
Lunchtime
Some Japanese high schools have central cafeterias (or a repurposed gymnasium), but quite a few don't. Even when the school does have a cafeteria, many students choose to eat lunch in their homeroom anyway.

PAGE 47
Mio-*shan*
–shan is just a cutesy variation of *–san* that expresses the intimacy of *–chan* without any of the condescension. The emotion being conveyed is sort of like "I'm not worthy of your friendship."

PAGE 48
"You must be tired."
The Japanese phrase "Otsukare-sama desu" (literally "You must be tired") is also a standard way of telling someone that you appreciate the work they've done.

PAGE 59
Yui's Constant Hugging
The Japanese word is *sukinshippu*, literally "skinship." Although originally used to

TRANSLATION NOTES

COMMON HONORIFICS

no honorific: Indicates familiarity or closeness; if used without permission or reason, addressing someone in this manner would constitute an insult.

-san: The Japanese equivalent of Mr./Mrs./ Miss. If a situation calls for politeness, this is the fail-safe honorific.

-sama: Conveys great respect; may also indicate that the social status of the speaker is lower than that of the addressee.

-kun: Used most often when referring to boys, this indicates affection or familiarity. Occasionally used by older men among their peers, but it may also be used by anyone referring to a person of lower standing.

-chan: An affectionate honorific indicating familiarity used mostly in reference to girls; also used in reference to cute persons or animals of either gender.

-senpai: Used to address upperclassmen or more experienced coworkers.

-sensei: A respectful term for teachers, artists, or high-level professionals.

K-ON!

The title *K-ON!* comes from the Japanese word *"kei-ongaku,"* meaning "light music" in the sense of casual or easy listening (i.e., not serious or innovative as in serious classical or jazz). In the context of school clubs in Japan, the term *"kei-ongaku-bu"* ("light music club") usually contrasts with *"ongaku-bu"* ("music club") in that it focuses on popular forms of music (pop, rock, folk, etc.) where the latter focuses on symphonic and choral forms.

kakifly

The author's name, "kakifly," comes from the Japanese word *"kaki-furai,"* meaning "fried oysters." It seems to be a running joke, as the author comments for this and future volumes reference his feelings toward oysters.

PAGE 2
Yui Hirasawa

Yui's last name is an allusion to Susumu Hirasawa, founder and former guitarist for the now-defunct Japanese techno band P-Model. Her first name means "only."

Mio Akiyama

Mio's last name is an allusion to Katsuhiko Akiyama, former bassist for P-Model. Her first name means "wake (of waves)."

Ritsu Tainaka

Ritsu's last name is an allusion to Sadatoshi Tainaka, former drummer for P-Model. Her first name means "meter (of rhythm)."

Tsumugi Kotobuki

Tsumugi's last name is an allusion to Hikaru Kotobuki, former keyboardist for P-Model. Her first name means "woven (silk) cloth."

Azusa Nakano

Azusa's last name is an allusion to Teruo Nakano, former bassist for P-Model. Her first name means "Japanese cherry birch."

Ui Hirasawa

Ui's first name means "gloomy/vexing."

Sawako Yamanaka

Sawako's first and last names are an allusion to Sawao Yamanaka, vocalist and rhythm guitarist for the Japanese alternative rock band The Pillows.

Nodoka Manabe

Nodoka's last name is an allusion to Yoshiaki Manabe, lead guitarist for The Pillows. Her first name means "serene."

PAGE 6
School Clubs

Participating in after-school clubs is a very big deal in Japanese high schools, as it's one of the only chances for students to interact outside of their fixed class groups.

PAGE 9
Japanese School Terms

The Japanese school year is divided into three terms: the first starts in early April and ends in mid July; the second begins in late August or early September and ends in late December; the third begins in early January and ends in late March.

Class Assignments

Japanese high school students don't move

PAGE 83
Azusa the Number Two
"The Number Two" (*ni-go*) is also a Japanese euphemism for "mistress" (i.e., one's "number two" gal), so the nickname sounds a bit sillier/cuter in Japanese than it does in English.

PAGE 84
Sneezing
Another common Japanese folk belief holds that sneezes are caused by people talking about you behind your back.

PAGE 95
One of These
Yui refers to Tsumugi as a household appliance using a quirk of Japanese grammar: when objects (nouns) are counted in Japanese, the nouns have to be marked with special particles indicating what type of object they refer to. Some examples are *ni-hiki* (two animals), *ni-mai* (two flat things), *ni-hon* (two long, skinny things) etc. In this case Yui says she wants *ichi-dai* (one appliance) of Tsumugi.

PAGE 105
Hot pot
A hot pot (*nabe*) is a hearty soup that's cooked and shared by all at the table. The ingredients can vary considerably, but usually it's a soy/miso-flavored broth containing meat, wild mushrooms, tofu, bok choy, scallions, and thick noodles.

New Year's Soba
New Year's *soba* (*toshikoshi soba*, literally "year-spanning soba") is a simple noodle dish eaten on New Year's Eve. The long *soba* (buckwheat) noodles represent long life, and according to tradition, everyone has to finish their noodles completely by the time the new year rolls around.

PAGE 106
Chopsticks Etiquette
Holding chopsticks in your mouth (*kuwaebashi*) is seen as bad manners in Japan.

PAGE 107
Kotatsu
The "heated table" is a typical piece of furniture in Japanese sitting rooms. It's a small coffee table with a space heater mounted to the underside of the horizontal surface and quilted material draped around the sides to trap the heat in the space underneath. When people sit at the table, they place their legs inside the heated space to keep warm. Sitting around the heated table eating tangerines and other winter foods is a stereotypical winter scene in Japan.

PAGE 112
Stomach Appeal
The phrase Ritsu uses, "*iroke yori kuike*" (literally "food over sex"), is something of an idiomatic expression in Japanese, made pithy by the symmetry between the words "*iroke*" (sex appeal) and "*kuike*" (eating appeal).

PAGE 115
Musical Instruments
The humor of this page comes from a bunch of puns based on the brand names of musical instrument makers: "*hen da*" (it's weird) becomes "Fender" (*fendaa*), a guitar and bass brand; "*tamatama*" (just a fluke) becomes *tama* + "Tama," a drum brand; and "*soo nanda*" (is that so) becomes "Roland" (*roorando*), a keyboard brand.

PAGE 3

describe the necessary physical intimacy between a parent and child, now it generally refers to physical contact between close friends (especially but not exclusively same-sex friends), engaged in for the purpose of friendship bonding, and sometimes as "practice" for later sexual relationships or even as an outright sexual act of its own. While hugging, friendly touching, and even kissing is practiced and accepted to varying degrees in many Western countries, the Japanese practice of "skinship" is sometimes taken to a level that many Westerners would regard as sexually intimate, although in Japan it's seen as a normal, healthy personal exchange between friends and often (as in this case with Yui toward Azusa) carries no explicit sexual overtones.

PAGE 64
Intonation
In musical terms, the intonation (called "octave tuning" in Japanese) of an instrument describes the degree to which the notes sound at the correct pitch (i.e., "in tune") independent of the player. In this case, warping of the neck of Yui's guitar has caused an effective shortening of the open string so that an open note now sounds a little too high compared to the same note played on the neck of the guitar. A problem like this is usually easily remedied by replacing the strings and making small adjustments to the action (height) and bridge (length) of each string until open notes match the fretted notes.

PAGE 68
"Miss" Tsumugi
The saleswoman in the music store refers to Tsumugi ("Tsumugi-ojousama") in the same obsequious way her butler does because Tsumugi's family owns the music store, making the saleswoman feel like an employee of the whole Kotobuki family, including Tsumugi herself.

PAGE 70
Gui-Ta
Yui's pet name for her guitar. Several Japanese male names end in –ta (Kenta, Kota, Ryota, etc.), so the name indicates that she thinks of her guitar as male. It's also an obvious pun on the Japanese pronunciation of "guitar" = "gitaa."

PAGE 72
Nosebleed
It's a common manga trope that young innocents get nosebleeds when they're exposed to an explicit sexual scene, presumably as a symbol of their sexual arousal.

PAGE 73
The Girlz
In Japanese, Ritsu says onna-gumi ("girl group"), but it's written in a way that makes it look tough, like the name of a yakuza crew. (Yakuza gang names generally end in –gumi; e.g., Yamaguchi-gumi etc.)

PAGE 74
The Recharge Round
Ritsu feels that Tsumugi's band name suggestion of "Juden Kikan" (literally "recharge period") would jinx the band because it implies that they're going to need to take time away from band activities to "recharge" (commonly used in Japan as a euphemism for recovering from a bad experience).

PAGE 76
Yukata
A lightweight cotton robe worn in casual situations (such as for shrine visits, cherry blossom viewings, or festivals) in the heat of summer, or around the house after the customary evening bath at any time of year.

PAGE 80
Colds
There's a Japanese folk superstition that says you can get rid of a cold by giving it to someone else.

"Who will face me!?"
Ritsu is using an archaic phrase from samurai times for humorous effect. According to tradition, when a samurai would visit another family's home turf, he would announce the visit by shouting out "I would ask this of you!" (Tanomou!), which in many cases was intended as a challenge to duel.

Can't wait for the next volume? You don't have to!

Keep up with the latest chapters of some of your favorite manga every month online in the pages of YEN PLUS!

MAXIMUM RIDE

DANIEL X

YOTSUBA&!

K-ON!

gossip girl

Visit us at
www.yenplus.com
for details!

YEN⁺ Plus

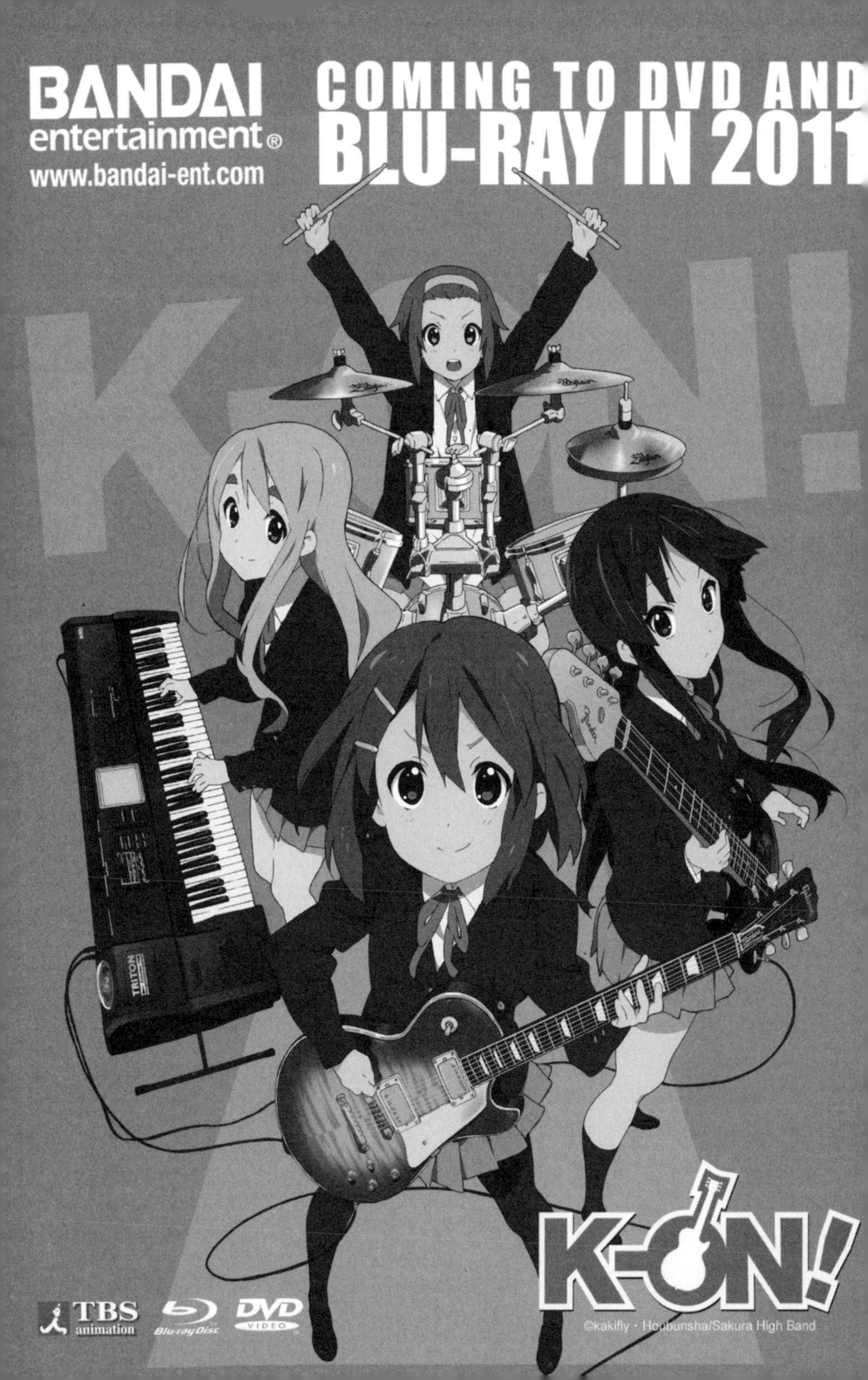
BANDAI entertainment®
www.bandai-ent.com
COMING TO DVD AND BLU-RAY IN 2011
K-ON!
TBS animation
Blu-ray Disc
DVD VIDEO
©kakifly · Houbunsha/Sakura High Band

K-ON! ②

KAKIFLY

Translation: Jack Wiedrick

Lettering: Hope Donovan

K-ON! vol. 2 © 2009 Kakifly. All rights reserved. First published in Japan in 2009 by HOUBUNSHA CO., LTD., Tokyo. English translation rights in United States, Canada, and United Kingdom arranged with HOUBUNSHA CO., LTD through Tuttle-Mori Agency, Inc., Tokyo.

Translation © 2011 by Hachette Book Group, Inc.

Yen Press
Hachette Book Group
237 Park Avenue, New York, NY 10017

www.HachetteBookGroup.com
www.YenPress.com

Yen Press is an imprint of Hachette Book Group, Inc. The Yen Press name and logo are trademarks of Hachette Book Group, Inc.

First Yen Press Edition: March 2011

ISBN: 978-0-316-11940-5

10 9 8 7 6 5

RRD-C

Printed in the United States of America